D1164687

My Life in Prison

My Life in Prison

Memoirs of a Chinese Political Dissident

Jiang Qisheng

Translated by James Erwin Dew
and edited by Naomi May

With a foreword by Andrew J. Nathan
and an introduction by Perry Link

ROWMAN & LITTLEFIELD PUBLISHERS, INC.
Lanham • Boulder • New York • Toronto • Plymouth, UK

Published by Rowman & Littlefield Publishers, Inc.
A wholly owned subsidiary of The Rowman & Littlefield Publishing Group, Inc.
4501 Forbes Boulevard, Suite 200, Lanham, Maryland 20706
www.rowmanlittlefield.com

Estover Road, Plymouth PL6 7PY, United Kingdom

Copyright © 2012 by Rowman & Littlefield Publishers, Inc.

All rights reserved. No part of this book may be reproduced in any form or by any electronic or mechanical means, including information storage and retrieval systems, without written permission from the publisher, except by a reviewer who may quote passages in a review.

British Library Cataloguing in Publication Information Available

Library of Congress Cataloging-in-Publication Data

Jiang, Qisheng, 1948–
[Yi sheng shuo zhen hua. English]
My life in prison : memoirs of a Chinese political dissident / Jiang Qisheng ; translated by James Erwin Dew and edited by Naomi May ; with a foreword by Andrew J. Nathan and an introduction by Perry Link.
p. cm.
Includes index.
ISBN 978-1-4422-1222-0 (cloth : alk. paper) — ISBN 978-1-4422-1224-4 (electronic)
1. Jiang, Qisheng, 1948– 2. China—History—Tiananmen Square Incident, 1989. 3. China—Politics and government—1976–2002. 4. Dissenters—China—Biography. 5. Political prisoners—China—Biography. I. Title.
DS779.32.J5313 2012
365'.45092—dc23
[B]

2011041694

∞™ The paper used in this publication meets the minimum requirements of American National Standard for Information Sciences—Permanence of Paper for Printed Library Materials, ANSI/NISO Z39.48-1992.

Printed in the United States of America

In order to confirm the right to speak out in this great land of China, and to establish a system under which dissent will not be considered a crime, there must be people who will continually struggle against the prohibitions of free speech and will challenge bad laws, using their own sufferings in prison to narrow and, in time, to block the road to "the crime of free speech." I sincerely believe that in this land, even among the docile common people, those with clear understanding, who are also inheritors of a profound belief in oriental culture, will surely find deep in their hearts the stirrings of humanity and the hope that the day will come when speaking the truth will be just like taking a walk in the garden, or going to a restaurant or a movie, and that this will no longer be the special privilege of a few brave individuals but will be something available to any ordinary citizen.

—Jiang Qisheng

Contents

Part II: In the Transfer Center

~

Foreword

Many Chinese writers, artists, and lawyers spend time in prison. It is a price paid sooner or later for saying what one thinks. But few besides Jiang Qisheng have managed to give us such a vivid impression of what life in a Chinese prison is like—the routines, the food, the ennui, the random acts of cruelty and kindness, outbreaks of violence and moments of humanity, and the surprising clarity of prisoners from all walks of life about the arbitrariness of the system that put them there.

To tell such a story requires sharp powers of observation, generous empathy, a philosophical disposition, and the courage to violate the rule against writing. Having written, the prisoner needs to make friends who will help smuggle the work out and enough good luck not to get caught, as Jiang Qisheng almost did. To serve his readers well, the author must honestly report the humiliating effects of detention on his body and mind, but also help the reader understand the spiritual resources the prisoner finds to resist such conditions. The writer must see the other prisoners in the round even though more of them are criminals than saints. And he must understand the guards and interrogators as workers doing their jobs in a complex organization.

Jiang Qisheng does all this in his account of four years of imprisonment in three different confinement facilities during 1999–2003—first a detention center pending trial, then a brutal transfer center, and finally the Beijing Number Two Prison where he finishes his sentence. He suffered all this for writing an article to commemorate the victims of the June 4th, 1989, crackdown in Beijing. Jiang is one of that small group of brave Chinese who persists in writing about the reality of authoritarian rule in China even though it means that he is not allowed to have a job and faces constant harassment with interludes of imprisonment.

Prison is a place where China's otherwise highly stratified society comes together. Jiang paradoxically learned more about the life of his fellow countrymen behind bars than he had outside them. His book gives a rich picture of life in China as seen from the bottom, through the experiences of peasants, religious believers, thieves, murderers, and innocent men, thrown together in unwanted intimacy by a common fate. He describes the little-known customs and jargon of jail life. With wry humor he reflects on the psychic and health benefits of life in prison and on the working conditions of the guards and interrogators. Through his experiences we see how punctilious and legalistic the Chinese system has become in its fundamentally extralegal work of criminalizing speech.

Through his writings the English-speaking reader will gain a new friend. Jiang is a vivid character, a strong, self-conscious man of principle, who speaks eloquently on the importance of speaking the truth. Tested by repression, he confirms his commitment to open inquiry, peaceful methods, and individual autonomy.

Andrew J. Nathan
Columbia University

Author's Preface

On 19 May 1999 the authorities threw me into the Beijing Detention Center and began political persecution against me by means of judicial procedures. On 1 November of the same year the First Intermediate People's Court of Beijing considered my case. In response to the official accusations I entered a plea of not guilty and unequivocally asserted that as a victim of literary inquisition I held no hopes of a fair judgment. Subsequently, almost five months elapsed before a decision was handed down. As winter passed and spring came I decided that I would gather the notes that I had written in the Detention Center and put them in order so that they could be sent outside the walls and made available to the world.

28 March 2000
Beijing Detention Center

Editor's Acknowledgments

I should like to thank English PEN for its contribution to the funding of the translation. I am also most grateful to Andrew J. Nathan and Perry Link for their generous support, to the author's agent, Joanne Wang, and to Ros Schwarz and other English friends whose initial hard work and enthusiasm were crucial to the project. Above all, I must thank James E. Dew both for his fine translation and for the courtesy, patience, and charm that made it such a pleasure to work with him.

Naomi May

Introduction

Jiang Qisheng (1948–) grew up in the Yangzi Basin city of Changshu. Gifted with an extraordinarily bright mind, he did not begin his life as a contrarian, but events made him into one.

A star in high school, and a Maoist Red Guard after that, he went in 1978 to Beijing to begin an undergraduate degree in aerodynamics at the Beijing Institute of Aeronautics. From 1985 to 1988 he was a lecturer in aerodynamics in an extension program of Tsinghua University, and in September 1988 he entered a Ph.D. program in philosophy of science and technology at People's University in Beijing. He became an activist in the prodemocracy student movement in spring 1989 and a leader of the student "dialogue delegation" that tried, unsuccessfully, to negotiate a meeting of minds with Communist Party leaders over the stand-off at Tiananmen Square. The massacre on June 4th, 1989, came as a life-changing shock to him. On 9 September 1989, the authorities sent him to Beijing's elite Qincheng prison for one and a half years. They did not formally charge him with anything but held him "in detention for interrogation" because of his activism in the democracy movement. After his release from prison People's University expelled him from its Ph.D. program.

During the 1990s he supported the Tiananmen Mothers group in its efforts to find and support victims of the massacre and their families. He also began to write articles on human rights issues for Chinese-language magazines published in Hong Kong and overseas. In early April 1999, he penned a piece called "Light a Million Candles to Commemorate the Souls of the

Heroes of June 4th." This attracted the attention of the authorities. Was Jiang going to spark a protest on June 4th, 1999, the tenth anniversary of the bloodshed? In any case it seems clear that the article was the main reason they arrested him again, charged him with "incitement of subversion of state power," and sentenced him to four years in prison. He spent two years in the Beijing Detention Center, two months in the Beijing Prison Transfer Center, and the remaining time in the Beijing Number Two Prison.

This book records some of his thoughts and experiences during those years.

Upon release he resumed an energetic program of writing, and in recent years, unlike the 1990s, has been able to reach readers inside China because of the Internet. In order to see his essays, Chinese readers must evade the regime's "Great Firewall," but at least some can do this. A Chinese-language Google search today produces a long list of hits on "Jiang Qisheng." A search on the government-approved Baidu search engine shows nothing.

Jiang's intellectual odyssey from Red Guard to anti-Maoist freethinker illustrates a common pattern in his generation. Liu Xiaobo, Zheng Yi, Su Xiaokang, Hu Ping, Bei Dao, Zhong Acheng, Zhang Zuhua, Chen Kuide, and many, many others of that generation's best and most independent thinkers learned to rely on their own minds when their Maoist ideals crashed on the realities of Chinese society during the late Mao years. Jiang Qisheng is vivid and honest in telling us exactly how the process happened to him.

He remembers, as a fifteen-year-old, wanting to answer Mao Zedong's call to "learn from Lei Feng," a soldier whom Mao exalted as a paragon of selfless heroism. In their afterschool hours, young Jiang and some of his classmates would look for the workmen in Changshu who pushed night soil carts through the city streets. The workmen needed help getting the carts over the city's arched bridges, so the young students waited there to help them do it. Their hands and clothing inevitably got splattered with liquid excrement, but that, to them, not only did not matter, it actually seemed "a badge of honor, not attainable any other way." However stinky the cart was, they thought, "it did not stink as much as the stink of our petty bourgeois class backgrounds."

When the Cultural Revolution arrived three years later, Jiang was classified, despite his Maoist ardor, "a little ox-ghost and snake-spirit." The unfair label disappointed him, but did not really disillusion him. The first crack of real disillusionment came when Liu Shaoqi, number two to Mao in the Communist pantheon, was declared a "renegade, traitor, and scab." This label bothered Jiang Qisheng—but not because of the idea that a top leader might be so evil. The point, to his sharp analytical mind, was that Mao himself must have had flawed vision if he worked so long and so closely with a man who, "in his heart," as the charges said, had been a traitor "from the beginning." Five years later, when Mao's next "second in command," Lin Biao, was also suddenly found to be a traitor, "I couldn't take it anymore," Jiang Qisheng recalls. The Lin Biao affair marked the beginning of his long career of voicing doubts about top leaders.

For Jiang Qisheng as for many others of the newly disillusioned in his generation, the hypocrisy of official language became a key issue. China, in his view, was "a republic on the surface, a dictatorship inside; a democracy in name, a Party-state in fact." In a 2011 essay he observes that the official language, although laughably false and utterly dead as of today, stays in place because "people just cynically pretend to obey, out of practical interest." And the regime, knowing that it is not getting—and cannot get—real allegiance, settles for fake allegiance as long as it keeps the lid on society.

Someone should write a book some day on how young people who embraced Maoist ideals in their youth came to be the sharpest critics of Maoism after they came to feel they had been deceived. Examples in China are legion, but even more interesting is the fact that there are examples of it all around the world, in veterans of the 1968 protests in France, the anti-Vietnam-War generation in the United States, and elsewhere. In all these places Mao today is criticized most sharply by people to whom he was a hero four decades ago. A similar pattern appears in an earlier generation of philosophical socialists—George Orwell, Arthur Koestler, and others—whom Stalin disillusioned and thereby made into some of the sharpest of the Soviet Union's critics. There is something about betrayal that supplies fuel for the most telling criticisms and most ardent opposition. A Big Lie stings most among people who once believed it. By contrast, people who never took socialist language seriously, one way or the other, but embrace only self-interested "realism," are able to support anticommunist wars in one era and be friends of Party elites in another. Henry Kissinger is a good example, but there are many others.

But if Jiang Qisheng illustrates a broad pattern, it is equally important to appreciate what makes him distinctive. In person he has a "presence" and charisma that commands people's attention. His astute opinions are expressed in crisp diction that emerges from a classically handsome face that bears sharp, angular features—all adding up to a powerful impression of natural "clarity." Most distinctive is his ability at—and obvious appetite for—rigorous logical reasoning, which he applies in every direction, toward friend and foe alike.

This talent sometimes isolates him, but it leaves no doubt in the minds of others that he thinks independently and also provides for himself an inner confidence that he always knows exactly where he stands, and why. We noted this talent, above, in the way the teenaged Jiang reasoned that Mao's finding fault with Liu Shaoqi implied that there had to be something wrong with Mao.

A more recent example is from 10 December 2009, when government prosecutors in Beijing handed down an indictment of Jiang's friend Liu Xiaobo (who was awarded the Nobel Peace Prize exactly one year later) on a charge of "incitement to subvert state power." Liu's alleged crime was his advocacy of the prodemocracy manifesto called Charter 08. On the day the indictment came down, 165 of Liu's supporters released a public statement that "if this man can be tried on these grounds, then each one of us belongs in the dock with him, and if he is judged guilty of a 'crime' then the judgment stands as a claim that each of us, too, has committed the crime." Within a few days, 600 more people had added their signatures. To sign was a courageous act, of course. Each signer was saying, "I am ready to go to prison, too," and everyone knew that the more people signed, the harder it would be for the regime to send them all to prison. So there was a certain moral pressure to join. But Jiang Qisheng did not. He had helped to draft Charter 08, including some of its most sharply worded passages, and had a proven record of willingness to go to jail for his beliefs, but in this case he withheld his signature on an independent principle. "Why volunteer to go to prison?" he asked. The best way to support Liu Xiaobo, he argued, was to remain in society and to continue pushing for Liu's ideals.

When the authorities learned that Jiang Qisheng had declined to sign the open letter, they instructed the young plainclothes police who were assigned to monitor him to express "encouragement" to him for his improved attitude. But that act only left Jiang with the task of disabusing the authorities of their misconception. The reason he declined to sign, he explained, was not to draw closer to the regime, but in essence to do the opposite, to remain in position for maximal continuing resistance.

Jiang's friends are accustomed to his gritty independence of mind even when they are its targets. Nobel Prize–winner Liu Xiaobo, Tiananmen Mothers founder Ding Zilin, leading exiled dissident Hu Ping, imprisoned rights-lawyer Gao Zhisheng, imprisoned AIDS-activist Hu Jia, and others have all been subject to Jiang's analytic deconstruction on certain points. But none of this seems to detract from the very high esteem in which he continues to be held.

Jiang not only enjoys thinking, but clearly relishes intellectual combat with adversaries. When he was brought to prison to begin his four-year sentence in May 1999, he met with a "preliminary interrogator" named Pang Jiang, and placed the poor fellow squarely in his crosshairs:

> *Pang Jiang:* In accordance with the law, you must respond truthfully to my questions.
>
> *Jiang Qisheng:* In accordance with human rights principles, I have the right to remain silent.
>
> *Pang Jiang:* Human rights principles are not what I do; there is no provision for silence in the law.
>
> *Jiang Qisheng:* This shows that China's legal code is backward and needs to be revised.
>
> *Pang Jiang:* But it has not yet been revised, right? So we go with what we have.
>
> *Jiang Qisheng:* That will depend on what questions you ask.
>
> *Pang Jiang:* I know what I'm supposed to ask.
>
> *Jiang Qisheng:* Everything I have done on the outside is within the rights of a citizen; there is nothing the police need to do or to look into.
>
> *Pang Jiang:* My assigned task is not for you to decide; I will ask and you must reply.
>
> *Jiang Qisheng:* And my right is to decide when I choose to pay attention to you and when I choose not to.

And so on. Jiang prevailed. He did answer some of Pang's questions, but declined on principle to answer, for example, any question that involved a third party.

At the end of his prison stay, four years later, a similar squabble occurred over whether Jiang would ride home from prison in a police van (the police insisted on this, and had a motive for their insistence but would not tell Jiang what it was) or in a car provided by his family and friends. After arguing his prison guards to a stalemate, Jiang said, "Please tell your superiors that whether or not they send a car tomorrow is none of my business and what car I get into is none of their business."

Jiang applies his logical powers not only to human rights but to theoretical physics. He has written dozens of papers with titles like "Bilateral Symmetry Still Holds True in Weak Interactions" and "On Experimental Tests about T Invariance." These are beyond me, so I cannot help to interpret them.

Political prisoners like Jiang are labeled "prisoners for special handling." Their numbers are considerably more than the few who are known in the outside world. Political prisoners are watched more carefully than ordinary offenders, and prison wardens subject their belongings to more thorough inspections to be sure they are not doing things like communicating with the outside or writing memoirs. On the other hand, political prisoners are generally treated with more respect than ordinary prisoners. Jiang Qisheng is able to resist certain humiliations, like having to stand with his hands on his head, not only because of his charisma and because he knows better how to demand his rights, but also because many in the prison, guards and fellow inmates alike, respect him for what he stands for. Young guards, who are no match for him intellectually, make it clear when they make him do certain things that they are "only doing our jobs." One official, a section chief, actually suggests that Jiang should complain about him more. Why? Because if Jiang does not complain, the higher-ups get the impression that the chief is being too soft on Jiang. "It would be better for me if you said bad things about me," the chief confides to Jiang.

Jiang experiences three different Chinese prisons (five, actually, if we count his earlier stay in Qincheng and a forty-five-day detention in 1994), explains some of the pros and cons among them, and makes it clear that all of them are dismal. We should note, though, that none of them is as harsh as the Mao-era prisons that Wang Ruowang, Zhang Xianliang, and other writers have described. In Mao's prisons, beatings, psychological torment, and chronic hunger were routine devices for controlling inmates. Jiang Qisheng is able to write with more "authorial distance" than memoirists of Mao's prisons could achieve. He can endure prison and reflect upon it at the same time, and the reflection brings him to insights about human rights, human dignity, and the relative importance of spiritual and material values that would have seemed luxurious thoughts to Mao-era prisoners, who of necessity were preoccupied with the next grain of rice (or yet-barely-green leaf, or captured toad). Jiang takes time to understand the life experiences of other inmates, who come from parts of Chinese society he had not encountered in his life outside of prison, and these exchanges extend his notions of the intrinsic dignity of all human beings.

Later people ask him if he has any regrets about choosing his course through life, when other routes obviously would in some ways have been much easier. He thinks it over and decides that, no, not only does he not regret his choices, he feels there is no doubt that they were better than the alternatives. By what other route could he have come to see the meaning of human life on this earth in such sharp relief? And what other values—how high an official position, for example, or exactly how many BMWs—could outweigh the appreciation of human dignity that his prison experience and human rights work have given to him?

In May 1991, shortly after Jiang emerged from his first stay in prison, he went home to Changshu to see his family and friends. In a moment of frankness one of his younger brothers said to him, "We know what happened in Beijing in 1989, and we know exactly what you did there. But I am your younger brother, and I would prefer not to see you do that again. I don't want to see you suffer again." Jiang answered his brother this way: "If I listen to you, and do as you say, then someone else will need to go do the things that I am no longer doing. But if that person has a good younger brother who advises him, too, not to do those things, and if he, too, listens, then who is going to do them?"

Perry Link

PART I

THE DETENTION CENTER

CHAPTER ONE

A Trip to the South

The year 1999 would not be a quiet one. As I put the finishing touches on my essay "Citizens' Movements: The Road to Freedom" and with my wife and son boarded the train in Beijing to go home to Wuxi for the New Year vacation, small waves of disturbance began to rise.

Soon after we had settled into our seats, I discovered that two plainclothes officers from the Beijing Public Security Bureau, who had been watching our home for some years, were also on the train. This had never happened before. I asked them why they were there, and they replied that the leadership had told them to escort us to Changshu. On arrival in Wuxi, where we stayed overnight with relatives, we found that the local police were on duty downstairs.

The next day, when my younger brother drove from Changshu to pick us up, two cars followed us closely all the way back. On the third day the authorities took the unprecedented step of sending a New Year's greeting letter to our door. Meanwhile, they contacted many of my old classmates and warned them not to see me. This unusual harassment led me to think that if I returned directly to the capital after the holidays, given the upcoming meetings of the National People's Congress and the Chinese People's Political Consultative Conference,* I would certainly be subject to special surveil-

* The NPC is China's legislative body but is usually considered a rubber-stamp entity that approves decisions made by the Communist Party. The CPPCC is a consultative body whose mandate is to advise the government. The two bodies meet in Beijing, usually in the spring and at the same time. When these meetings take place, security is tightened in Beijing and officialdom becomes more tense than usual.

lance of a more severe degree than in the past. Yet, like any normal person, I wanted freedom—freedom to move about and to see my friends, to be able to breathe without fear. So we decided that my wife and son would go to Suzhou before returning to Beijing, while I would visit friends in Shanghai, and then slowly continue my trip southward, fulfilling an ordinary citizen's dream of a March vacation.

On the morning I left alone for Shanghai, my brother drove my wife and son to Suzhou. The police, assuming that I was also in that car, tailed it all the way, and not until late in the day, when they had seen no sign of me, did they begin to spread a net to find me.

My own journey passed smoothly, and as soon as I arrived, I telephoned my friend Jiang Danwen. But when I went to his house the next morning, I discovered that the Shanghai police were now following me. So my "freedom excursion" was no sooner begun than it was brought to an end, and I sighed in deep disappointment.

At noon I went to a restaurant with several Shanghai friends. This was a new experience for them—eating a meal under the gaze of plainclothes special agents. Reluctant to cause them any further trouble, I decided to return to Changshu and think things over; if the police wanted to follow me, let them follow me to back to Changshu. As we finished our meal, we said goodbye and I calmly took a taxi to the Gongxing Road long distance bus station. As luck would have it, the flustered special agents were unable to track me. When I confirmed that I had once again regained my freedom I decided to go south to Hangzhou.

At eight o'clock in the evening I walked out of the Hangzhou train station and boarded a double-decker bus, and, in a seat on the upper level, I made my way westward at a relaxed pace under the beautiful night sky. Not wanting to use a telephone, I decided to go directly to friends' addresses. Although this might be more troublesome, it allowed me to enjoy their company unsupervised. Three days later I left for Nanchang and, while reading on the train, I was noticed by an assistant manager of a local factory who had been making cell phone calls one after another to conduct his business. We struck up a friendship and I was invited to move into the Nanchang Hotel that evening.

The next day, having bought a train ticket for Guangzhou, I began my first stroll through the streets of Nanchang. I went to Teng Wang Pavilion and had a taste of the famous *lihao* vegetable from the waters of Boyang Lake, and in the farmers' market I chatted with a cousin about family affairs. Coincidentally, I happened to see a copy of *Southern Weekend*, the front page of which featured photos of the chief of the Nanchang Public Security Bureau, who had just been arrested. At 4 p.m. I boarded the overnight southbound train to Guangzhou. In contrast to the relatively quiet bustle of Nanchang, as soon as I emerged from the Guangzhou train station I was in the midst of noisy crowds of people. After taking a moment to gather my wits, I caught a minibus for Shenzhen and reached the Nantou barrier at about 12:30 p.m. To enter Shenzhen one has to show an identity card and a border pass. I had two choices. Either I had to pay eighty yuan* to be escorted by one of the agents wandering about in front of the barrier looking for business, or I could contact a friend to come out and take me in. As I didn't trust the first option, I chose the second and called a People's University alumnus, Xia Hongyue, who came with his border pass and took me in with no difficulty.

This was the first time since my visit to Shenzhen in June of 1992 that I had set foot in this ever-changing city. Xia was my Ph.D. classmate from the class of 1988. He had received his Ph.D. in 1991, when he was only twenty-six years old. Since moving to Shenzhen he had worked in the United Front section of the Municipal Party Committee, in the Municipal Bureau of Industry and Commerce, and on the *Shenzhen Business News*. Thus he could be considered a *tiaocao boshi*, a Ph.D. holder who moves from one job to another to improve his position. Since I had arrived on the day of the Lantern Festival, I had dinner at Xia's home in Jingmi New Village with his parents and his wife and daughter. That night Xia arranged for me to stay at the Zhongshen Dasha on the North Ring Road.

My plan for Shenzhen was to get together with friends, do an interview, and in an easy and relaxed fashion enjoy myself and learn about the area. I wasn't on a dissident's trip; it was just a citizen's trip. The only friends that I would seek out would be People's University alumni; the only person I wanted to interview was He Qinglian, the author of *The Pitfalls of Modernization*; and my tourist activities would be simply to go wherever my footsteps led me.

One morning Xia and I had breakfast at the Xiangmi Lake Vacation Villa, then headed for Shenzhen University. The taxi entered the campus by the north gate and passed through grassy slopes and green trees, finally coming to a gentle stop. I got out, and without thinking about it, watched a motorcycle overtake the taxi and go around to our right, where the rider turned off the engine and leaned the cycle on its stand. When I glanced around again I saw a man who looked like a student, wearing glasses and carrying a book, who was standing behind us with a smile on his face. I was puzzled, but had not yet thought of special agents following me once more.

Xia and I set out on a small path, chatting as we walked. At this time of year Shenzhen was green and fragrant. As we reached a dormitory area of the campus, I looked around and saw that about thirty meters away there was that student-like man again. I knew right away that I was being followed, but

---

* The exchange rate at this time was roughly eight *yuan* (or *renminbi*) to one US dollar.

when I mentioned it to Xia, he couldn't believe it. This *tiaocao boshi* friend of mine had only seen student spies and special agents in movies set in the pre-1949 era; he had never witnessed the real thing. But I was battle-weary from my years of experience. I said I knew how to put him to the test. We could simply go to someplace where there were not many people about, then make several rounds from one place to another, and if this person was still behind us, then he was without doubt a tail.

In less than a minute we had the answer. We were both very angry. When would the authorities give up this silliness of thinking every bush and tree was an enemy soldier? Once again my dream of freedom had been spoiled by the specter of human rights violations.

As we left the Shenzhen University campus the two of us decided to see if we could lose the tail. As our taxi set off at a high speed, taking us eastward on University South Avenue, Xia saw in the rearview mirror that the agent was right behind us on his motorcycle. Xia told me that motorcycles were prohibited on this street. I said, "The rules don't apply to special agents." Later we stopped at the *Shenzhen Journal of Law* offices, and when we came out we again we took a taxi and purposely drove blindly from one place to another in the busy downtown area of the city, but the motorcyclist, and now also a Toyota minibus, still followed us like a shadow. At noon the two of us went into an underground fast food restaurant for lunch, and the agents came in quickly and looked around to see whether there might be another way out. When we finished eating I suggested that we separate and I would deal with the agents by myself. I thought I could trick them by running back the way I had come and taking unexpected turns on the pedestrian overpasses, but because I was not sufficiently familiar with the lie of the land, I finally gave it up in defeat and went back to my room. Over the next few days the two of us did succeed in losing the tail, but I still couldn't see my other old classmates, nor was I able to interview He Qinglian.

On the day I left Shenzhen, while I was buying a ticket for the boat to Zhuhai, where I wanted to get together with friends, I was detained by the authorities on a fabricated pretext and locked up in the police station. I immediately began a hunger strike to protest my arrest, and for the next three meals did not eat a single grain of rice. At 2:30 p.m. the next day three policemen arrived from Beijing under orders to "accompany" me in my travels around Guangdong and Guangxi and to see that I did not return to Beijing until the National People's Congress and the CPPCC meetings were concluded.

At certain times, "freedom," for those leading the quest for freedom, becomes the very thing that is most lacking.

CHAPTER TWO

~

Dark Clouds Appear

In the evening of 19 March I returned home. According to past practice, once the meetings of the "Two Congresses" were over, the plainclothes police from our district would be withdrawn and would not return to continue their surveillance until the middle of May. But it was different this year. Beginning in late March they would often appear, but from early May they were no longer below my apartment on the nineteenth floor but were hanging out around the gates of Capital Normal University. I did not assume that these inauspicious dark clouds were especially focused on me. In fact, not long after the Lunar New Year they had driven one of my close friends away and threatened another. The June 4th Incident was a big knot of anxiety for the authorities. As the tenth anniversary of the incident approached, they would surely do their utmost to prevent any protests or commemorations from taking place. But my conscience told me that we had no choice. No matter how great the risk, we must continue to seek justice, commemorating those who died and denouncing the murderous authorities.

In early April, I had drafted an open letter to all fellow citizens, titled "Light a Million Candles to Commemorate the Souls of the Heroes of June 4th." Meanwhile, an attempt by some eminent scholars and the mothers of students who had died in the June 4th crackdown to bring suit against Li Peng in the International Court of Justice* was being accelerated. The

* Li Peng was premier at the time of the June 4th Incident, and it was assumed that he gave the order for the military crackdown on the students who were demonstrating for democracy in Tiananmen Square.

distribution of my letter, together with June 4th signatory activities of Chinese people around the world increased the anxieties of the already nervous authorities, and the dark clouds of suppression began to move in.

Around the 7th of May, fellow activists brought a petition to my home. They had already gotten signatures from Xu Liangying and Wang Ruoshui, and I readily added my signature. I told them that I felt there was no turning back from my duty to take part in the commemoration of June 4th, and I would be happy to be liaison for Wang Dan's campaign for a million Chinese signatures. On the 11th of May my friend Cao Jiahe suddenly disappeared. Then on the 14th he came to my house again, having been beaten black and blue. He had been secretly taken by the authorities to a Beijing Public Security Bureau hostel and humiliated and beaten, leaving wounds and bruises all over his body. On May 12th, Yu Zhenbin had been taken to the same hostel and tortured in an effort to extract confessions and then forcibly taken to his hometown in Jiangxi. His entire savings from his past years of labor had been confiscated. When he returned to Beijing from Jiangxi on the 17th he recounted to me the details of the violence and violation of human rights that he had suffered at the hands of the police. In addition to feeling indignant, I was also somewhat puzzled because I thought that the authorities had in recent times given up such hypocritical use of physical violence against political dissidents. Now, after the signing of the International Human Rights Convention, were they going back to their old habits of vengeful ferocity? Was it anxiety? Insanity? I was determined that whatever happened, I would be neither humble nor arrogant but would go my own way.

Thinking back on it now, I should have seen that the arrival of two policemen who came to arrange an interview with me on 17 May was a veiled omen of unpleasant things to come. I was prepared to engage them in debate about the Falungong and the Kosovo incident, but they didn't say a word about these two matters. I gave them copies of several of my articles, including "Light a Million Candles" and "Thoughts on Reading the Newspapers on the Eve of May 4th." They accepted the essays but made no comment. Then they asked me, "with concern," if I was planning to leave Beijing in the near future? I assumed that this was something that their superiors had told them to ask me. Perhaps because of a guilty conscience, their attitude was very serious. Of course they knew that action was going to be taken against me, but if they disclosed this, they would lose their rice bowls, so they really couldn't speak out. They didn't know, or perhaps knew but couldn't believe, that I had been told that I would be arrested and that I wouldn't hide or run away. I didn't have the heroic feeling that to be arrested or locked up would fulfill my desires, but I did hold the belief of basic citizenship that "when it was time to go to jail I would go to jail." That is to say, when the time came for me to go to jail I would never shrink from it, but I would also not purposely seek arrest and declare "the more severe the punishment the better." Of course when one is in prison it is necessary to curry favor with those in charge and try to accommodate to the system; one must try hard to find a way to get by, regardless of how one disdains such actions.

CHAPTER THREE

~

A Sleepless Night

The 18th of May began as an ordinary day with clear blue skies of early summer. In the forenoon I studied and read aloud from *The World of English* magazine. In the afternoon Wang Linhai came to the university for a class and stopped by my place for a brief visit. A fax arrived from another friend in Xinyang, Henan. Shortly before 5 p.m. I went to the table tennis room and played ping pong with physical education teachers until six o'clock. On my way back home I paid special attention but saw no tail. At nightfall I put several articles in envelopes for friends in Changshu and Changsha, preparing to mail them out the next day. And I picked up the postal notification slip for the tea leaves that Fu Guoyong had mailed to me and stuck it into my pocket so that I could retrieve the package and have some of this year's fresh tea from Zhejiang. After 9 p.m. Chu Yanqing stopped by and while we were chatting I accepted a telephone interview call from Free Asia Television. As Chu Yanqing was leaving I gave him some copies of "Lighting the Candles," and around eleven o'clock I went to bed.

Before I had drifted off to sleep there was a knock at the door. I turned on the light and glanced at the clock on the wall: it was 11:30. A visitor in the middle of the night was sure to be the police. It was a People's Policeman named Gao from the Enjizhuang station. Since both my family and I were used to my being taken away in the middle of the night, I opened the door without hesitation. To my surprise, five or six police quickly crowded into the apartment. Then I realized that this was not good; they were really taking action now. I calmly got dressed, suppressing self-reproach and anguish about a recent diary that I now had no chance to hide. This would cause trouble for friends, especially those who had secretly helped us. As I walked out of the bedroom and went to the front of the apartment, I saw that my wife was already sitting up on the bed. Obviously aware of the seriousness of the situation, she called out, "When will you be back?" I wanted to say, "It won't be long," but then I saw that the group included a female police officer. They were going to undertake a search, and this meant that I would certainly not come back home soon. So I smiled but said nothing. I looked back at my wife, and my son, who had been awakened by the commotion, and I walked out of the apartment.

When I came down the stairs I saw that in addition to the four or five policemen closely surrounding me, standing out in the darkness were more than twenty others. I asked officer Gao, "Is it really necessary to mobilize such a big force just to deal with one little scholar?" He said, "Who knows what the higher-ups are thinking?" After a few minutes a convoy of seven or eight cars was organized and we arrived at the Enjizhuang police station. At the entryway I saw Chief Yu, head of the First Section of the Haidian District Bureau, but he pretended not to recognize me. As we passed the Criminal Affairs office, I was surprised to see that Chu Yanqing was being held there. They had brought him in more than an hour ago. I was taken to a room far back in the interior of the station. Soon an assistant chief named Zhai came in and solemnly read a formal summons for detention, and four or five officers started taking pictures. With the magnesium lights flashing, I allowed myself a slight sarcastic smile. Afterward, Song Aixin from the First Section of the Haidian Bureau began a routine interrogation, while personnel of Section eleven of the Municipal Bureau wandered back and forth.

After about an hour I was moved to the Criminal Affairs office, where I faced two people who said they were from the First Section of the Municipal Bureau. The one who began questioning me was a man of about fifty who wore glasses, was rather short, and didn't have much hair. He looked very civilized and had a leisurely manner of speaking. I speculated that he had long experience in police political affairs. I figured that he had just been busily going through the things taken from my home and was now ready to confront me. Although I despised the profession of political police, my habit had always been to show appropriate respect to every officer with whom I had contact, and our verbal exchange continued until daylight.

He began by saying that he had recently read my essay "Citizens' Movement: The Road to Freedom." Then he mentioned other essays of mine that he had read. When he said with a sigh, "I'm surprised that you seem so young," I responded, "That is why there is no need for me to say things that I don't believe. What do you think of my essays?" He looked away in embarrassment and changed the subject, saying that I was highly educated, able to use my head, and a prolific writer; surely I had written other essays. There must be a lot of articles that I had published under pseudonyms. I laughed aloud at that, and he continued his cross-examination, repeatedly coming back to two articles, my "Light a Million Candles" and Li Xiaoping's "Reflections on Peacefully Bringing about Fundamental Change in China's Social System." From his questions I quickly confirmed that they had found my diary, and this made me very anxious. I could only pray that my friends would forgive my carelessness, and at the same time, I swore that I must never again say anything that would bring harm to them. It was also clear to me from what he was saying that his boss was very angry about this "guiding principles" essay of Li Xiaoping's and that they were determined that the author must be exposed.

Around two or three o'clock in the morning someone called him out to "have a bite to eat." A People's Policeman named Zhang Hongyan came in and handed me my white jacket, saying, "It's late and getting cold. You'd better put it on." The People's Policeman Gao, who had been ordered to knock on my door, brought me a bowl of noodle soup, looking sheepish. After half an hour the "chief interrogator" came in again. His focus was still on Li Xiaoping and the tenth anniversary of June 4th. Right away he said that on careful consideration they had discovered that my views were extremely similar to his and they were forced to conclude that I was in fact Li Xiaoping. He then asked how I could explain this. I laughed and said, "You must know the expression 'heroes have similar views'!" He came right back with, "Can you introduce me to that hero?" I told him, "He is a professor, who knows me well but is younger than I am." "Well, what's his real name?" He was hoping I would speak frankly. I said, "He uses a pseudonym because he hopes to be promoted and he wants to keep the privilege of being able to leave and reenter the country freely. He and I are good friends. If I told you his name, it would harm him and I would lose my integrity. I wouldn't get mixed up in organizing a party, but I draw a line that I won't cross." Irritated, he immediately started to ridicule me, saying, "Do you think what you have done is not an important offense? Wang Dan is abroad promoting the campaign to get a million signatures for June 4th. As for yourself, quite apart from your writings, you are taking the lead as the contact person within the country. Are you a normal law-abiding person?" I said that I felt duty bound to commemorate June 4th; was this not very normal? When it comes to setting a limit on what one will do, an honorable man is not afraid of boiling water. He said sarcastically, "You came out of the philosophy department; I know I can't get the best of you in an argument." Then he started talking about the "scandals" of "those who are involved in the democracy movement abroad." Suddenly he mentioned several Changshu friends of mine who are now in ministerial level positions in Beijing. He mentioned their names one by one, watching to see how I would react. I thought to myself, they're really shrewd; they have gone through the name card box that I keep at home. My only comment was, "We all have our own aspirations," and he started talking about other things.

The interrogation went round and round, but all without result, and a dim daylight began to appear. He abandoned his gentle manner and, somewhat flustered and frustrated, said, "There are two final questions I want to ask you. First, we have all along suspected that Li Xiaoping is your pseudonym. Is it? Second, if we let you go home now, will you persist in commemorating June 4th?" I gave clear and definite answers to the two questions: "No," and "Of course." "Hai!" he retorted. "So you still want to go ahead with the commemoration!" And he turned and walked out.

CHAPTER FOUR

~

In Section Seven

The sleepless night of 18 May had passed and the sun was shining into the small courtyard.

At a little after 10 a.m. the man who had interrogated me all night came into the room and said, "We'll move to a different place and continue our chat," and I left through the front gate of the station with three men from Section One of the Municipal Police Bureau. We got into a light blue sedan and, with the hazard lights flashing, sped away southeastward through the city. On the Second Ring Road South the car turned north into a narrow neighborhood lane, and suddenly high walls, electrified netting, and a sentry box appeared before our eyes. I immediately speculated that this must be the so-called Number 44 Banbuqiao, where suspects in important cases were held. The car entered the compound through the west gate, which was standing wide open, and drove another forty meters before stopping outside a big iron gate that was shut tight. There were two signs hanging on this gate. One read "Beijing Detention Center," and the other "Branch Office of the Beijing Municipal Procuratorate." I waited in the car for more than half an hour, then Section One personnel took me to a small iron gate for entry on foot, and under the gaze of armed police I stepped into a world where I would be completely without freedom.

I was quickly taken to a preliminary hearing room on the second floor of a building. The Beijing Public Security Bureau's Preliminary Hearing Unit, also known as Section Seven, is within the Detention Center. "Section Seven" is commonly used to refer to both the Preliminary Hearing Unit and the Detention Center. I remember that when I was locked up in the Westside Jail in 1994, people in custody there would turn pale at the mention of being "posted to Section Seven." This hearing room was not very big and was dirty and disorderly. While a policeman who appeared to be in his late twenties watched me, the several officers from Section One who had been escorting me turned and left without a word and did not reappear. Missing my family and feeling concern for my friends, I looked around and sat down on a wooden chair.

Suddenly something unexpected, though quite reasonable, happened. The man who was watching over me asked what I was in for. I said that I had written an essay about the tenth anniversary of the June 4th Incident. I saw a change in the expression on his face, and right away he said, "To tell the truth, I really respect you fellows who are willing to go to jail for your beliefs, like Wei Jingsheng and Wang Dan."* He spoke with a sincerity that left no room for doubt, though I was very surprised at his boldness. I was completely unknown to him, yet he dared to speak so frankly to me. I said to him, "Yesterday evening I told foreign interviewers that I was willing to go to jail to promote freedom of speech." Then I asked him his name, but he mumbled, "Let's talk about it after you get out." After a little while he brought me some fried cakes and some beef, and I realized that I was indeed hungry.

In the afternoon I was taken into custody by the Criminal Police.

At nightfall, my belt, wallet, and leather shoes were taken away and my key ring and driver's license booklet were confiscated. Then after passing through yet another iron gate guarded by armed police, I entered the inner courtyard for detained criminal suspects and was taken to cell 313 in area three, and I began another special life as a prisoner.

---

* Wei Jingsheng was sentenced to fifteen years in prison for his leadership in the short-lived "Democracy Wall" experiment in Beijing in 1978. Wang Dan was one of the leaders of the June 4th, 1989, Tiananmen protests. Arrested twice, he gained early release, earned a Ph.D. in history at Harvard, and now makes appearances around the world in support of democracy for China.

CHAPTER FIVE

~

Maintaining One's Dignity

Anyone who has just been thrown into the Detention Center is faced with three problems. First is the matter of how to deal with interrogation tactics designed to wear you out by using a revolving team of interrogators who question you at any time of the day or night. Second, you must learn how to live peacefully with your fellow prisoners. And third is to find a way to minimize the damage to your health from the sudden decline in living conditions. Of course I was no exception to the rule, but there was another special problem for me, namely, how to maintain the dignity of a prisoner of conscience.

Section Seven had a special policy requiring that whenever a prisoner was taken out of his cell he could not walk erect and look straight ahead but must clasp his hands over his head and wear an expression of wretchedness, maintaining this posture all the way to the interrogation room. This demeanor must also be maintained on the return trip, right up until his cell door clanged shut behind him. I learned this when I entered the lockup at nightfall on May 19th, and I immediately felt that I could not accept this policy. Such a rule would injure the dignity of any criminal suspect, not to mention its effect on someone who was purely a political prisoner. That evening when I was taken out, at 9 p.m., I decided that I would not obey the rule. I stepped out the door and stood in the hallway. The guard escorting me turned around and barked an order: "Hands on your head!" With my reaction already prepared, I smiled and quietly replied, "I'm here for writing an essay. Is this really necessary?" He grunted a quiet acknowledgment and said no more.

The next morning I made a formal request to one of the interrogators, saying that this rule was an insult to human dignity and asking him to inform the wardens of my opinion. In the afternoon, Warden Wang came to take me out of my cell and asked, "Do you really consider this matter important?" I said, "Yes. I cannot accept it." Appearing embarrassed, he said, "We have many guards here and they are all used to this procedure. It wouldn't be convenient for me to speak to each one of them." I told him that I could handle it myself. Over the next few days each time I encountered a different guard I used the same method to counter their shouted orders. After I got to know them they would chat a bit with me each time we came together. My fellow prisoners were very envious of the way I was treated, but they didn't dare to try my methods themselves.

One other thing that I could not comply with was recitation of the "Detention Center Regulations." It was a rule in Section Seven that every prisoner must endure this. Even those who were illiterate had to get help from others to do it. One or two days after entering the prison they would take you out for a test, and every morning at eight o'clock (except on weekends) prisoners would gather for a group recitation, going through it twice. On May 20th I carefully read the set of prison regulations that was posted in a wooden frame on the wall. It was exactly the same "edition" as what I had seen when I was in the Qincheng prison ten years ago, still preserving the same misprinted characters that offended my eye then. But even more questionable was that these regulations were based on the principle of "assumed guilt," treating all detained persons as "criminals." For example, rule number two is: "I must strictly abide by the study system, try hard to rectify my thinking, maintain an upright attitude, thoroughly confess my crimes and seek out the reasons for them, and actively expose all criminal behavior. In order to gain compassionate treatment I will renounce all past evil and become a new person."

I said to the interrogator, "These regulations are long out of date and should be revised. Asking me to recite something like this is like telling me to eat a dead fly; it really turns my stomach!" His response was, "Well whether you recite it or not is up to you, but we can't do anything about revising it."

I also made the request to the wardens. Warden Wang said that they wouldn't demand that I recite it but they still had to require it of the others. Thereafter, every time I heard the recitations, which sounded like elementary school students chanting their morning routine, I would close my eyes and try to refresh my spirit, involuntarily thinking of my fellow citizens' slave mentality. They were still unwilling to take a half step forward on behalf of their own rights and dignity. I thought: They actually don't want to recite, but they don't dare refuse to do it. Why couldn't they at least lower their voices a bit? Or couldn't they play at being Mr. Nanguo (a man of the Warring States period, 475–221 BCE, who couldn't play an instrument but faked his way into the king's orchestra by pretense)? Or at the very least, they shouldn't put so much effort into it, enunciating so clearly, as if each one of them wanted to show more obedience than the others.

CHAPTER SIX

~

Verbal Tussles during Preliminary Examination

At 2 p.m. on 19 May Examiner Pang Jiang and Secretary Song Junjie arrived for duty and with some relaxed conversation began the opening scene of the "battle to exhaustion."

Pang Jiang remarked, "You look very much like Wang Jiawei. Oh, no, I should say Wang Jiawei looks like you." I laughed and said, "If we look alike, it's probably because we are both southerners. He grew up in Shanghai and I grew up in Changshu, so we were both subject to the influences of that area." Then after some more bantering about how I looked much younger than my real age, and so on, his expression turned solemn and he showed me the order for my detention. It was not until later, June 26th, that he showed me the warrant for my arrest, also in connection with some light conversation. But to tell the truth, I felt that he was really not bad, nor was he especially leftist. However, the role that he was playing determined the fundamental key of our conflict and the way our verbal tussles would continue to play out.

One of the focal points of our verbal battles was the question of whether I must "respond factually" to all of his questions. Because current law stipulated that I had the duty of responding factually, he was sure he had the answer to this question. My response was that according to the concept of human rights, I had the right to remain silent. He said, "I'm not concerned about human rights; there is no such provision in the law." I demurred, "This shows that China's legal code is backward and needs to be revised." He replied, "So far it hasn't been revised, so we have to act accordingly." "But that," I pointed out "will depend on what questions you ask." He said, "I know what I should ask." I answered, "Everything I have done on the outside is in accord with the human rights of a citizen; none of it was anything that the police should question or be concerned about." He then snapped, "What I should or shouldn't do is none of your business. My responsibility now is to question you, and you have to reply." I said, "I have the right to decide when I should pay attention to you and when I needn't listen to you."

The second point of contention in the verbal battle was whether I should say anything that involved other people. My aim was to say nothing. Whether I knew the answers to questions involving others or not, I would not respond. Pang ridiculed this attitude, saying, "This is just an excuse for protecting yourself." I objected, "You can think so if you like, but for my part, I cannot betray my friends." In a further effort to provoke me, he said, "You don't really believe this; you're being hypocritical." I replied, "You don't understand me, but I am clear about the following: if I show the 'proper attitude' and talk about other people's affairs, the price I pay will be that for the rest of my life I will not be at peace with my conscience. Do you think I could do that? You can think what you like about whether I am hypocritical or not, but there is one thing I want you to remember: for this 'attitude of resistance' I am willing to spend additional years in jail." It must be acknowledged that he later compromised on this and apologized, saying, "You aren't a hypocrite. I was wrong about you. You don't have to talk about other people's affairs. You can just talk about your own."

The third bone of contention was whether I should be willing to discuss matters that concerned only myself. His view was that a real man dares to act and has the courage to take responsibility for his actions; once having acted, he should be willing to talk about his actions. My view was that it depends on whom I am speaking to. I said, "If you and your colleagues are impartially carrying out the law, of course I can speak to you. But if your aim is deliberately to harm me, then wouldn't I just be helping you do this? Do you think I would be so foolish?" His response was, "Haven't your actions been undertaken openly? Therefore why would you not speak of them?" I said, "The fact that something doesn't have to be kept secret doesn't mean that it necessarily must be told. The key to whether I speak of something is whether I think it is necessary, whether I want to tell it. In court there is an 85 percent chance that I would tell." He asked, "Then have you determined not to speak here?" I replied, "You have my diary. What else do you need to ask?" He said, "Those are two separate matters." Later, under the force of his combined soft and hard tactics, there were several times when I gave in and told him of the signed articles that I had written.

The fourth point was whether I could see my lawyer. On the afternoon of 19 May Pang told me that according to the law, I now had the right to retain a lawyer. I immediately asked for pen and paper and wrote a full power of attorney and handed it to him. What I wrote was, "I hereby authorize my wife, Ms. Zhang Hong, to retain Messrs. Zhang Sizhi and Li Huigeng as my defense attorneys." I asked him on the 20th and again on the 21st whether he had sent out my power of attorney. He mumbled something but did not give me a direct answer. It was clear that they were simply holding my document. I angrily protested: "What kind of game are you playing? You are trampling on my rights and hypocritically using this as a fig leaf to cover your shame!" He shrugged this off, "According to the law, you may retain a lawyer, but we have other rules." I said, "What are your rules? Your rules cannot contradict the law!" He said, "Don't ask me anymore. No matter how often you ask, I won't tell you anything." My right to retain a lawyer had been illegally taken from me by bullying and power politics.

The fifth point of contention was whether they were "handling the case according to the law" or indulging in illegal political persecution, carrying out a literary inquisition. The interrogator claimed repeatedly that his only objective was to "handle the case according to the law." If this were really true, then he could examine his conscience in the stillness of the night without feelings of guilt and self-recrimination. But if he was being used to carry out a literary inquisition and create new cases of injustice, that was a very different matter. As a political prisoner, I was determined to uncover the realities of the case and launch a counterattack against the persecutors. The interrogator was my true target, the one who must bear my criticism and attacks. I felt that the term "literary inquisition" named the crucial point of this case and would stir up both the interrogator and those behind him who heard his reports. Before dawn on 21 May the interrogator and his superior officer came to me and demonstrated their irritation. The interrogator said in a pitiless voice, "This time we will deal with you!" His superior added with even less mercy, "We wanted to deal with you several years ago. Those who are trying to organize a democratic party have to be caught, and you also have to be caught! You have no freedom of speech here! Taking forceful measures against you has been carefully considered. You'd better understand this!" I replied, "I quite understand. But I haven't closed my eyes for sixty-eight hours. I've decided that from now on I will not answer any of your questions!" Then I closed my eyes and pretended to sleep. I heard them continuing to make useless speeches back and forth, and finally the battle to wear me out drew to a close.

CHAPTER SEVEN

Peaceful Coexistence with Fellow Prisoners

There were already twenty-one detainees in cell 313 when I came into it. Although I had had the experience of being locked up in the Westside Jail, conditions here were not entirely the same. The biggest difference was that most of the men held in Section Seven were facing one of three sentences: life imprisonment, suspended death sentences, or death. These were people such as I had never before encountered. In addition, those who were in for murder or rape wore four- or five-kilogram iron shackles on their ankles twenty-four hours a day. This was the first time in my life I had eaten and slept with such people. There were nine men who wore shackles. Of these nine, three were charged with injury resulting in death, five with premeditated murder, and one was charged with murder during a robbery. There was also a second year high school student named Wang Hui who was accused of causing injury leading to death. Because he was not yet an adult he was not shackled. Of the nine men who wore shackles, Wang Yan had also been fitted with metal handcuffs that held his two wrists closely together. Once handcuffed, he could not dress or undress himself. Furthermore, the handcuffs were linked to his shackles with a chain so short that he could not stand up straight but had to move around in a stooped posture. Making a man live curled up like a shrimp this way was the ultimate in punishment by restraint. Wang Yan had been involved in a violent fight that occurred in cell 310 at about two o'clock in the morning on 29 March 1999. After the fight was stopped, all of those involved were severely beaten and then moved to other cells. By coincidence, there had also been a violent fight in cell 313 back in 1993 in which a prisoner had been killed by an armed prison guard. We could still make out faint scars from the bullets on the north wall of the cell.

Aside from the ten men listed above, others were charged with kidnapping, drug dealing, theft, and possession of stolen goods. There were also five men charged with serious economic crimes, of whom Zhang Liming and Huo Haiyin were appointed monitor and assistant monitor by the disciplinary officer to keep order in the cell.

As a mere scholar and an ideologue, how could I achieve peaceful coexistence with them? Amid the clanging of their chains, I felt a certain self-confidence. I would explain my status and act honestly, hoping that I could turn bad luck into good and everything would be all right.

When I told them that I had been arrested because I had written an essay commemorating the tenth anniversary of June 4th, they immediately gave me a bold and resonant sobriquet: Political Prisoner! What the authorities were painstakingly determined to eliminate, here received unequivocal and unanimous support. I understood that this appellation carried special respect. As they expressed it, "You are the only one who is not here because of money!" It also showed their understanding. As they put it, "We always need someone who dares to stand up and speak out!" And it implied sympathy, saying, "We were caught because our turn had come, but you are really suffering injustice."

As we were eating the next day, the Uighur, Ablimit, sat close on my right side. In awkward Mandarin, he said, "Wang Hui told me that you are different from the rest of us; you are not a bad person."

When we were let out for exercise, they all crowded around to talk to me. Zou Guigen, who had made his living at a fruit stand in Chongwen District, talked to me about Radio Free Asia. He could recite the toll-free phone number of the station backwards and forwards. Huo Haiyin talked about his trip to Paris. He had had dinner there with the Wan Runnan family. Sun Baocang talked about Tiananmen Square ten years ago. His work unit had sent many truckloads of food and drinks to the square for the students. Ma Huijun told me about his time in the Number Two Prison, where some years before he had met Wang Dan. Others talked about the possibility of a general pardon. They really hoped that the Communist Party would declare an amnesty in honor of the fiftieth anniversary of their coming to power. But I couldn't deceive them, and when I said, "There is no hope for an amnesty; what is more likely is a severe crackdown," they suddenly jumped up and angrily shouted, "American missiles hit the embassy in Yugoslavia. Too bad they didn't do it right and strike the headquarters of our corrupt officials!"

Several days later Chen Jun told me about his impressions when I first came into the cell. He said that when he saw a man who appeared to be thirty-some years old come in holding his head high he at first thought I was a policeman making a surprise check of the cell. But then he noticed that I was carrying my clothes and other items, and decided I must be a secret agent planted by the authorities. I asked him why he would have these strange ideas, and he said it was because I wasn't holding my head in my hands and looking down at the ground. "If you had had the pitiful sheepish look of the rest of us, I wouldn't have thought anything of it." When he finished talking, we looked at each other and had a big laugh.

CHAPTER EIGHT

~

Avoiding Self-Pity

Beginning on the 19th of May my living conditions underwent a precipitous decline.

First was the question of food. At home, for breakfast I would have pickled vegetables in rice porridge with a poached egg. Lunch would be scrambled eggs and tomatoes, pickled-vegetable soup, and a big bowl of noodles. The whole family got together for dinner, which would usually be three dishes and a soup, with rice. The three dishes would be either two meat dishes and one vegetable, or two vegetable dishes and one meat. I did the cooking. Sometimes I would also have a little liquor with American ginseng soaked in it. But what did we eat in prison? Breakfast was a bowl of cornmeal gruel with a coarse cornmeal bun and two or three pieces of salted vegetable. The noon and evening meals were the same: two cornmeal buns and a bowl of cabbage soup with a few spatterings of oil floating on it. If we were lucky we might find a few pieces of ground pork about the size of a mung bean. Tuesday, Thursday, Saturday, and Sunday were better, with two steamed wheat-flour buns replacing the cornmeal buns. This food was not as good as what I had in the Qincheng prison ten years ago, and it was far inferior to what a lot of pigs and dogs eat nowadays. For someone who had just come into the Detention Center and had no money of his own to buy something to eat at the prison snack shop, his intake of calories and nutrition took a sharp drop, and the resulting damage to his health is easy to imagine.

Sleeping arrangements were as follows: The cell was 11 meters long by 3 meters wide, providing 33 square meters of space. Within this, the raised sleeping platform was 11 meters by 2 meters, for 22 square meters of space, and the remaining 11 square meters was concrete floor. Of the twenty-two men in cell 313, sixteen of them slept on the platform and six on the floor. I was told to sleep on the platform. However, the quality of sleep was not by any means guaranteed. The first problem was that two light bulbs burned day and night. And then there were always people getting up in the night to relieve themselves, creating large or small disturbances. And there was the snoring, alternating from one fellow to another. Zhang Liming was especially bad. His snoring was like thunder, and it seldom stopped. In my quiet home I hardly ever had trouble sleeping, but when I suddenly found myself in these circumstances I tossed and turned and had great difficulty getting some peaceful sleep.

The question of space for activity was also very important. Locking a person up in jail is like putting a jungle animal into a zoo. The space for exercise is extremely limited, putting a great strain on both body and mind. I am a very active person. In the summer I swim every day, and in spring, fall, and winter I like to play an hour of table tennis. Sometimes on a Friday evening I would go with my wife to the Number 304 Hospital dance hall and dance. During our son's summer vacations, the three of us like to go on sightseeing excursions. We have been to Mt. Emei, Mt. Wutai, the Changbai mountains, and Mt. Wuyi, and we have taken trips to the Three Gorges and Jiuzhaigou National Park. We have visited the Yongding Hakka Village and Chrysanthemum Island in the Bo Sea. Now I am confined in a steel cage and let out for exercise at most twice a week. And this "outdoor" exercise space is actually another cage, 5.5 by 3.5 meters, and covered by steel mesh at a height of 2.8 meters, so that even if one could sprout wings, it would not be possible to fly away.

After a few days my health began to deteriorate. I lost my appetite, eating only one cornmeal bun at each meal. I became constipated and had only one bowel movement every three days, and my anus became irritated. My eyelids were heavy all day long. I had been mentally prepared for prison, but that did not stop the steady decline of my physical health. In order to reduce the harm to my health as much as possible, and especially to avoid any possible irreversible effects of these conditions, I settled on two measures. First was to buy some supplementary food so as to improve my nutrition a little. Second, I established an attitude of acceptance of my imprisonment so as not to fall into a state of self-pity. The first ten days, I would remind myself every day that I was not a person easily deflected from my course by good or bad fortune, and therefore I should be able to bear jail time.

Later on, the hemorrhoids subsided without treatment, and my eyelids were no longer heavy. At the beginning of October, every morning before breakfast I would exercise with "dumbbells"—big soda pop bottles filled with salt—and over a period of a couple of months my chest muscles became noticeably more prominent. And because I was eating apples, I was no longer constipated. Whenever we were let out for exercise I practiced *mogao*—jumping and reaching as high as possible. This was good exercise for my legs, and I was soon one of the two best at *mogao* in the cell. By March 2000 my thighs were not noticeably thinner than before. On the first of March I was happy to see that I could stand a cold water bath without grinding my teeth. However, the hair on my right temple was turning gray, probably due to lack of certain vitamins, and fishtail wrinkles began to appear at the corners of my eyes. All of this was a part of the price that one had to pay for being in prison. I would have to go on living, as my family and friends wanted me to do, trying to get a good night's sleep every night and get through the day with strength. I thought of a line from a song: "Each day without you, I treasure you even more." The future would confirm that I succeeded in this.

CHAPTER NINE

~

Death and Life by the Wall

I sensed that I would be in cell 313 of the Detention Center for a long time, probably right up until I was transferred to prison. I reasoned that because the authorities did not want me to come into contact with more prisoners, they would not transfer me to another holding cell. Therefore I decided to make use of my time by interviewing my cellmates one by one. Aside from those who were in for economic crimes, all the others came from the lowest or most marginal levels of society. I felt that whether from the point of view of accommodating to the environment or for social studies significance, I wanted to know them, to understand their inner worlds and hear their views on life and society. And they were happy to talk with me, taking advantage of this opportunity to give voice to their confusion, suffering, hatred, and repentance, and, finally, raising the question of how to succeed in their trials. These talks could only be held after dinner, when we were no longer required to sit in our assigned places on the sleeping platform.

When I was not engaged in the interviews I began to take part in making a Chinese chess set. There was already one set in the cell so I worked on a second set. The procedure was to cut toothpaste boxes into small squares and write Chinese characters on them. I was very good at this. The chess board was drawn on a small piece of cloth. After a few days, when my wife brought me some money, I bought some bedding for a hundred yuan, and when it arrived, replaced the two quilts that I had been using with the new ones, and I felt that I was "settled" in cell 313.

At 1:30 in the afternoon of 16 June the cell door was suddenly opened, and Warden Wang announced that all but five of us should pack up our things. Five minutes later, I said some quick good-byes and, together with the sixteen others, set out for area four with our belongings. Area four was also known as the "death area" where inmates charged with capital crimes were detained. We wondered why we were being brought here. After trekking through a long, deathly quiet corridor, the sixteen of us were brought to a stop in front of cells 401 through 404. After a brief wait, Wu Chaoyang, Liu Shihai, Chen Jun, and I entered cell 404, but Chen Jun was soon moved to another cell because one of his accomplices was in this one. It soon became clear that cells 401 through 404 were treated as an extension of area three. On April 19th, the twenty or so inmates in 404 had been moved as a group from cell 306. The ten cells from 405 to 414 held inmates charged with capital crimes. Each cell held eight to ten prisoners, all of them wearing shackles and handcuffs, regardless of whether they were charged with violent crimes, economic crimes, selling drugs, or trafficking in human beings. In addition, in order to guarantee tight control over the prisoners charged with capital crimes, they were paired, one by one, with "partners," convicted criminals who were serving relatively short sentences, usually for complicity in major cases, such as harboring criminals or possessing stolen goods. In cell 404, I was so close and yet so far from the capital inmates of 405, separated only by the wall. Later I learned that we had been moved to area four because cell 313 had been reassigned to hold juvenile inmates, and I had thus wound up beside the real life-or-death wall, the border between darkness and light, and I would spend a period here that would be an unforgettable life experience.

I was not surprised to find that the cell monitor, assistant monitor, and all the men in cell 404 openly welcomed me and accepted me into the group. The assistant monitor, Hu Xuezhong, a husky fellow around forty years old, was charged with "harboring," that is, covering for wrongdoers or hiding stolen goods. As soon as I sat down on the sleeping platform, he started talking with me in a loud voice about Wei Jingsheng and the Xidan Democracy Wall. Later, on the afternoon of 29 September, he was released without having undergone criminal punishment. Only one or two percent of the prisoners in Section Seven achieved this good fortune. An inmate named Hua Yan was accused of smuggling Ericsson equipment. When he heard that I had studied atmospheric dynamics in college, he wanted to talk about Base Number 29 of the National Defense Science and Engineering Institute in Mianyang, Sichuan. His parents had worked there and he had lived in Mianyang for more than ten years when he was growing up. The

Chinese Research Center for Atmospheric Dynamics was there. When he had returned to Beijing with his parents, his father had gone to work at the *Science and Technology Daily* newspaper, and there he had gotten to know Mr. Sun Changjiang. Sun was now teaching at Capital Normal University and living in building 24 and was thus a neighbor of mine. In the summer of 1998 I had gone together with professors Ding Zilin and Jiang Peikun to call on him. Wang Kequan was charged with falsifying contracts. He had spent some time together with Fang Jue in cell 307. He told me, "Six months after Fang Jue was arrested, the authorities told him that if he would sign an affidavit of repentance he would be released, but he firmly refused."

Later the authorities found another solution to the problem and sentenced Fang Jue to four years in prison for unlawful operation of a business. Our chief monitor, thirty-five-year-old Tie Qi, was charged with financial swindling. He said to me, in a quiet voice, enunciating every word clearly, "Don't we have freedom of speech? How can someone be arrested just for telling the truth?" What he said was almost the same as what was said by Zhang Lei of cell 313, who was brought in later. Zhang Lei, a twenty-five-year-old from Fengtai, had been brought into Section Seven, charged with causing injury to others. Several days earlier he had said to me, "It's only guys like you who can be counted as having guts. We only express our hatred to ordinary people, but you dare to say no to the bigwigs." The next day I told them how on the night of June 4th, from midnight till 3:00 a.m. I had stood in silent commemoration of the June 4th martyrs. Then I recited for them my letter to the nation, "Light a Million Candles to Commemorate the Souls of the Heroes of June 4th." After listening to this, many of them asked me, "Teacher, after I get out, can I come back to be a political prisoner with you?"

CHAPTER TEN

Looking on the Bright Side

Serving time in jail is not necessarily all bad. To me, there are four important benefits in prison life.

First is the matter of regular hours. We always hear that early to bed, early to rise is beneficial to one's health, but this is very hard to achieve on the outside. For many years I went to bed late and got up late in the morning, and I couldn't change this habit. But inside, we always go to bed at nine and get up the next morning at six thirty. This is the same for everybody, with no exceptions. And I was secretly happy that 12:00 to 1:30 p.m. was obligatory naptime, making it possible for me to continue my noon nap habit.

Second was sleeping on a hard surface. I had always liked to sleep on a hard board, but my wife didn't like it, so as a compromise we used a firm mattress. Once in prison, there was only the hard board, and as the under-quilt was very thin, I got what I wanted at no expense.

Third was bathing in cold water. Drinking water was brought to us twice a day, and there was not so much as a drop of hot water for washing our faces or bathing. Throughout the four seasons everybody had to bathe in cold water. On the outside we often hear about the benefits of taking cold baths, but how many of us actually do it? Even in the middle of the summer, we take hot showers, yelling out if the water is just a little bit chilled. But here we had no choice. From May to September I was happy with the cold baths, but from October to the following March I bathed only once every ten days or more because the water in Section Seven was really too cold—you couldn't splash water on yourself without grinding your teeth. Still, although bathing was painful, once you dried yourself off, you felt very refreshed. And no one ever caught a cold from bathing.

The fourth benefit was that I couldn't eat anything that would burn my mouth. From my childhood I had loved to eat my food very hot. I felt that some foods just didn't have any flavor unless they were hot. But my wife didn't approve of this habit of mine; she said it could cause throat cancer. Of course I accepted her reasoning, but it was very hard for me to change my habit. Sometimes I would burn my tongue into insensitivity. After that I would be careful for a few days, but then before long I would forget about it and go back to my old ways. Now I didn't have to worry. Hot vegetable soup was poured from the cooking pot in the kitchen into large containers to be delivered to the cells, then poured through a big funnel into the buckets provided by each cell, and then dipped into each prisoner's plastic bowl. After this process, we were lucky if the soup retained even a little warmth. There was no danger of burning our mouths, and of course any anxiety about throat cancer vanished like a mist.

In prison we often heard, "The Public Security Bureau cures all illnesses." Of course this was an exaggeration, but it was not entirely without logic. As I understood it, for those who were addicted to cigarettes or alcohol, and who couldn't resist sensual pleasures, or people who couldn't bring order into their daily lives, spending time in prison was very effective in curing their afflictions. There were more than a few of them who actually gained weight while in jail.

Aside from these four benefits, I also gained a special appreciation for the saying, "It's better to do something yourself than to ask others for help." When you're in prison your fingernails and your whiskers keep growing. What can you do about your fingernails? Use nail clippers. But when would the guards give you nail clippers? Sometimes they wouldn't bring them for a whole month, and when they did come, with more than twenty people in the cell, the clippers might be taken back before your turn arrived. So we would use a more primitive method—file our nails on the concrete walls. Harmless and painless; very efficient. But what about the whiskers? You wouldn't want to go into court with stubble on your face. This could be seen, favorably, as "letting one's beard grow for a special purpose" or else as "a scruffy rat in a cage." But the problem of whiskers was different from fingernails. The guards would definitely not give us a razor. So we developed a special procedure—plucking the whiskers. Each cell had a homemade "whisker pluck," made by fastening a pair of toothpaste tops tightly together with a rubber band, creating tweezers of two tiny disks. The first time my whiskers were plucked, it was done by my cellmate Chen Lianmin. Since my whiskers were those of a thirty-year-old, the stubble was quite coarse, and after the plucking was done, the follicles where the hairs had been pulled out oozed blood, and especially in the most sensitive triangular area under the lip, for each whisker plucked, a tear rolled down my cheek. I could only grind my teeth and bear it. After that, I did it myself. Soon after a fine hair broke through the skin I would pull it, reducing the pain considerably. Thus, except for haircuts, I could take care of matters of personal hygiene myself, with no need to ask others for help. Plucking whiskers and bathing in cold water were linked together as two painful aspects of cell life.

CHAPTER ELEVEN

~

The White Hole of Human Rights

According to Einstein's theory of relativity, the universe contains black holes from which matter cannot escape. There are also supposed to be white holes, where matter cannot be confined but completely dissipates. A white hole of rights is thus a state in which no rights can be retained. The men held in Section Seven were in a white hole of human rights.

First was the question of personal rights. Needless to say, personal freedoms had been stripped away by the law. Then what about the right to keep one's person inviolate? In truth there was no guarantee of this. We should acknowledge that men in Section Seven were not often beaten during detention or preliminary investigation; however, this was not because the guards were concerned about human rights but rather because beatings were no longer needed. The great majority of men held in Section Seven had already suffered severe beatings administered by the arresting police, or in the precinct or drug investigation unit, "as necessary to solve the case," and had already had their confessions recorded. Once they arrived in Section Seven, as long as they didn't recant their confessions they would not be beaten by the preliminary investigators. However, if they did recant their confessions, the interrogators would do whatever was necessary "to bring the case to a satisfactory conclusion." For example, Chen Xianglong recanted his confession and suffered cigarette burns inflicted by the interrogators, and when Li Jiting withdrew his previous statement, the interrogators whipped him on the back with bamboo strips until he once again accepted it. Usually beatings in the Detention Center would occur if inmates broke prison rules, as when Li Yaping received fifty or sixty slaps on the face for climbing on the water pipes in the toilet, while Zhang Tieying was severely beaten for breaking a window.

And then there is the privilege of reading books and newspapers. In the lockup there was hardly anything to read, only a few martial arts novels that had been sneaked in by the work unit. Now and then there would be some books that inmates' family members had simply mailed to Section Seven and the wardens, in a merciful mood, and after inspection, had allowed them to be kept in the cell. A special absurdity was that there were no texts having to do with the law. There were not even any copies of *The Penal Code* or *Criminal Lawsuits*. (We were, however, allowed to see television presentations such as *Criminal Law* and *Criminal Lawsuits*.) Under ordinary circumstances, in any given week we could see two or three days' newspapers. But whenever there was anything that was "inappropriate for inmates," the wardens would withhold those pages. From late October 1999 to late March 2000, because the authorities were cracking down on Falungong, arresting those who did the exercises and locking them up, there were no newspapers to be seen in the prison. During this time, television was also almost entirely shut down for us. Even in ordinary times, we were only allowed to watch the movie channels; we were seldom allowed to see news programs.

Third is the privilege of being let out of the cell for exercise. With more than twenty men crowded into one cell, the odors from our sweaty bodies, farts, and the toilet were really hard to bear. Therefore our outdoor exercise time was especially important. And in fact the law stipulated that we should be let out for one hour every day. But in actuality, we were never let out on Saturdays and Sundays, and seldom on Mondays and Fridays. On average we could only expect to be let out twice a week for an hour or so each time. In other words, five-sevenths of our exercise time was taken from us. On December 1st, 1999, the door from cell 404 to the exercise pen became stuck and could not be opened. Getting it repaired should have been a very simple matter. The Detention Center could simply have placed a phone call and gotten a man to come and fix it. But it was not until the 16th of the month that someone was finally called to do the repairs. This shows that our exercise time was considered quite insignificant. If the problem had been that the door couldn't be *closed*, allowing us to go in and out at will, everybody in the cell knew that a repairman would come running within minutes to ensure that we fulfilled our duty to stay in the cell.

Fourth, consider the right to see a lawyer during the investigative phase of confinement. Section 96 of *Criminal Suits* clearly states that persons under arrest have the right to seek legal assistance. But 99 percent of arrestees are deprived of this right. Furthermore, the responsible parties know that they have nothing to fear and don't care in the least about it.

Finally, let's have a look at the Ministry of Public Security's *Standards of Behavior for Persons Held in the Detention Center*. The section on rights is very strange. In the forty-three "standards" clauses, the word "must" appears fifteen times, "must not" appears twelve times, "not permitted" thirty-seven times, and "strictly forbidden" once. Prisoners are forbidden even to give anything to each other. In order to ensure that these "standards" are maintained, two surveillance devices are installed in each cell—one in the speaker box of the cell and the other on the wall in the toilet, both of them in operation twenty-four hours a day.

Then in this "white hole of human rights," what rights do prisoners enjoy? As I see it, the only rights that they have are, one, to hire a defense attorney after receiving their indictment, and two, the right to appeal if they refuse to accept the first court decision.

CHAPTER TWELVE

~

A Brief Look at Evidence of Corruption

The single appearance of "strictly forbidden" in the *Standards of Behavior* was in the rule against smoking. From the time the Standards went into effect on the 1st of May 1999, this was forbidden for the inmates of Section Seven, and they could no longer have their "smoke out." (For the "smoke out," they would stand in the exercise cage and a warden, on the catwalk above the cage, would throw a few lighted cigarettes down to them. They would take turns smoking them for quick relief of their nicotine craving.) The no-smoking policy applied to the wardens, guards, preliminary examiners, and the work unit, as well as the inmates. The entire Section Seven was made a smoke-free zone. However, promulgation of the policy didn't really stop cigarettes from coming into the section. What changed was their price. Previously, inmates could buy cigarettes at market rate and have them kept in the warden's office; now there was a steep rise in price and inmates secretly used "spirit money"—scrip printed by the Detention Center—to buy their cigarettes from the work unit. For example, a pack of Dragon brand cigarettes sells for less than two yuan outside, but the work unit sold them for fifty yuan—a better profit than reselling heroin. In the year 2000, prison personnel bought six packs of cigarettes for three hundred yuan. A number of men who had been transferred from Section Six to cell 404 told me that in Section Six the wardens managed this business. Each warden was responsible for five cells. Eight packs a month for each cell comes to forty packs a month. Just from this one line of business, he made more than two thousand yuan a month. I knew only too well how an addicted smoker was willing to give up several packages of instant noodles for a single cigarette. Therefore, this sort of exorbitantly profitable cigarette trade could easily be kept up indefinitely. When the cigarettes came in we used a primitive method to get them lit. A little laundry powder was scattered on some cotton batting and the cotton rolled into a spill, which was pressed down hard with the sole of a plastic shoe and rolled quickly back and forth until sparks and soon a flame were produced. The smokers would then gather in a corner not covered by the surveillance camera and enjoy for a while the beautiful comfort of a living immortal.

Another kind of transaction that made the cigarette trade pale into insignificance was *zoutuo*, or "finagling" various ways to get help from others to accomplish one's goals. Combinations with the term *tuo*—"to entrust (a task) to someone"—were used frequently in the lockup—for example, "to arrange *tuo*," "have *tuo*," "direct *tuo*" and "reverse *tuo*." Whenever possible, family members or friends of criminal suspects would spare no effort in undertaking various *zoutuo* measures. First, they would try to find a way to bribe public security officials to seek favorable resolution of a case. If this was not feasible, they would then go for the next best solution: Could they ensure that the individual would not be beaten? Or have the case resolved more quickly? Or get him out of the Detention Center to begin serving his sentence as soon as possible? Could they at least give him something good to eat? And so on. The motto "With facts as evidence and law as our guide" is openly mocked by the prevalence of *zoutuo* deals. At certain times and places the principle that was obviously used was "Money is the evidence and personal relationships are the guide."

Many *zoutuo* deals involve bribery that truly perverts the law. They reach a level of corruption that could be labeled "invest one yuan for a ten-thousand-yuan return." The father of a man named Liang who was moved up from the Chaoyang Detention Center spent sixty thousand yuan on *zoutuo* and the bribery was so effective that more than ten charges of robbery were "shrunk" to two. But another man, who was moved up from the Battery detention center, said that his family had spent sixty thousand yuan but it was ineffective and did not succeed in preventing his move to Section Seven. Liu Deguo told me that his accomplices had "sowed seeds" multiple times in the Chaoyang and Fengtai precincts. When their "big brother," or gang leader, shelled out money for *tuo*, if the case was relatively light, the accused were often released immediately. Xiao Haijun of Miyun County had been arrested many times there and his family had always managed to "bail" him out using *zoutuo*.

This bribery is typical systemic corruption. Far from being secret, it is openly known as an everyday occurrence. If one just looks at the oily fat prosecutors, investigators, and judges, it becomes very clear. When cases have not yet been cleared up and the *zoutuo* process is under way, they are very closemouthed, while for suspects in cases of economic and drug-related crimes, the mouths are closed even tighter. The little transactions that I have mentioned here are not even the tip of the iceberg.

CHAPTER THIRTEEN

~

Longing for Books

On 8 August 1999, the beginning of autumn on the lunar calendar, I turned in two reports to the Detention Center. The first report was a request for "sick list" meals. Because I was beginning to develop hemorrhoids, I wanted to improve my diet, so I requested a "soft" diet for two weeks—noodles cooked very soft with a small amount of egg in them. This request was quickly fulfilled. The other was a letter requesting books, as follows:

> Warden Song, for forwarding to the Detention Center:
>
> Books are very important to me, but there is hardly anything to read in the Detention Center. At home, I have subscriptions to the journals *Methods*, *Readings*, and *The World of English*. Could I ask my family to bring them in for me to read? Books are an important pleasure in life and, if one has good reading material, cornmeal buns are better than wheat-flour buns. I would be infinitely grateful if this request were approved.
>
> Cell 404 Prisoner of Conscience
> Jiang Qisheng
> 8 August 1999

After the report was passed from the study unit to the warden, it was as if a stone had been dropped into the ocean; nothing more was heard of it. More than a month later Warden Song told me that the Detention Center was planning to set up a library. This sort of passing the buck didn't surprise me, but I was perplexed. Why couldn't they go ahead with their plans for a library while I read my own materials? For something that could be done so effortlessly, why not do a good deed and accumulate some merit?

My request for books having met with failure, I turned my attention to the dictionary. Fortunately there was a copy of the *Xinhua Zidian** in the cell, so I began to browse through it character by character. This way I gained a first-time nodding acquaintance with many obscure characters that one seldom sees in ordinary daily life. But then I realized that I really remembered only ten or twenty percent of these characters, while on the other hand I now gained a much clearer understanding of many terms of common knowledge which I had known only vaguely. In addition, as a southerner I had an innate weakness with regard to standard Mandarin. There were many colloquial terms that I did not know or didn't know how to use, or if I could use them in speech, I couldn't recognize or write the characters for them, so now I achieved a real breakthrough in this regard. And I was pleased to discover that certain Wu dialect terms had been included in the dictionary, such as *xuetou* ("tricks designed to elicit amusement"), *dayang* ("to close a business for the night"), and *gangtou gangnao* ("crude, rash").

On entering the Detention Center my contact with hearing, speaking, reading, and writing English had been completely broken off. Later, through certain connections, I was able to get a copy of the *Oxford Chinese-English "Shuangjie" Dictionary*, with definitions in both languages, and thus once again had a little contact with the English language. A few months later Warden Song finally brought me a copy of Mark Twain's *Tom Sawyer* from another cell, and my English study became at least a little better than nothing.

In December of 1999 Wang Feng's father sent me a copy of *The Romance of the Three Kingdoms*† by special delivery from Jinan, and Warden Song sneaked it in to me. I was happy to have a chance after more than thirty years to reread this famous work of classical literature. However, it was the first time I had seen the annotations and commentaries by Mao Zonggang and his son. This work from our past describes the world's constant changes and the experiences of human life with such clarity and strength that one can fully savor them, and Mr. Mao's commentary is the height of perfection. It is clear that the Chinese people attained a thorough understanding of hu-

* A small but comprehensive character dictionary, inexpensive and ubiquitous, used by all schoolchildren and most adults throughout China.

† This perennially popular historical novel recounts the breakup of the Eastern Han dynasty (25–220 CE) and the division of China into the three competing kingdoms of Wei, Shu-Han, and Wu.

man nature from a very early time. Without listing examples of intelligence, wisdom, craftiness, and deceit, I would only raise three points: (1) They opposed the emperor, not the system. When "heroes" rose up, they all wanted to be emperor, but the system could not be changed, nor did they have to worry about such things as human rights. They just toyed with the existing political autocracy. This demonstrates that the Chinese lacked intelligence and wisdom in regard to creative political change. (2) Sun Ce* did not believe in the supernatural but depended on his intuition, and his ability to stay on course in the face of opposition was admirable. However, in present-day China many people believe in the supernatural; even among my contemporaries, there are many who do so. In this matter, obviously, we can only leave it up to individual choice; people's beliefs cannot be forced. (3) "We should make plans according to our mental state or mood." This maxim covers so many things in human affairs, from the great affairs of the nation to such minor matters as playing chess. Anyone playing cards or chess should understand this. Annoyance or anger can lead to an unsettled mood, resulting in miscalculations or omissions. The longer one plays cards, the worse the cards get, or the chess game deteriorates more and more, and it becomes difficult to save oneself. When one's mood is unstable, the brain doesn't work well. This principle should be recorded in our hearts.

---

* Sun Ce (175–200) was a military leader in southeastern China late in the Eastern Han dynasty. He was assassinated and on his deathbed turned his command over to his younger brother Sun Quan (181–252), who later established the kingdom of Wu.

CHAPTER FOURTEEN

~

Chess and Cards

If one were to say that the thing most lacking in the Detention Center is freedom, then the thing that is most in surplus is time. When a case is under way there is not much to think or talk about, and once it is concluded and one is waiting to go into prison, one is faced with even more enforced idleness. I often thought that if there were no chess or cards in lockup, one would really not know how to pass the time. And how much more anxiety, entanglements, and irregularities would then ensue. Every afternoon and evening from five to nine o'clock the majority of the inmates passed the time playing chess or cards. The main theme of these vacant hours was to forget one's worries and seek entertainment. Of course the quest for happiness often gives rise to sorrow, and sometimes the inmates' sour moods would lead to fights.

The cell's playing cards were bought from the Detention Center's shop with money from the "common" fund, which derived from monthly contributions from cash sent to the inmates by their families for daily-use articles such as laundry detergent, dish washing liquid, and toilet paper. Usually each person contributed twenty yuan each month to the fund to ensure that those with no money would be able to take care of their personal hygiene. If somebody got nothing from home and had no friends on the outside he would not even have toilet paper to use and would have to wash his bottom with water.

The card games that were most often played were *gongzhu* and *qiaosanjia*. After the evening meal was finished and things were put in order, the men would form separate pairs or spread out in two straight lines on the sleeping platform. They were often evenly matched and would enter into the game with such enthusiasm that they would forget their circumstances, and sometimes the yelling and laughter would bring a guard to the door with a warning.

Usually they would just play, without betting. But if some of them had bought instant noodles during the day, they would bet noodles. The loser in a game of *gongzhu* would give up his noodles like a good sport. And what would those who had no money bet on? They would bet to see who would have to take a drink of cold water, who would get thumped on the noggin by the others, or who would have to get down and do push-ups.

When I was on the outside I had not touched cards for many years. In the lockup I would sometimes play a little *da shengji*, which I remembered from my youth, and I would really do my best at the game. Between two equal players it can be a contest of intellect and determination, a very interesting competition. One winter afternoon I encountered a probability situation that one might see only once in fifty years. We were playing "ten," and I was dealer. Among the twelve cards dealt to me and six more drawn, there was not a single card of the lead suit. I thought I would certainly lose. But sometimes "the flowers show brightly in the shadow of the willow" and the positive is hidden in the negative. On rearranging my hand I discovered that I held eleven clubs, lacking only the 2, and I had kept the ace of spades. I played my ace of spades, and on the next hand spread out my eleven clubs and reaching out with both hands, "shaved" my opponent clean. The men in the cell let out a startled cheer. In all of their card-playing experience this was the first time they had seen such an unusual display of cards.

We had a complete collection of the varieties of chess. Chinese chess, Western chess, *weiqi*, or *go*, and even five-in-a-row chess, or *gobang*. Aside from the chess set cut from pieces of paper that I mentioned earlier, all the others were made from "*wotou mian*," which was made by crumbling cornmeal buns and adding a little bean-milk powder and cotton fibers to make the *mian*, or dough. Saiyide, a Uighur, shaped Western chess pieces that in the dusky light of the cell could pass for the genuine thing. I could play two kinds of chess. I had played Chinese chess since childhood. My hometown of Changshu was known in the Jiangnan area for its "literati arts," music, chess, calligraphy, and painting. Hui Songxiang of Changshu won fourth place in a national Chinese chess tournament, and Yan Mujiang, an instructor in the Jiangsu Province Chess Academy, is from Changshu. My fourth younger brother, Jiang Huasheng, was recognized as champion of the Jiangsu Province workers and staff members' *weiqi* tournament. I learned to play Western chess in Qincheng prison in the spring of 1990, where I was taught by my cellmate Chen Jianxing, who was a graduate student in the English Department of the Foreign Languages Institute.

In the lockup I mostly played Chinese chess. I spent far more time playing chess in one year than I had on all board games in the previous fifty years. On the outside I had watched the live television broadcasts of "fast" chess contests on Saturday mornings from 10:00 to 11:30. Aside from that I played once every month or two with friends in Capital Normal University's chess association. Now I was considered the best player in the cell, and there was lively competition for second place, with frequent challenges and players forced to drink cold water or suffer thumps on the forehead for losing their bets. I remember that Duan Xingchang, who was in for human trafficking, had lost so often to Wang Feng that the bumps on his forehead were half as big as a chicken's egg.

CHAPTER FIFTEEN

~

Litigation Records

On Saturday the 26th of June I had been in Section Seven for thirty-eight days. Whether the arrest warrant had been prepared or not, the mystery should be resolved today. In the Detention Center, just as on the outside, every other week we had a "big weekend," and the inmates did not have to sit in ranks and files on the sleeping platform but could move about freely in the cell. June 26th was a sweltering hot day. Most of the men had taken their shirts off and were frequently in and out of the cold showers. Li Gang from Guizhou and I spread out the chess "board" and sat down to play. About 10:30 the cell door opened and a guard called my name. I pushed the chess board away and got up. Just as I had expected, my call had come.

A few minutes later I had taken my seat in the preliminary examination room. Pang Jiang turned on the air conditioning and poured a cup of hot water for me. Knowing that the arrest warrant was going to be issued, I sat quietly, waiting for him to speak. Soon he began in measured tones, saying that the Procuratorate had issued the authorization for arrest only yesterday and therefore they were executing the warrant today. The charge was suspicion of inciting subversion of state power. He asked whether there was anything I wanted to say. I said I knew it would come to this, and I had nothing further to say. I had the feeling that they could easily tamper with the record of the inquest, and therefore I did not want to leave evidence of my attitude. After I had signed the brief record of the inquest, Pang Jiang brought out the arrest warrant for me to sign. I carefully read the warrant, including the large red seal, "Qiang Wei, Chief of the Public Security Bureau."

Then in the signature column I wrote in bold characters "victim of literary inquisition" and on the following line signed my name. Pang Jiang watched, looking very unhappy. He asked why I hadn't expressed my attitude earlier. I laughed and said I had planned to do it like that all along. Perhaps leaving this record on the arrest warrant would have some historical significance. I told him that when I had received my arrest warrant in Qincheng prison in October of 1990 I had written a large character for "injustice" on it. That warrant bore the seal of Su Zhongxiang. Of course "literary inquisition" was much stronger, but it was not directed at him. He would only have to pass this message up the chain of command. He helplessly mumbled a few words and sent me back to my cell.

On the 25th of July there was another fierce heat wave. At a little after 2 p.m. Secretary Song Junjie asked me about the fax that my friend An Jun had sent me on the 18th of May. Two individuals in civilian clothes were also present in the hearing room, Pang Jiang having gone out on an assignment. Now I realized that An Jun from Henan had also been arrested and the two strangers sitting in front of me were from Public Security in Henan. An Jun had shifted from anticorruption to antiauthoritarianism, and the authorities, thinking they had the matter in their grasp, were taking action. I was now worried that friends in Xi'an and Changsha might also have been jailed.

On the 9th of September a woman from the First Branch of the Beijing People's Procuratorate came into our corridor and told me that my case had been transferred from the Public Security Bureau to the Procuratorate. She also informed me that I had a right to retain a lawyer.

On the afternoon of 22 December I walked out of the front gate of the Detention Center for the first time, wearing handcuffs. I got into the prison van of the Procuratorate's First Branch and was taken to Babaoshan Branch for examination. The examination room was in the basement, next to the parking area. Prosecutor Li Leisen was more than fifty years old. Bai Xin from the secretariat had bleached hair. After I had taken my seat, Li Leisen told a bailiff to remove my handcuffs and said, "We can talk better this way." All of the questions had to do with two articles. The first one was Li Xiaoping's "Reflections on Peacefully Bringing about Fundamental Change in China's Social System," written in February 1996. The other was "Light a Million Candles to Commemorate the Souls of the Heroes of June 4th," which I had written in April of 1999. From their questions I could see what the content of the indictment would be. When they finally mentioned the matter of retaining a lawyer, I immediately accused the Public Security Bureau of illegally depriving me of my rights. When Li Leisen heard my accusation, his expression didn't change and he said nothing and showed no emotion at all. I realized that this was what the common people of China often have in mind when they say "to speak is a waste of words." But my attitude was that even if it was a waste of words I still wanted to speak. If enough people would speak up, maybe it would have an effect. I informed Li Leisen that I had given my wife *carte blanche* to hire a lawyer for my defense. Who she would hire was entirely up to her.

On the afternoon of 11 October 1999 I met Attorney Mo Shaoping and his assistant, Wang Gang, in the attorneys' building of the Detention Center. I had not previously met Attorney Mo, though I knew that he had defended Fang Jue and, trusting in my wife's choice, I signed the power of attorney document without hesitation. I quickly discovered that communicating with a lawyer was not at all difficult. We talked about feelings, principles, and the law. I was rather surprised to learn two things. First was that my wife had never been informed of my detainment and arrest. The second was that the lawyer had found nothing in my dossier about the questioning that I had undergone in the preliminary hearing process. However, they had not dared to remove or replace my arrest warrant, and the "victim of literary inquisition" that I had inscribed on it still showed in the copy of the warrant like an emblem of shame on the historical record. Finally I read in the "suggestions for charges," which the Public Security Bureau had forwarded to the Procuratorate, that my criminal punishment should be based on the two "Reflections" and "Candles" articles. Attorney Mo had already formed the opinion that these "facts of the crime" would not stand up in court and he was prepared to enter a "not guilty" plea for me. "Of course," he said, "the plea will have to be based on the formal bill of charges from the Procuratorate."

Given that my case was purely a matter of political persecution by the authorities, the relevant adjudicative procedures were in essence no more than an interlude in the overall process, and it was not really necessary for me to hire a lawyer. Not only could I defend myself in court, I could also strike back in self-defense and reprimand those who had instigated the literary inquisition. So why did I decide to retain a lawyer? My main objective was to make it more difficult for the authorities to revise or obfuscate the record and to leave a more objective and just historical record of my case. I hadn't really held any extravagant hopes that a lawyer would take the risk of speaking with complete honesty and openness. Therefore, Attorney Mo's calm and composed attitude on that autumn afternoon filled me with gratitude. I was sure that Attorneys Mo and Wang could see this in my expression and in my eyes even though I didn't come right out and say it.

On October 20 I gave Warden Song my letter of complaint for transmittal to the Detention Center's public prosecutor. I accused the Public Security

Bureau of trampling on my right to retain a lawyer, my wife's right to be informed of my arrest and detention, and her right to hire a lawyer on my behalf.

The next afternoon a secretary from the First Intermediate People's Court of Beijing came to the door of cell 404, gave me a copy of my indictment and said that at some time after ten days from that date I would be summoned to court.

CHAPTER SIXTEEN

The Trial

My cellmates had a great deal of worldly experience, but they had never seen a written indictment of a political offender. As soon as I returned to the cell they clamored to pass it around and read it, and a lively discussion began immediately.

"What kind of a crime is this!"

"If you didn't see it you wouldn't know. Once you see it, it's really scary. For writing an essay, they put such a frightful hat on a person!"

"Human rights, human rights! We don't even have a right to speak!"

"If I hadn't seen it with my own eyes, I really wouldn't believe the Communist Party would deal with a person in such a deadly fashion!"

On the morning of 29 October Attorney Mo came to the Detention Center again and told me that my case would be heard in court on the 1st of November. I felt that the court's hearing the case right on the tenth day after issuing the indictment was an indication that the authorities had made up their minds for a quick trial and a quick decision. Actually I had also hoped for an early confrontation in court so that I would be able to see my family and would have an opportunity for an examination that would result in a historical defense.

After saying good-bye to the lawyers, I returned to my cell and contemplated the mental drafts of my plea and closing statement that I had already gone over so many times. The demand that I had placed upon myself was that my plea must be dignified and to the point, clear and with tightly formed logic, concise and comprehensive, and designed to hit hard at injustice. My closing statement must come from the heart and must be expressed with calm conviction of the righteousness of my cause. In order to avoid interruptions by the presiding judge, I must be appropriately reserved and not speak impulsively.

The 30th and 31st of October were days of rest. During these two days I carefully prepared the final versions of my plea and closing statement. I decided that I would not take any paper into the courtroom. With right on my side and skillful legal argument I would reverse the positions of host and guest and put the persecutors on the stand as defendant. My cellmates got busy washing clothes for me, finding a fitting pair of shoes, and even arguing over how to make a necktie for me. Someone assumed night duty to ensure that I would get a good night's sleep and be prepared to win the case.

On 1 November 1999, just after I had finished breakfast, the cell door was opened. Even though I was already neatly dressed, Wang Feng handed me a wool vest and Zhang Zhili put a cotton coat on my shoulders. I raised my right hand with a V sign and turned and strode out of the lockup.

There were six people whose cases were to be heard in the First Intermediate Court that day. After the judicial police took us out of the north gate of the Detention Center, a man wearing a leather jacket, who was addressed by the others as Lao Da, or "Eldest Brother," told me to wait while the other five got into an Iveco prison van. Shortly thereafter, I was put into a police car with two judicial police guards who complained that because of me they had missed their breakfast. They said that a police contingent had arrived at the First Intermediate Court before seven o'clock and set up police lines inside and outside the court building, then had sent this car to the Detention Center to pick me up. I realized that the authorities' phobia about political offenders had flared up again. Getting into the driver's seat, Lao Da told me that he must carry out the task assigned to him without a single glitch. A policeman sitting beside me said that Lao Da, forty-eight years old, was the chief of their Judicial Police unit. Lao Da made repeated calls on his cell phone, waiting for the order to set out. Finally about 8:30 the three police cars and one van left the Detention Center with their sirens screaming. As traffic controls had been implemented and all lights were green for us, our passage was unimpeded and swift. At each intersection that we passed, long lines of cars and pedestrians were waiting impatiently behind the red lights that had brought them to a halt. They had no way of knowing that this imaginary fear and waste of manpower was all due to one prisoner of conscience who dared to speak the truth.

Arriving at the court compound, in order to avoid the crowd of my friends and supporters, as well as reporters, the motorcade did not take the usual route of entry through the west gate but went in through the main north gate of the First Intermediate Court and stopped at a side door of the main building. After the five men in the van were led into the building, I got out of the police car and was taken to a holding room, where my handcuffs were removed. I took off my overcoat and slowly paced back and forth. Although I was about to see my family and would soon enter a courtroom for the first time in my life and be a *defendant*, my mood was extraordinarily calm.

A few minutes later a judicial policeman opened the steel-grating door of the holding room to take me into the courtroom, which was very close by. I took a step into the courtroom and saw that my wife was on the right-hand end of the row of five people in the visitors' seats. Wearing glasses and looking gaunt, she nodded at me. I nodded in response and swept a glance at the other four "audience members" who had been selected to act as visitors, then with a slight feeling of lightheartedness, I walked directly to the defendant's seat. Court personnel, the public prosecutor, and attorneys Mo and Wang were all sitting stiffly with their eyes straight ahead. A useless, hypocritical "open" trial was about to begin.

About two hours later, as I was wrapping up my closing statement, there was a sudden burst of applause from the visitors' seats. I knew at once that this came from my dear wife. Furious, the female presiding judge immediately ordered the bailiffs to take her out of the courtroom. After turning to see her leave, I suppressed my anger and continued with my statement. In the end I filed a strong objection to the rude removal of my wife from the court.

When the hearing was completed I was taken into the corridor leading to the holding room, where Lao Da allowed me to use the duty officer's desk and chair for the final procedure, which was to read the "court record." This was handwritten and I could see that the court recorder had not been able to keep up with the trial proceedings, especially the defendant's defense and final statement, which were recorded only in outline form. After mentioning this to the recorder, in order to give her some face, I signed with the notation "generally accurate." As soon as I put the pen down, I saw that the judicial policeman wanted to take me back to the Detention Center. I asked, "Aren't we going to wait for the other five men, whose cases are not yet complete?" Lao Da said, "If we don't get you back right away, there are many police on the streets who won't get to eat." Smiling, I objected, "If I go back now, Section Seven's mealtime is long past. As a rule, when someone is brought here for a court session, the First Intermediate Court provides meals. So now they must feed me." Lao Da chuckled: "You've really learned the ropes. OK, as a special favor I'll get you a *baozi** and an egg."

As traffic controls were once again in effect, after emerging from the court compound's north gate the two police cars entered what seemed like unoccupied territory and quickly reached Banbuqiao. Soon the judicial police turned me over to the guard on duty at the entryway to area four. As we walked down the long corridor, I chatted with the guard about the court session. He sighed and said, "Hai! You're really hard to deal with. Don't you know that 'the people should not struggle against officials'?" I replied, "When officials stop struggling against the people, then there will be hope for China."

When I entered cell 404 my cellmates were on the sleeping platform for their midday naps, but with my arrival, they couldn't lie still. Nor did I feel at all sleepy; so I began a detailed description of the court session. I recounted the evidence of the guilty consciences of the officials in charge of the literary inquisition. First, they had had me ride in a police car rather than the van. Did they think I might steal the van, or were they afraid of the media? Second, we had entered the court compound by way of the north rather than the west gate in order to avoid reporters and the crowd of people. Third, they had removed all but five visitors' seats in the courtroom in order to have what was in reality a secret trial. I said the way to make it fair and satisfying would have been to have a live broadcast of the proceedings, but the officials were very cowardly, afraid of openness and refusing to hold an open trial. At this point, Zhang Chunhua of Shunyi said that he and his accomplice had been taken to the Superior Court today for questioning, and when they entered and left by the west gate there were crowds on both sides of the street. (The Beijing People's Superior Court and the Beijing People's First Intermediate Court are in the same compound.) I said that in those crowds there were surely many of my friends.

I mentioned that the prosecutor was completely without confidence and had blushed with embarrassment in the face of the refutations that my lawyers and I had offered. The judges had treated the case as routine and glossed over the facts, but my lawyers had spoken in loud, clear voices and with reason and clarity, saying that the bill of charges was unclear and the law cited was not appropriate. I described my defense and recited part of it for them. I said that because the presiding judge had repeatedly interrupted me, I had had to speak more rapidly and there were a few shortcomings in

* Steamed bun with meat or vegetable filling.

my refutations of their “facts” and charges. Finally I spoke of my wife’s applause in the courtroom, making my cellmates click their tongues in wonder, and thus winding up an account of a courtroom story such as they had never before heard. There was a loud round of applause, shouts of admiration, and knocking on hard surfaces, whereupon the Detention Center’s control room discovered the storytelling gathering in cell 404 and we heard hurried footsteps in the corridor. A guard rushed up and knocked on the door and, opening the small observation window, said to me, “All right, that’s enough. It’s time for your nap.”

CHAPTER SEVENTEEN

Falungong Adherent Sun Wei

In early May of 1999, while I was writing "Thoughts on Reading the Newspapers on the Eve of May 4th," I mentioned the astonishing demonstration of 25 April when more than twenty thousand Falungong practitioners sat quietly outside Zhongnanhai,* and I noted that the authorities immediately retaliated by confiscating Falungong books.

Subsequent circumstances made it clear that in regard to any protest activities of the masses—even silent protests—any actions that the masses organized on their own rather than under government control, the Communist Party even today had no new ideas or policies. They always hauled out the same old response: suppression.

After the Complaints Office of the State Council attempted some deceptive measures to placate Falungong practitioners, large-scale naked suppression was unveiled. On July 22nd Falungong was labeled an "illegal organization" and was officially banned. Then in October, Falungong was capped as a "perverse religious sect" in an attempt to bring an end to it. I knew that the day when we would see Falungong disciples in the Detention Center was drawing near.

On 9 November 1999 Sun Wei, a believer in Falun Dafa, or the Dharma of the Wheel of Law, came into cell 404. We knew then that arrests had

*Falungong, or Falun Dafa, is a semireligious organization that teaches truthfulness, compassion, and forbearance and promotes *qigong*, gentle calisthenic exercises, for spiritual and bodily health. Zhongnanhai, just west of the Forbidden City in central Beijing, is the residential compound of party and government leaders. This peaceful demonstration was a shocking affront to the country's political leaders.

begun some time ago. Sun was a 1997 computer science graduate of Liaoning University. After graduating, he had worked for a computer company in the Zhongguancun area of Beijing and, after taking part in the 25 April sit-in at Zhongnanhai, he was quickly detained on criminal charges and locked up in "the Battery" (the Beijing Public Transportation Precinct detention center). After being detained for thirty days, he had been released to a guarantor while awaiting trial. Then at the end of October he had downloaded some Falungong materials from the Internet, made about two hundred copies of them, and mailed them to the Beijing Public Security Bureau and its precincts and local police stations; he also mailed copies to a few friends and relatives. For this, he was picked up again and sent directly to Section Seven.

Young Sun was rather small and thin. He wore glasses and had a friendly expression on his face. Cellmates gave him the nickname "Wheel." When asked why he was so foolishly fascinated with Falungong, he said that when he was studying at Liaoning University he had suffered seriously from insomnia. Someone had suggested that he try Falungong exercises and when he did the insomnia quickly subsided. He then went more deeply into it and read Falungong materials that encouraged people to do good deeds and avoid evil or harmful actions. This persuaded him to return the bicycle that he had been riding to the place where he had stolen it. Step by step he became completely convinced that "Teacher Li" (he never referred to the Falungong founder just by his name, Li Hongzhi) was superior by many levels to ordinary people. We believed what Wheel said, but we were very skeptical of his obsession with the Dharma of the Wheel of Law and his extreme admiration for Li Hongzhi. The inmates had always shown a petty arrogance that led them to make fun of anyone from the emperor above to movie stars, so one would not expect them to easily accept claims to superiority for Li Hongzhi, and questions were fired at Wheel like a string of firecrackers.

"What is your wheel of law really like? How much does it weigh?"

"Is it true that Li Hongzhi can heal a hunchback?"

"Can you get Li Hongzhi to bring us some pork buns?"

"If Li Hongzhi has higher standing than the Buddha, why did he change his birth date?"*

"When a disciple gets into trouble, why doesn't Li Hongzhi come and rescue him?"

"When Catfish Mouth says such mean things about Falungong, why doesn't Li Hongzhi make it rain and get him soaking wet when he inspects

---

* The government says Li Hongzhi changed his birth date to correspond with that of the Buddha. Li says the government misprinted his birth date and he just corrected it.

the troops in the October 1st ceremonies?" (The inmates had given President Jiang Zemin this nickname after noticing that his mouth looked like the mouth of a catfish.)

Still one had to admire young Wheel's calm patience in the face of all these questions. Without showing any excitement or anger, he would just continue his devout explanations. Even after we lay down for the night he would spend hours in detailed responses to either curious questions or taunts from fellow inmates.

On the evening of 11 November 1999 Wheel and I had our first serious conversation. However, we hadn't talked long before I found my attitude of tolerance and compassion changing. Because our differences were so great, I frequently became impatient. I felt compelled to suggest that we put aside some of our differences and not debate them, and I took up my pen and listed fifteen disagreements that we should reserve for later discussion. I told Wheel that there were many Falungong doctrines that I could not easily accept, including the principle of *ren*, or patient endurance and acceptance. If someone tramples on your human rights or insults your character, would you accept it? There are limits to what one can endure. There must be a time when one is no longer able to bear the offenses; otherwise one becomes a slave. Of course the four charges that the authorities had laid on Falungong were unjust accusations deliberately designed as persecution. Falungong may be worrisome to society and to humanity, but to say that it is antisocial and inhumane is extremely unjust; these are charges deserved by Nazism. Falungong has not opposed the government; it has only attempted to petition it. Furthermore, in my eyes, opposing the government is not a crime; it is a citizen's right. Didn't the Communist Party gain power by opposing the government of the Republic of China? As to the charge of being antiscientific, there is some truth in that. But science doesn't enjoy any special exemption from being opposed; it is not a crime to be antiscientific. Wheel heard me out and then said, "Although the two of us have major differences, your attitude toward Falungong is much more objective and fair than the government's. Suppression of Falungong is certainly a great injustice. When snow falls in June in Weigongcun we will see the proof of that."*

After that, Wheel and I had several more debates on the questions of whether Falungong was antiscientific and whether Falungong was a perverse religious sect. On 12 January 2000, Wheel was transferred to the Haidian

---

* The legend of snow in midsummer as a sign from heaven of injustice on earth is first seen in the thirteenth-century Yuan dynasty opera *Dou E Yuan (Injustice to Dou E)*. The story, and the opera in several modern forms, has remained popular down through the ages. Weigongcun is near Zhongguancun, where Sun was working, and is possibly where he was arrested.

district detention center. As he was leaving, we wished each other good luck and agreed that when we got out we would continue our discussions.

Fifteen Points of Disagreement

Sun Wei	*Jiang Qisheng*
1. At birth, people are naturally good.	At birth, good and evil both exist in our nature.
2. Consciousness is also substance.	If so, how do you define substance?
3. Plant life is superior to human life.	Just the opposite.
4. Culture existed before historical times.	Possibly.
5. The moon was created by prehistoric man.	Idiotic nonsense.
6. The theory of evolution is completely wrong.	There are flaws in the theory of evolution.
7. Extraterrestrials are the source of humanity's most important hi-tech achievements.	The source is human discovery and invention.
8. Qigong (deep-breathing exercises) is supernormal science.	Qigong is unscientific or pseudoscientific.
9. The basis of evidential science is wrong; to take observation and experiment as the basis of science is wrong.	It is extremely reasonable.
10. Beyond the four dimensions of time and space, another dimension certainly exists.	If it exists, it exists on a tiny scale and has nothing to do with Li Hongzhi.
11. Truth, goodness, and tolerance are the inherent qualities of the universe and all things have these qualities.	Evidence that we have so far only indicates that the nature of the universe and all things is movement.
12. There are many, many kinds of life that are higher than human life.	We can speculate that this might be so.
13. Humans definitely have supernatural abilities.	This remains to be confirmed or disproved.
14. A person's life is mostly predestined. Only small parts of it can be changed by individual struggles.	I don't agree with the idea that a person's life is predetermined like a part in a play.
15. The disadvantages of evidential science are greater than the advantages.	The advantages are greater than the disadvantages.

CHAPTER EIGHTEEN

~

Gao Shuo of the Electric Saw

On the afternoon of 11 November 1999 the sky was heavily overcast. Around three o'clock two men wearing shackles were brought into the cell. One of them, Liu Bo, transferred from the Haidian detention center, was suspected of murder and robbery. His whole body was scarred with ringworm. The other, Gao Shuo, from the Western district detention center, had lived in the dormitory of the Xiao Xitian Electric Trolley Company. He had killed a man and then dismembered the corpse with an electric saw and thrown it into the city moat. The arrival of "Ringworm" and "Electric Saw" in the cell caused a fair amount of disturbance. Cellmates' attitude to the former was dread and wanting distance from him, and toward the latter was a mixture of fear and curiosity. A number of guards also came later in the afternoon and stood at the door of 404 looking in, wanting to see what sort of a person Electric Saw was.

When Gao Shuo came into the cell he was wearing a gray down coat. He had a blank stare and didn't say much. However, he did not look like a bad person. Born in 1975, he was fairly short, pale, with clearly defined eyebrows and big eyes. He had completed the three-year program at a private college in the Western District of Beijing and was working in a China Youth Travel securities company, not making a lot of money. We asked him, "So you're the one who stirred up the capital with an electric saw?" With a blank expression he nodded but said nothing. A few days later he got more used to us and began to relax, and gradually he told us his story.

The people he came into contact with in his work were all much wealthier than he was, and in time the itch for more money became unbearable. As his passion for getting rich burned more and more brightly, he decided to follow the adage "when on the mountain, live off the mountain" and began to steal and sell clients' stocks. In May of 1999 he sold two hundred thousand yuan* worth of a client's stocks and hired an employee of a bank to withdraw the money. But when his hired agent saw the money, he got greedy and wanted to raise his cut from the agreed upon five thousand yuan to fifty thousand yuan. Gao took the agent to an apartment in a building in Chegongzhuang, and after two days of negotiations without reaching an agreement, he decided to bring an end to things. Waiting until late at night when the agent was sound asleep, Gao beat him on the head with a hammer until he was dead. After the corpse had lain in the house for two days, he borrowed an electric saw and set about dismembering it. After ten o'clock in the evening he wrapped up the two legs, went out and flagged a taxi and went to Yongdingmen, preparing to throw them into the moat. But just as he left the taxi a Joint Defense Forces squad appeared and he was unable to talk them out of taking him to their security post. At this unexpected turn of events, he initially broke out in a cold sweat, but then for some reason quickly grew calm. Several times they asked him to open the packages for inspection, but he managed to put them off. Finally he said he wanted to go to his grandpa's place to get his ID card and would come right back to get his packages. He walked calmly out of the office and down the street. As soon as he rounded a corner, he took off running. After running for about the distance of a bus stop he stopped to catch his breath, and caught another taxi and went back to Chegongzhuang. Rushing up the stairs, he wrapped up the torso and the head and immediately ran down the stairs, and again caught a taxi and headed straight for Deshengmen, where he was able to get rid of the remains in secrecy.

We said that just listening to his story we were trembling in fright, and asked wasn't he scared when he set about cutting up a body with an electric saw. He said that he couldn't carry the whole body out by himself, and if he asked someone else for help there would be even more trouble. He had thought about it for two days and got a terrible headache, unable to work out a good solution. Finally he braced himself and went ahead with it. We said surely the Joint Forces men would unwrap the packages after he had left their post and then it would be all over for him. Didn't he go crazy with fear? With his usual blank expression, he quietly replied, "Yes, of course." After we

* At eight yuan to one US dollar, this would be about $25,000.

had talked with him face to face this way and looked into his eyes, we were still very perplexed. The human creature is really something to ponder. Even today I still can't come to terms with the vision of this expressionless young man, in a frenzy, killing a fellow human being.

Later I talked with Gao Shuo twice with just the two of us present. He told me that his parents were of my generation. He was an only child and this episode was a devastating blow to them. Why had a thirst for wealth brought him to commit murder? He said there were two reasons: First was worship of money. The lust for riches had occupied his mind to the exclusion of everything else. The second factor was that the great majority of those he had met who had "gotten rich first"* had made their fortunes through force or trickery, and the injustice of this had been a powerful stimulus for him. He added that if I wanted to write about him, I should include both of these factors; I could not omit either one of them.

On 24 January 2000 Gao Shuo received his certificate of indictment. As expected, it was imprinted with the phrase, "One special factor and two extremes." This meant that the result would be extremely severe. It was often said in the Detention Center that with "one special factor and one extreme" the result was uncertain; for "two special factors and one extreme," the death sentence was definite. Since his certificate was labeled "one special factor and two extremes," he faced certain death.

In the middle of February he stood trial in the First Intermediate Court. An uncle attended the proceeding. His father and mother were brokenhearted and did not want or dare to go to see him. On the morning of March 20th he went back to court to receive the written verdict. Before he left we all understood that it would be his death certificate. In the afternoon, when he was unexpectedly permitted to return to the cell to gather his belongings (he had arranged *tuo* with one of the guards), he already wore the manacles of a prisoner sentenced to death and was on his way to death row, where he would spend his final months. I pulled his bedding from the pile on the sleeping platform and handed it to him. As I signaled good-bye with my eyes, he responded with a gloomy and bitter smile.

In late April when the Superior Court reviewed his case, Gao tried a clever ruse. He fainted and fell to the floor, forcing an adjournment. On June 14th the court convened for the case again and Gao again fainted, bringing about adjournment once more. Cellmate Hao Weijun, who was on the docket in the Superior Court that day for his appeal, was in the same car

* This is an allusion to top leader Deng Xiaoping's statement that "we must let some people get rich first."

with Gao, both going and returning. He said that after Gao was taken back to the "cage" (a holding room in the court that resembled a cage), he quickly "revived" and started yelling, "Honored Judge, I am unjustly accused!" And on the way back from the court, he was conscious and clear, even asking young Hao, "Has Teacher Jiang received his sentence?"

At the beginning of July we knew that he had "set out on his journey to the Western Heavens."

CHAPTER NINETEEN

~

Treated as Guilty Even without Evidence

Chen Xianglong was from Fuping in Shaanxi. We all called him Big Brother Long. In late December of 1999 he had been sentenced to death with a stay of execution and was transferred from the Chaoyang center to Section Seven and assigned to cell 404. This unprepossessing little fellow was one of only two criminal suspects I had met who refused to admit guilt either in the preliminary hearing process or in his court trial. (The other was Hu Xiupeng, also an unassuming fellow, who was ill-tempered and had the nickname "One Knife Hu.") On 6 August 1998, Chen Xianglong had been arrested by the criminal police of the Fengtai District, and on the same day, under torture, he made a deposition saying that he had killed his roommate Li Heping. But then he immediately withdrew the confession and subsequently maintained his innocence. He was taken to the Beijing Municipal Detention Center, where he was severely abused for continuing to deny that he had killed anyone.

Section Seven officers took him out of the cell for a preliminary hearing and did not allow him to return for three days and four nights. During this time the only food he was given was one fried dough-cake and one egg. He was not allowed to lie down to sleep or rest and was made to stand facing the wall, with his nose almost against it, for more than six hours at a time. While standing in this position he was not allowed to move an inch, and was burned on his shoulders and neck with hot cigarette butts several dozen times. After the preliminary hearing was unsuccessful, the wardens took him again and, seeing that he still refused to admit guilt, they put restraints on him and told us in the cell to "think of a way to make him face reality." This one little sentence could do nothing but add to his suffering. Brother Long told me that he had ceased to care about dying. He had been tormented till he felt that death was better than life and that he had already died several deaths.

A few days later I asked him to show me the written verdict from his preliminary hearing. I was shocked to see that there was absolutely no direct evidence that he had killed anyone, and the indirect evidence only showed that there was serious suspicion against him, but nothing to prove he actually was a murderer. I thought that if the court had acted on the evidence, there was no way this verdict could have been reached. Still there was no mistaking the fact that the Second Intermediate Court had indeed handed down this verdict. I thought that the deciding judges surely must not have clear consciences. If the evidence was really "ample and conclusive," with the defendant so adamant in refusing to admit guilt, why had they not sentenced him to certain execution rather than giving him a suspended sentence? Some of the cellmates knew about such cases. They said this was called a "conservative decision." It left Brother Long alive, and if on the off chance he had not in fact killed anyone, the verdict could be reversed. But I felt that this "conservative decision" violated modern legal principles, as it amounted to treating a suspect as if he were already convicted. According to the principle of "innocent until proven guilty," if the evidence was not sufficient to prove guilt, the suspect should be freed. He could not be found "probably guilty." I told Brother Long that he should appeal. I asked what basis did they have for convicting him of murder? He gave me a reproachful look and heaved a big sigh. Then in his Shaanxi dialect he slowly explained that if they were arresting such good-hearted and harmless people as Falungong practitioners, what hope could he have? He had decided not to appeal. His heart was already like cold ashes, and it would be useless to appeal. A small-time hoodlum could never get the best of a big gangster.

On February 24th, 2000, Chen Xianglong ate only half of a bun and didn't say a word. Through the next three days, he ate nothing, didn't speak, and didn't seem to hear anything that was said to him. On the 28th he again ate no breakfast or lunch, and in the afternoon a warden took him out, and he never came back to the cell. We all felt that Brother Long did not seem to be consciously on a hunger strike, protesting his fate. It was rather as if mental illness was taking hold of him. Why? For four days he didn't eat as much as a grain of rice, his cheeks became gaunt and dark and his eyes were sunken, but the strange thing was that in his facial expression he never exhibited the slightest bit of pain and suffering. Without exception we all felt great sympathy for Brother Long, and at the same time extreme grief and indignation. What a great tragedy it was if unfounded accusations had caused a good and innocent man to lose his mind.

CHAPTER TWENTY

Precious Messages

When a person is thrown into the Detention Center his communication rights are stripped from him. This is especially true of prisoners awaiting trial, who are not even allowed to write to their families. The only exception to this rule is that once a month a prisoner is allowed to write to his family or friends requesting funds. And the only communication from family that an inmate is allowed to see is the signature of the person who sends the funds. Naturally this prohibition doesn't apply to prisoners who have made *tuo* arrangements. An "air *tuo*" can carry oral or written messages in either direction, while a "water *tuo*" can bring in food or arrange meetings, and a "solid *tuo*" can turn big problems into small problems or make small problems disappear.

I had neither *tuo* nor any magical abilities, so my longings for family and friends could only be a silent inner torment. Still, there was the old saying, "There is always a way out." There were men in the cell whose homes were far out in the suburbs or even in another city, and when they received funds it was by postal money order. Certain detention center personnel were assigned the duty of bringing these to the prisoners for their signature. The money order slip had a space for a "brief message," which was usually left blank. But I had seen that Hu Xuezhong once received a money order from his wife on which she had written a few precious words of endearment, and suddenly the idea struck me that I could have my wife mail money to me rather than bringing it by hand to the detention center.

On the afternoon of 20 December 1999 a female police officer who was delivering money orders came into the lockup and called my name and two others. I received the slip through the steel bars of the door and saw that the "brief message" space was densely crowded with tiny characters. I scanned it quickly and then without thinking, I tore the message off. After signing the slip I handed it back to the officer, and when she took it she frowned and said, "What happened to the message space?" Never any good at making things up, I was tongue-tied. Fortunately, cellmates came to my rescue. Several men standing at the door with me chimed in, "When you brought the slip, that part was already missing." The officer let it pass and I was able to keep the precious message (though I never dared tear off any subsequent money orders).

After the officer left, I took the message out and read it carefully. My wife had written, "Why haven't I received your request for funds this month? The high walls separate us, but they cannot separate our hearts. No matter what happens I will always be with you, forever. We are fine. Jiang Feng works hard at his studies, so don't worry. Our friends are all thinking of you." As I finished reading, tears were streaming down my cheeks. When one is locked up in prison, "a letter from home is worth ten thousand pieces of gold." This letter had passed through four successive steel doors carrying my wife's love and had bound our two hearts even more tightly together. That night the tides in my heart rose and fell and I was not able to sleep. The twenty-four years that my wife and I had known each other, and the twenty years that we had accompanied and depended on each other in marriage unrolled again before my eyes.

My wife was born in Changshu, Jiangsu, in December 1950. When she was in preschool her parents were transferred to Suzhou and the family moved there. In 1966, when the Cultural Revolution began, she was in her second year at Suzhou's Number One Middle School. Because her parents were deemed capitalist roaders, the best she could hope for was to be considered a member of the "uninvolved faction." After spending four years in a production brigade in Kunshan County, she returned to her hometown of Changshu and joined the local Tangqiao production brigade as an "educated youth returned to the home area." At the end of 1974 she went to work in the Changshu County textile machine factory as a lathe operator. Her registration was still in the countryside and she was still an "educated youth." In the spring and summer of 1975, after energetic string-pulling by my high school classmate Lu Zhengfang, I got to know Zhang Hong and we began a legendary, circuitous romance. Even today, the girls with whom she worked in the factory delight in recounting our story. In the spring of 1978 I enrolled in the Beijing Institute of Aeronautics as a member of the "class of '77."* In the summer of 1978 Zhang Hong was transferred from the Changshu bed sheet factory back to Suzhou to work in the Southgate Trade Building.

At the end of 1978, as a thirty-year-old college student, my application for permission to marry received the stamp of approval from the Beijing Institute of Aeronautics. On the eve of the Lunar New Year in 1979 we picked up our marriage certificate in Suzhou, and on Lunar New Year's day in 1980 we were married in a lively unconventional wedding ceremony in Changshu. In the spring of 1981 Zhang Hong was able to work out an exchange of work assignments and move to Beijing, and on 10 November 1981 Jiang Feng arrived. From the spring of 1982 we were together morning and evening through both difficult and happy times. In her after-work hours she completed technical secondary school and then passed stiff exams and earned a three-year college degree.

For the past twenty-four years we have walked together in wind and rain, with our understanding and love for each other constantly growing. For twenty-four years, living in frugal simplicity, we have together sought the truth, accepting our lives and knowing that we will accept death when it comes.

In the middle of January 2000 I received the second message, which I remember as follows: "Did you receive my 26 November transmittal of funds? I don't like winter, but winter is here and therefore spring is not far off. I miss you and wish I could see you. Our friends all ask after you. Our parents, siblings, and friends back home all understand what you are doing."

Near the end of February I received the third message, saying, "I went home for Spring Festival;† everything is fine. On the third day of the new year I got together with some of our friends. They all miss you and are concerned about you. Baba ("Dad") has trouble walking, but his mind is still clear. He insisted on giving me some money. My mom's health is so-so, and your mother is in pretty good health. Younger brother and sister are fine. Jiang Feng will take the TOEFL‡ on February 26th."

---

* In the fall of 1977, after the death of Mao and the arrest of the Gang of Four, a nationwide college entrance examination was administered for the first time since the Cultural Revolution began eleven years earlier. Successful applicants in this unprecedentedly competitive examination began their studies after the Lunar New Year in 1978 but were known as members of the "class of '77," for the year of the examination.

† Spring Festival, the first two weeks of the first lunar month of the year, is by far the most important holiday of the year and is the time when everybody tries to go home for visits with their families.

‡ Test of English as a Foreign Language. This US-administered test is required of all foreign applicants for admission to American colleges and universities. But because English language competence has been considered very important in China since the 1990s, many high school students take it even if they have no immediate plans to go abroad.

At the end of March I received the fourth message: "I have already let our friends read and appreciate the five documents,* and on 10 November I mailed a copy to the Madman.† Someone told me recently about your circumstances inside. It's been exactly ten months since we last saw each other."

On the morning of 29 April 2000 I saw attorneys Mo Shaoping and Wang Gang. Attorney Mo told me that because my time had exceeded the legal limit for detention without a decision, he had submitted a brief to the First Intermediate Court requesting that my detention status be changed from "held in custody" to "under bail, awaiting trial." Attorney Wang gave me the news that Jiang Feng had passed the preliminary college entrance exams with two grades of "Excellent" and the remainder "Good."

That afternoon I was happily surprised to receive a message from my son. It was carefully composed, with neat and clear handwriting: "Baba, I have passed the preliminary entrance exams and am beginning to prepare for the formal exams. At Spring Festival we went to the old home place. The relatives expressed their concern for you. It's been almost a year since I've had our traditional meal of scrambled eggs with tomatoes and noodles with pickled vegetables, but I will never forget that flavor. Mom and I are doing very well; don't worry about us. Baba, I will always support you! Your son, Jiang Feng, 17 April."

When I finished reading my son's message my eyes once again filled with tears. My son's understanding of me exceeded my expectations. Now 1.83 meters tall, he was beginning to exhibit intellectual maturity and a splendid character. This was an immeasurable comfort to me.

The adage "No one knows a son like a father" made me feel ashamed. I had been too concerned about myself; I was not concerned enough, didn't worry enough, about my son, and didn't have sufficient understanding of him. I could name three of his virtues: honesty, independence, and frugality; but beyond that I didn't know much. As to shortcomings, I only knew that he was reluctant to exert himself, and not sufficiently hardworking; but that was about all. I didn't know his opinions or his evaluation of what I had done. I had only hoped that my misfortune would encourage him and urge him on, helping him grow into a real man. After a year now, he had unexpectedly brought me a pleasant surprise. Now my jail time was even more worthwhile.

---

* The five documents that made up the author's self-defense in court.

† There was a current folk rhyme that called Jiang Zemin "the Actor," Li Peng "the Fool," and Zhu Rongji "the Madman." At the time of writing, Jiang was president of China, Zhu was premier, and Li was chairman of the National People's Congress.

CHAPTER TWENTY-ONE

~

Occasional Loneliness

Among the men who were locked up, the political prisoners were the steadiest. Not only were they calm and unperturbed, their arrests had not brought a halt to their cause. Still, although I was respected both for my status and my friendly approach, while I continued my efforts, there were times when I was perplexed, or worried, or lonely. After a period of careful observation and quiet thought, I came to realize that the crux of my situation was my respect for nonviolence and the advocacy of peaceful evolution, while the people around me were wedded to China's violent culture and the Communist Party's devotion to the philosophy of struggle.

In the lockup, if one talked about the self-indulgence of bureaucrats or the degeneracy of scholars and famous individuals, one wouldn't be lonely. If one brought up the gap between rich and poor or the injustices of society, one wouldn't be lonely. If one denounced the use of torture to force confessions or corruption in the justice system, one definitely wouldn't be lonely. Once, to my cellmates' delight, I recited a poem on bureaucratic corruption, a parody of Mao Zedong's 1935 "Long March," which, in the early decades of the PRC [People's Republic of China], all schoolchildren were required to memorize. But when the conversation turned to "how to reform China," my advocacy of nonviolence elicited no support. Rather, everyone wanted to talk at the same time, saying that violence must be repaid with violence, and rebellion is justified. The following is typical of conversations that I had with my cellmates:

Cellmates: To deal with the Communist Party without violence is hopeless.

Jiang: But it worked in Eastern Europe and the Soviet Union.

Cellmates: In China there is definitely no hope.

Jiang: How about Taiwan's movement to democracy?

Cellmates: That's because the Nationalist Party is more open-minded. It won't work in the mainland.

Jiang: Suppose the people once again revolt against official exploitation and bring about regime change? Would that be significant?

Cellmates: Never mind whether it's significant or not. Make the change and then let's see.

Jiang: Even if they can ignore one call for reform, eventually it will be unavoidable. Don't we have to face up to the prospect of peaceful transformation?

Cellmates: Well, we'll leave it for future generations to do.

Jiang: Why shouldn't we begin it?

Cellmates: You are educated and can write essays, but how can we begin anything?

Jiang: Between submission and rebellion there is something that everyone can do. We can gradually withdraw support for the rulers, causing the backward system to lose its ability to function. This is called using the power of the powerless.

Cellmates: If the system stops functioning, won't they arrest people?

Jiang: If we nonviolently reduce our cooperation, or cease to cooperate, the great majority of people won't be arrested. The few who will be caught should be willing to serve time in jail.

Cellmates: If you are arrested and get into a life or death struggle with them, and you use speech while they use force, it will be very uneven and unfair. If you get out and write another "Letter to the Whole Nation," "Light a Million Candles" won't work. You must write "Pick Up Your Swords and Spears, Axes and Guns," and remember that "political power grows out of the barrel of a gun."*

Deep-rooted habits are very difficult to change. In the cell, martial arts books and movies were very popular. Aside from myself, there was hardly

---

* This is a reference to one of Mao Zedong's most famous statements. In his 1938 article, "Problems of War and Strategy," he said "Every Communist must grasp the truth that 'political power grows out of the barrel of a gun.'"

anyone who did not read such books or watch those movies. I believe that the savage lust for blood and violence has long inhibited the development of new sensibilities and the spread of understanding. To a lot of Chinese the notion of "the power of the powerless" was an entirely new concept. Without effective enlightenment, there would not be a critical number of people who would identify with this idea. After I get out I must intensify my efforts.

CHAPTER TWENTY-TWO

~

Victims of Injustice and Crackdowns on Criminals

When men in the cell talked about their own cases, the term that was heard most often was *dianbei.** "Injustice," or "wrongly accused," was also often heard, as in "The punishment is too severe; it's not just." But if second- or third-timers heard these complaints, they would rebuke the speaker: "You think you've been treated unjustly; if it was in the crackdown of 1983, you would have been 'dragged out.' I'll tell you the truth. Back then, everyone in this cell, except for the economic criminals, would be 'dragged out.'" That meant to be sentenced to death with the sentence carried out immediately. I had heard quite a lot about the 1983 crackdown and felt that what the second-timers said was true.

The crackdown of 1983 was a result of the personal whim of high officials. In the summer of 1983 Deng Xiaoping, as chairman of the Military Commission, took direct control of the government. He summoned Liu Fuzhi, minister of public security, and ordered that within three years three campaigns were to be carried out, and he wanted this done with *yan*, that is, strictly and severely. The crackdown began at once. In that "model movement of personal rule," the solemnity and fairness of the law were recklessly set aside. Legal criteria were ignored, minor offenses were severely punished, abnormally severe sentences were commonplace, and confessions forced by torture were routine. Treating human life as not worth a straw was the order of the day. The ghosts of victims of that crackdown and the resulting proliferation of "punishment that does not fit the crime" are still moaning today.

---

* This is a colloquial expression, similar to the more common *daomei*, that registers helplessness and despair at the bad luck that has befallen one.

Mu Yongshun told me that in 1983 he had taken an old telephone from his work unit to use at home and was punished with fifteen days of administrative detention. But then when the crackdown got under way he was arrested again and given a four-year sentence. He said that this unjust arrest and punishment had ruined his life. Hao Weijun knew a man who in 1983 had stolen a box of welding electrodes worth a little more than ten yuan and was sentenced to nine years in prison. He also knew about a couple who had been caught by a joint defense squad while they were having a romantic meeting in a park. Out of embarrassment the woman lied and said she had been "forced," and the man, who was tortured until he falsely confessed to "taking liberties" with her, was sentenced to eight years in prison. Hu Xuezhong knew someone who was suspected of stealing something from his girlfriend's home. The man "confessed" under torture and was sentenced to fifteen years. Several years later the circumstances were clarified and he was released to return home, but his health had been ruined. Hu Xuezhong also knew of someone who had been executed for stealing half a cartload of cucumbers. Shang Jianguo told me that when he was serving time in Gansu's Number One Prison in 1983 there was a man in his cell who had stolen a pocketbook containing only five yuan and was sentenced to fifteen years. Later he had witnessed two cases of revised judgments. One was a case of rape, and the other of taking liberties and harming a woman. In both cases the men were sentenced to ten years, and had already served four years when the crackdown got under way. The judgments were then changed to death sentences and all of the four men involved were taken out and shot.

From the fragments that I have listed above, one can see how far the "crackdown of 1983" strayed from the spirit of the rule of law. Of course laws undergo change over time, but the justice and solemnity of law must not fluctuate with changing circumstances. One set of laws cannot be enforced strictly at some times and then lightly, or even ignored, at other times, so that when "problems pile up and the situation becomes grim," a battle strategy can be organized, which will proceed strictly, severely, and quickly, sentencing and executing people left and right without discussion or reprieve. Yet, more than fifteen years after the dark curtain of the crackdown of 1983, officialdom is careful to avoid the subject and the media keep silent about it. Not only that, they still consider "crackdown" a magic weapon that can be brought out and used at the slightest provocation. Of course subsequent crackdowns have not been as reckless and frantic as in 1983, but the use of torture continues, while administrative organs still interfere with the judiciary, and special treatment for those with *tuo* goes on. I think that as long as personal rule persists instead of the rule of law, when the climate demands it and a political need arises, the dark curtain of 1983 will once again be drawn down.

CHAPTER TWENTY-THREE

~

The Clank of Chains at Dawn

The Beijing Municipal Detention Center has a year-round capacity of eighty death row inmates. The closest one was half a meter from me, and the farthest was fifty meters. Almost every week someone received a death sentence in his initial trial and joined the ranks of those on death row, and almost every week death sentences were confirmed in second hearings and someone was taken out and executed. This was the so-called ironclad rule of death row, including the turnover. On the day of an execution, the prisoner was usually brought out of the cell around eight o'clock in the morning. But because prisoners who were being called for ordinary investigations, court appearances, or other administrative reasons were also taken out at this time, we had no way of knowing whether someone had "set out on their final journey" on a certain day. However, if before breakfast on a given day we heard the steel door of the cell next to us open and then we heard the clank of chains in the corridor, we could be pretty sure that there was going to be an execution on this day.

December 8th, 1999, was overcast and cold. We had just gotten up when we heard the door of the adjacent cell being opened. This was quickly followed by irregular, rising and falling sounds of chains. We figured that at least six or seven men were being taken out. On the 13th of December Xiao Haijun had been brought into cell 404. He said that on the 9th of the month, when he was in the Chaoyang detention center, he had read in the *Beijing Daily News* that nine men, including Chen Lianmin, had been executed on the 8th. Chen Lianmin had been in cell 404 and had slept right next to me. On the morning of 23 September, the day before the Mid-Autumn Festival, he had gone to the First Intermediate Court for his initial trial and had not returned to the cell. Two and a half months later his spirit had now returned to the Western Heavens.

There is an old saying, "To be in different professions is like being separated by a mountain range." In the detention center it was "To be separated by a wall was like being cut off by a mountain range." Aside from the news that was conveyed by the sound of the chains in the morning, we had no way of knowing what was going on in the next cell, among the men sentenced to death. Our curiosity often led us to guessing and debating such questions as how these men passed their final hours. Were they given prior notice of the day of their execution? Were they given a special final meal the day before their execution? Were the authorities afraid of the prisoners' screams, and did they have some way to keep them from screaming? If it weren't for two things that happened later, even if we had stayed in cell 404 for a year, these questions would have remained a mystery.

The first incident occurred on 21 January 2000 when I was in the lawyers' building and met Yang Shubin who had been sentenced to death for robbery and confined in cell 413, wearing shackles and handcuffs. That day he had been taken out of the cell to see his lawyer for an appeal of his case. I took the opportunity to ask the questions that I had long wanted to put to someone, and he answered them one by one. He said that inmates were never told when they would be taken out for execution, and of course they were not given an "improved" last meal. At 8:00 a.m. on the day of execution (or 6:00 a.m. if it was a publicly announced verdict) the cell door was opened and a warden came and called the names of the men who were to be taken out. Court police were waiting outside the door. As soon as the condemned man stepped outside the cell a rope was tightened around his neck to prevent him from crying out. Then he was taken for a blood test to make sure of his identity. After he was taken to the court, his handcuffs were removed and his arms and hands were tightly bound behind his back. Then the shackles were removed, and after the judge read the appeal decision, the prisoner was taken to the execution ground. Yang also said that all the chores in the cell were done by the condemned prisoners, including washing their cell partner's clothes. The cell partner took a 30–40 percent "cut" of any money that the condemned man had received from his family or friends. Yang said that his own appeal was hopeless. Only 5 percent of the death row prisoners were taken back to the cell after their appeals.

The second incident occurred on the afternoon of 22 June 2000, when Li Shoulong, an ethnic Korean economic criminal, was transferred into cell 404. He had been partnered for eight months with a condemned man in cell 411. Then he had submitted a request that he be allowed to serve out his sentence in his hometown, and as a result he was transferred to 404. As soon as he arrived, we asked him whether the answers that I had gotten from Yang

Shubin were true, and he confirmed all but one of them. He said that the entire amount of an executed prisoner's money was now kept in the wardens' office; the partner didn't get to "cut" it.

Yang also told us that a condemned man was called the "heavy" and the formal term for the "partner" was "jail guardian." The partner had to write a "guardian's report" every week, but since there was really nothing to report, these reports were like something made up by elementary school students. Cell 411 had seven partners and eight heavies. For the most part, the partners slept on the platform, though the "night watches" were entirely their responsibility. Night watch was divided into first and second shifts, with one man taking each shift. The atmosphere in the death row cells was much more solemn and constrained than in the ordinary cells. The heavies were not allowed to talk in a loud voice and were not permitted to sing or even to hum a tune. They often contemplated their situation, with the two main topics being *dianbei*, or bad luck, and how they had let their families down. They very seldom felt repentance for their criminal actions. This made me think of the so-called quasi-condemned men I had known in cells 313 and 404—that is, inmates who were expected, by themselves and others, to be sentenced to death. Among the ten men I knew in this category, I had only heard Sun Baocang express repentance for his actions. And among about a hundred prisoners I had known and talked with, only two had repented their actions. Can we say from this that Chinese people lack a consciousness of regret and repentance?

Of course we had still other questions about condemned men. For example, where was the execution ground? After a person was executed, were his organs removed, and by whom? But it would be hard to get answers to these questions in the detention center; I would have to wait until I got out and then look into the matter further.

Regarding the questions to which we had found answers, my cellmates had two comments. First, the fact that condemned men were not given a good meal prior to their execution indicated that the Communist Party was not as generous-hearted as the old emperors. Under the emperors, on the night before the autumn executions, the turnkeys would bring a few dishes of food and soup and a jug of wine to the condemned prisoners. Now they get only a couple of cornmeal buns and a bowl of vegetable soup. Second, in the matter of not allowing a prisoner to speak out prior to his execution, the Communist Party was clearly not as magnanimous as the Nationalist Party. In the movies we had often seen condemned communists shouting slogans as they were led to execution. Obviously their windpipes had not been choked, nor had they been strangled by ropes around their necks. Nowadays a condemned man could not open his mouth and speak; he was totally cut off.

CHAPTER TWENTY-FOUR

~

A Sketch of the Detention Center

The address for all of the inmates held in Section Seven was uniformly Number 44, Side Gate, Banbuqiao, Xuanwu District. In 1989, eleven years ago, when I was in the Qincheng prison and my family sent me money, clothing, or books, they used this same address. At the time, I had no idea where Banbuqiao was or what sort of place "Number 44, Side Gate" was. Now as I set pen to paper to write this account, I have lived at this "Side Gate" for thirteen months and seventeen days, and I am very clear about Section Seven's overall arrangement and management.

Anyone walking on Banbuqiao Street would see the West Gate of Section Seven. Family members who have received a request to bring money would arrive at the reception office just inside the West Gate. About forty meters beyond this gate is the main North Gate. Here there are two placards, "Beijing Municipal Detention Center" and "Branch Office of the Beijing Municipal People's Procuratorate." There is a large electrically operated iron gate, which, except for the occasional entrance and exit of vehicles, is tightly closed all day. Beside the big iron gate is a small iron gate for pedestrian entry and exit that is guarded by a policeman with a loaded rifle on his shoulder. After entering the North Gate, one sees the outer yard of Section Seven. In this yard are the administrative office building, the preliminary hearings building, and two further buildings for the lawyers and the police. A hundred meters to the south, on the west side, is another big iron gate guarded by armed police. Inside this gate is the inner yard of Section Seven.

Having eaten prison fare for more than a year, I feel that I am well qualified to speak of it. Beginning in early December 1999, breakfast every Monday through Friday consisted of one cornmeal bun and one bowl of cornmeal porridge, with the addition of two small pieces of *xian geda* (lumpy-noodle bread). Lunch was two wheat-flour buns and a bowl of vegetable soup, and dinner was two cornmeal buns and a bowl of vegetable soup. On Saturday and Sunday the morning meal was two wheat-flour buns and a bowl of vegetable soup, and the afternoon meal was two cornmeal buns and another bowl of vegetable soup. Through the year there were three main vegetables: from late October till late April we had Chinese cabbage; from early May to early July it was ordinary cabbage, and from mid-July to mid-October it was potatoes. Every year we also had squash and celery about ten times each, and turnips about five times. We had some kind of bean product once a year, during Spring Festival, and we had *jiaozi* dumplings on the first day of the Lunar New Year. There was usually a small amount of ground meat in the vegetable soup, and on New Year's Day, May Day, Mid-Autumn Festival, and October 1st National Day, we had slow-cooked pork. We also had slow-cooked pork twice during Spring Festival.

In March of 2000 the foods that were available for purchase in the prison shop suddenly improved. The thirty-some items that had been available were expanded to more than seventy. No matter that the foodstuffs that were brought in at wholesale prices were sold to us at a markup of 30 to 80 percent above the retail prices on the outside; the inmates weighed the pros and cons and welcomed this exploitation, saying that if they couldn't buy anything and had to depend on the meals that were provided for us, their eyes would long ago have turned green.

There were four things that met with universal complaints in Section Seven. First, every Monday, Wednesday, and Friday morning the loudspeakers broadcast the "Detention Center Regulations" and the "Standards of Conduct." Each spiel was broadcast twice. This foolish action met with total rejection on the part of all the inmates. It had absolutely no positive effect and just resulted in a round of curses. Second, there were five occasions during the year—New Year's Day, Spring Festival, May Day, the August 1st anniversary of the establishment of the army, and the October 1st National Day—when a "savage" cleaning of the prison occurred. Of course it was necessary to keep the prison clean, but what was the point in coming in like foreign devils or bandits invading a farm village. Each time one of these cleanings occurred, all the inmates were first driven into the exercise cages, then the guards and wardens came in dressed in dark green smocks and rooted through our bedding, clothing, food, and personal articles, leaving everything in a disorderly jumble. While this was going on, other guards would undertake personal searches of the inmates in the exercise cages. After twenty minutes or so, the cells were left looking like a disaster area, and the guards swaggered away with only our newly purchased playing cards in their pockets, having failed to find our homemade antenna in the TV room or the drafts for *My Life in Prison*. Of course everybody roundly cursed this behavior of "government employees."* Even the men who were in for robbery were bitterly indignant, saying, "How are they any different from us?"

The third object of loathing was the rampant formalism that accompanied the "specially designated struggles." Beginning on 3 July 2000, there was a two-week period of "informing and exposing," when we had to remain in our assigned seats on the sleeping platform from dinnertime until 10 p.m. We were not allowed to watch television, play cards or chess, or engage in any kind of entertainment activities. With twenty-six men jammed together in the midsummer heat, having sat still through the day, when evening came we especially needed some relaxation, and to be subjected to this kind of nonsensical and formalistic rule was inhumane and could not have any good result.

Fourth was that at Mid-Autumn Festival and the Lantern Festival,† the prison did not give the Chinese prisoners free mooncakes and sweet dumplings, though they did distribute these treats to the foreign prisoners. The Chinese inmates unanimously denounced this absurd and mean-minded way of doing things. On Chinese holidays the Chinese prisoners were ignored and provoked, while the foreign prisoners wouldn't necessarily appreciate the attention that they received. In the first place, they didn't celebrate the Chinese festivals, and besides, knowing that the Chinese inmates did not receive the treats, they would feel very perplexed and embarrassed.

At festival time, Section Seven followed the standard Communist Party line of inviting people to submit essays and broadcasting discussions to entice and force inmates to "reveal their inner feelings." Although many people were fed up with this sort of thing, they still complied with the requests. For my part, I continued to hope that everyone could gradually come to understand that to refuse to cooperate was actually a better choice. If you don't dare to be a hero of resistance, that doesn't mean that you have to debase yourself to a position of slavery. Without being either obsequious or arrogant,

---

* Government jobs are highly prized and government employees are supposed to be models of good behavior.

† The Lantern Festival (*Yuanxiao*) occurs on the night of the 15th of the first lunar month, that is, on the first full moon after the Lunar New Year. Like mooncakes for Mid-Autumn Festival, consumption of *tangyuan*, sweet dumplings made of glutinous rice flour, is de rigueur for the Lantern Festival.

you could say a few words, or you could laugh and not say anything. Still, listening to the all-encompassing slavish pronouncements on the loudspeaker, I felt more sympathy than resentment. These inmates were no longer the ignorant dupes of the 1970s; they now understood that they were speaking against their own convictions. Still, I could detect that their self-deprecatory speech was playacting, done on the surface in order to cope with their environment. I wrote only one piece on cell 404; the title was "A Brief Analysis of Riots and Fighting in Prison." But because it made no attempt to fawn on the authorities, and in fact expressed disagreement with the Detention Center's "strike at prison bullies" policy, it was not accepted for publication.

Then should we say that the policies and personnel of Section Seven only received adverse criticism from the inmates, never gaining favorable comment? No, that is not true. For example, everyone approved of such policies and actions as the guaranteed supply of cold water, hiring of workers to replace prisoners for cooking and distributing food, and always promptly delivering to inmates the money that was brought or sent to them. And there were some guards, as well as doctors, who were universally praised by the inmates. Take Dr. Wang, for example. The reason for our praise of her was basic and very simple: she treated us humanely.

Here I attach my essay on fighting in Section Seven:

A Brief Analysis of Fighting in the Detention Center

Everyone knows that prison bullies used to be a scourge of prison life. Individuals or small cliques would form gangs and purposely take advantage of people, humiliating and abusing them. The existence of such jail bullies has been common. They meted out inhumane treatment to others. They would act recklessly and were often savage and cruel. Such behavior was possible only because it was openly or covertly permitted. Now, because of various measures and policies that have been put in place, although such things still happen occasionally, they are no longer typical or representative of Beijing's detention centers. Today the thing that is most commonly harmful to good order is fighting among the inmates.

This occurs when two inmates attack each other or a larger number of people become involved in personal violence. These fights usually occur for some specific reason, in contrast to the way prison bullies provoked trouble or attacked people for no reason. Also, these fights usually take place between men both of whom are to some extent problematical individuals, neither of them being a really virtuous person. The better fighter is likely to be a worse person, but the weaker one is almost always also at fault to some extent. This is different from the bullies who used their strength against the weak, flaunting their evil to oppress the good. Also, these fights burst out suddenly, with two men unexpectedly mixing it up with each other. And there is often the danger of escalation. The loser in a fight will always look for an opportunity for revenge, usually at a higher level of violence.

Fighting has become a prominent and frequent phenomenon. On the surface, the principal causes are as follows. First, there has been an argument and neither side is willing to give in, each man challenging the other. For example, two men are sitting quietly playing chess, when one of them is unwilling to accept that he is losing the game. Each accuses the other of being a poor player, and pretty soon they are hitting and kicking each other, noses are bloodied, and faces are swollen. In a second kind of situation, someone feels that he has been cheated by a cellmate. It might be that two men share this feeling about each other, and the rancor between them builds up until one day it explodes. Or the feeling of grievance is on only one side, one person feeling that another is unbearably hateful, always trying to cheat him. He reaches a point where he can't stand it any longer, and fists fly. Third, a man might be moody or depressed and suddenly fly off the handle. Or someone has received his statement of charges and finds the wording too severe, and his psychological resistance suddenly drops to the point where he can't stand even the harmless chatter of other inmates: so he starts attacking people.

Fourth, sometimes joking or teasing is overdone and shame turns to anger. Someone throws a peanut or a clove of garlic, then a shoe is thrown, and anger grows until they are fighting. Fifth, a monitor is seen as being unfair or carries out his duties in a slapdash manner. In all of these circumstances, a spark ignites and a fight gets under way within a minute. First, something is said that hurts another person, then the language becomes abusive and obscene, antagonism quickly heats up, blood vessels swell, dark bile wells up, and a man loses control of himself. Fists and feet go wild and a fight is under way.

At a deeper level, the causes of fighting are the following: First, the men lack a moral standard of respect for others' character and dignity. This can be clearly seen in the coarse and abusive language that often comes out as soon as a man opens his mouth. Second, a basic concept of respect for an individual's rights and interests is lacking. A man will purposely take advantage of others in an underhanded attempt to gain "face." He never admits to being a scoundrel, but sees himself as being entirely upright and proper. Third is an excess of vanity, recklessly seeking to build self-respect. And fourth is a habitual dependence on violence and a deep-rooted inclination to cause trouble.

There is absolutely no doubt that this problem of fighting should be carefully monitored and measures should be taken to control it and bring it to an end. Generally speaking, the inmates are in the Detention Center because they have broken the law, and they all have had a rough life and are depressed. But for the great majority of them, one cannot say that they have no conscience or have lost their ability to distinguish between right and wrong. Therefore, promotion of good and suppression of evil, while remaining on guard, should encourage them to give up violence, adopt reason, and develop an atmosphere of peaceful coexistence. This would greatly reduce fighting, and it should be entirely feasible. In concrete terms, the following measures could be undertaken:

1. Launch practical and effective educational activities to help the inmates develop standards of civility and the concept of the rule of law. Teach them that cursing is shameful and fighting is unlawful. Once they have these standards and concepts in their hearts, once they have absorbed the moral norm of respect for people and their rights and interests, curses and dirty language will no longer flow from their mouths, and utterances of tolerance and forgiveness, and heartwarming speech, will naturally come forth. The inclination to take advantage of others will be greatly reduced. How can this be done? In some cells fighting has already been stopped. The key is that a standard of civility has been established.
2. Act with more fairness; leave a margin for self-respect. Monitors must be fair in their criticism and correction of others, and their methods must be appropriate, leaving a margin for self-respect.
3. Respond quickly so as to prevent trouble from spreading. When a fight breaks out in a cell, it must be stopped immediately. Don't let the men go into the bathroom to settle the score.
4. Distinguish perpetrator and victim, and mete out punishment fairly and impartially. Strict criticism should be based on who was right and who was wrong in the fight, and punishment should be fair and should cause the perpetrator to sincerely repent and earnestly reform himself.

11 May 2000

This essay was given to Warden Song on 13 May 2000.

CHAPTER TWENTY-FIVE

~

The Campaign for Democracy

Chapters 25–29 are random thoughts, which I wrote down as they occurred to me.

"Campaign for Democracy" is a good term. In actual practice, however, except for such short-lived surges as the fifty-odd days of the 1989 democracy movement,* it has reached only a few people. Those who have been active in this movement are belittled as people who make their living off popular discontent. Thus the democracy movement has not found much sympathy among the masses and is still struggling to develop a closer relationship with the people at large. One finds the following attitudes toward the activists in the movement.

1. Keep a respectful distance†

There are many who express respect for the democratic activists but feel that these are exceptional people who come from a different mold and whom they would not want to imitate or become involved with.

2. Caution

While it is recognized that the democratic activists are dedicated to their cause, the general public does not fully understand their motivation, or, for

* "The 1989 democracy movement" refers to a series of demonstrations throughout April and May 1989 that eventually led to the government crackdown beginning on the night of June 3–4, which came to be known as "the Tiananmen massacre," or, in official Chinese terminology, "the June 4th Incident."

† This is an allusion to Confucius's (551–479 BCE) famous response to a question about his attitude toward gods and spirits: "I respect them but keep my distance from them."

fear it might harm their own interests, they are very cautious and reluctant to get involved.

3. Indifference

There is the traditional indifference to political matters and the fact that most people's energies are directed to other concerns—worldly materialism, for example. Many people don't even listen to the Voice of America or Radio Free Asia.

4. Avoidance

Some see the democratic activists as politicians and think they are not much better than the bureaucrats of the Communist Party. Others go further, perceiving them as even worse than the latter, and therefore strongly disliking them.

Aside from the authorities' suppression and defamation and the constraints of traditional concepts, another important reason for the difficulty in promoting a democracy movement is that the activists themselves lack a thorough understanding of the democratic process. One way to solve the problem would be to bring in people more focused and better informed so as to improve the image of the movement. Another way would be to initiate a movement based on the idea of citizenship, promulgating a new concept of politics and government.

For a citizenship campaign there must be a clear understanding that the objective of those involved is not to change their status from ruled to ruler, but to hold their heads up and be real citizens. Ordinary members of such a movement would not need to be seen as "participating in politics"; rather that they are just acting according to their conscience and living a decent, ethical life.

23 February 2000

CHAPTER TWENTY-SIX

~

Reading the Newspapers

The *Beijing Daily* cannot be compared to the *Southern Weekend*,* but in the lockup we could only see the former, and even it was allowed into the Detention Center on a very limited schedule. From late October 1999 to the present (February 2000), we were only allowed to see about ten days' papers. To tell the truth, though, the *Beijing Daily* was not entirely propagandistic nonsense. The "Notes on Beijing Culture" column in the 30 July 1999 issue included an item, "A Life Guided by Intelligence," which was actually a very good article.

With quotations from a foreign journalist and an editor at a publishing house, it argued that China's problem was a matter of ideological backwardness and a deep-seated lack of political awareness. Of course the writer could not point out that this was the result of the authorities establishing restricted zones that thinkers were not permitted to enter; but newspaper readers could easily understand this.

The foreign journalist had protested to the writer, Fang Gang, "In Beijing I cannot get up-to-date information or buy the books that I need. I can't live an 'intelligent' life here."

---

* *Southern Weekend* (*Nanfang Zhoumo*), a weekly newspaper published in Guangzhou, is generally considered the most outspoken newspaper in the country, considerably more bold in criticizing the government than other publications. It is periodically shut down by the censors, and its reporters are occasionally ordered to be relieved of duty. The *Beijing Daily* (*Beijing Ribao*) is much preferred over the official Party mouthpiece, the *People's Daily* (*Renmin Ribao*), because of its more lively style and reporting of local news.

While having dinner with the writer, an editor of an academic publishing company had complained that an extremely important book by the most advanced thinker of the century was, for a number of reasons, not available in China. He said, "Many of us scholars spend our most valuable time pursuing an important question which might already have been solved by our colleagues in the West." Some Chinese scholars who have spent a few years in the West return to China and don't dare to take their studies further, but change their profession and turn to business. "They realize that no matter how hard they work, it won't be possible in this generation to reach a high level of scholarly achievement, so they might just as well do something practical."

In China, people used not to dare to talk freely at a dinner party, but now it is more common to speak out among friends. If this progress could continue so that what is said around the table could also be printed in newspapers and spoken on television, it would then no longer be impossible to pursue an "intelligent" way of life.

Though the inability of the Chinese to embrace democracy can be blamed on those who govern us, it is also related to a tolerance of the system on the part of the governed. Generally speaking, Chinese people's spiritual or mental pursuits have always taken second place to their material interests. Furthermore, the distance between the two is immense. This is perhaps the main reason why China has fallen behind Eastern Europe and Russia.

29 February 2000

CHAPTER TWENTY-SEVEN

~

The Taiwan Question

The Taiwan question was created by the failure of the Nationalist-Communist civil war to reach a thoroughgoing conclusion in 1949. The Communist Party was unable to "liberate" Taiwan with military force, and the Nationalists, who had retreated to Taiwan, refused to surrender. Therefore for more than fifty years the territory of China has had two national titles, with the mainland called the People's Republic of China and Taiwan the Republic of China. When the United Nations recognized the latter, the mainland did not give up its designation, and after the UN shifted recognition to the PRC, Taiwan continued to fly the flag of the ROC. If Lee Teng-hui's* "theory of two nations" expresses this actuality, it must be considered as valid.

The bizarre historical fact is that it was the mainland authorities' sworn brother Kim Il-sung, who provided the first impetus for the shattering of the Chinese Communists' dream of "liberation." On 25 June 1950, in defiance of world opinion, Kim Il-sung ordered his army to cross the 38th parallel and, in an all-out surprise attack on the Republic of Korea, brazenly started the Korean War, which was to take the lives of several million people. Later the United Nations armies, seeking justice, drove him back. Then he dragged his mainland Chinese comrades and brothers deep into the quagmire of a much larger war. At the same time, his aggressive actions inflamed American public opinion to such a pitch that the Truman administration ordered the Seventh Fleet into the Taiwan Strait. Thus, before Kim Il-sung's "dream of

* Lee Teng-hui, president of the Republic of China (Taiwan) from 1988 to 2000, led democratic reform in Taiwan and argued for recognition of Taiwan's independent status.

unification" (of North and South Korea) could succeed, he caused the Chinese Communists' "dream of unification" (of mainland China and Taiwan) to come to nothing. The people of Taiwan were thereby saved from suffering under Communist totalitarianism and were able to bring about their world-renowned "economic miracle" and to establish the first successful democratic government in the five thousand years of Chinese history.

It is not hard to understand that the decades of separation alone might have brought about profound alienation, not to mention that the values and norms of behavior of the two sides are now fundamentally different. Therefore there is no avoiding the strength of the feeling for Taiwan independence and the desire to maintain separation from China. Furthermore, for each additional day that the mainland's system persists, the movement for Taiwan to retain its independence will be further strengthened.

However, there is also a desire for unification in Taiwan, asking that all of China be unified under a democratic system. For example, Lien Chan, Soong Chu-yu, and Ma Ying-jeou* have often said that their policy is not "one country, two systems" but rather "one country with a *good* system." Up to the present, this tendency has been as strong as the demand for Taiwan independence. The ideas of both of these trends are incompatible with the Communist Party's proposals for unification under the flag of dictatorship. The mainland authorities say repeatedly that unification is the greatest benefit; for its sake, all other advantages can be set aside; for unification, we are willing to go to war. But I am very suspicious of this idea. Are the mainland authorities really so eager for unification? That anything and everything can be said and done to bring it about? If that were really the case, the solution would be easy. There would be a route to unification with no need to start a war—the mainland authorities could give up their autocratic rule and convert to a democratic system. This way, the vested interests would only have to lose their special privileges, which in any case should have been abolished long ago, and indeed, without the use of a single rifle or bullet, without the death of a single ordinary citizen, a peaceful outcome would be achieved. If this democratic, peaceful road to unification were taken, the fuel for the Taiwan independence movement would be removed, leaving it helpless to interfere with the process.

---

* At the time Jiang wrote this piece, Taiwan's year 2000 presidential election was just coming to a close. Lien Chan and Soong Chu-yu split the pro-unification vote, and on 18 March Taiwan independence advocate Chen Shui-bian won the election. This news would not yet have reached Jiang when, on 18 March, he wrote this piece. Ma Ying-jeou, mayor of Taipei at that time, became president in 2008.

Now if the mainland and Taiwan go to war (assuming that America does not intervene), not only will Taiwan be destroyed, but such cities as Beijing, Tianjin, Shanghai, Chongqing, and Guangzhou will be razed to the ground. The people will be plunged into the depths of misery, and great wealth destroyed, while enmity will be created among the Chinese people that could last for generations to come, and would cause a great regression in the strength of the Chinese nation. Compare this with the democratic and peaceful unification described above. If we assume for the moment that the mainland authorities do indeed want unification but that they would choose a despotic, military route over democratic and peaceful means, this clearly indicates that, in their minds, their own vested interests are all-important, and the present system, which enabled them to gain those benefits, is the most beneficial.

The mainland authorities have begun naked intimidation of Taiwan: "If you want to talk, all right; if you don't want to talk, that's OK too. Whether you talk or not, we'll do it our way. If you don't agree with our proposals, we'll go to war." How can this be called peaceful negotiation? It is clearly a threat of war, a forced agreement. Fortunately, the power of democracy in the world today is much greater than the power of autocracy. While autocracy can for now win out over smaller and weaker reform movements, it must take into account the much stronger force of worldwide democracy that hangs over its head.

Therefore, with the mainland authorities not daring to play with fire, there will be no war in the Taiwan Strait in the next eight or ten years.

18 March 2000

CHAPTER TWENTY-EIGHT

"Give Birth Early and Often"*

Today we were joined by a new prisoner, Li Jiting. He had been sentenced to seven years for helping to transport one hundred thousand yuan in counterfeit money. Growing up in a village in Henan Province, he had gotten married when he was fifteen, had a son when he was sixteen, and now had three sons and a daughter, now two years old. He said that in his hometown there were some youths who got married at age fourteen and had a baby at fifteen. For someone to marry at fifteen, as he had done, was not at all unusual. He was sure that by the time he was thirty-two he would have a grandson, while in the cities there might be many people who were thirty-two years old and didn't even have a son. Li Jiting also told me that in his area it was very common for a family to have four or more children, in contrast with the cities, where the great majority of people had only one child. It is reasonable to assume that in family planning, this practice of enforcing the one-child policy in some places and ignoring it in others was prevalent throughout the system and that it would lead to China's population structure becoming unbalanced and unhealthy. While the authorities brag about slowing global population growth, the Chinese people are swallowing the bitter results of the Communist Party's earlier policy of encouraging births, the seriousness of which has far from completely run its course.

20 March 2000

---

* "Zǎo shēng duō yù" is the author's ironic word play, reversing the meaning of the official slogan "Shǎo shēng yōu yù," "Have fewer children and provide superior nurturing for them."

CHAPTER TWENTY-NINE

Teachers' Low Self-Esteem

Since the Communist Party took control of the government, the relative social status of teachers has fallen to the lowest level in history. Over the past two years, the Zhu Rongji* administration, with its motto of "rejuvenating the country with science education," has not changed this basic state of affairs.

The *Beijing Daily* of 22 March reported on a study of the mental health of 2,292 teachers in 168 elementary and middle schools in the cities and villages of Liaoning Province. The results of the survey indicated that approximately 50 percent of the teachers had psychological problems. This is thirty percentage points higher than in the general population. Especially notable was the fact that 69 percent of those surveyed had relatively serious inferiority complexes. The salaries, meanwhile, of many teachers in the countryside were heavily in arrears.

An inferiority complex is something that cannot be hidden from oneself or from others, and that reflects a person's low status in society. For many years China's farmers have been the group with the lowest self-esteem. In recent years the self-esteem of blue collar laborers has fallen precipitously (not to mention laid-off laborers). Since 1949, teachers have not been accorded preferential treatment by the Communist regime, so it is not surprising that they have relatively strong feelings of inferiority. Here we have to note that the thing that one most hates and despises is the hypocrisy of officialdom: Those who are trumpeted as "the masters of the nation, the owners of the

* Zhu Rongji was premier of the PRC from 1998 to 2003.

land and the engineers of the human soul," actually have the most severe inferiority complexes, while those who modestly call themselves "public servants" have the greatest sense of pride and self-esteem. Over the past decade, when public servants have compared themselves with the tycoons, a sour feeling of inferiority has arisen. However, many of the tycoons were previously public servants. And furthermore, the present tycoons still don't dare not to do favors for the public servants, so both parties are kept happy.

26 March 2000

CHAPTER THIRTY

~

The Joy of Books

The Detention Center was not completely bereft of books. No cell was without copies of violent and bloody martial arts novels. Sometimes other books would also appear, for example, famous Chinese classics like *The Romance of the Three Kingdoms*. However, really good books were sorely lacking, and profitable reading material was hard to come by. Furthermore, when a year had passed, no good books had appeared in the library of Section Seven.

On 19 July 2000 attorneys Mo Shaoping and Wang Gang came to the Detention Center to tell me that Jiang Feng was leaving the next day to go to America to study. After explaining several goals that I held for my son, I then asked them to tell my wife that I wanted her to mail some books to the Detention Center so that my time in prison would not be completely wasted. I said that she should first mail the journals *The World of English* and *Readings*, which I had subscribed to at home for a long time. (Another good journal that I had subscribed to, *Methods*, had been arbitrarily closed down by the authorities in the spring of 1999.) I had in mind that if the Detention Center confiscated my journals, I would just consider that I had donated them to the Center so the personnel could get acquainted with some of the few good periodicals of contemporary China.

Much to my surprise, the first try was successful. At the beginning of August, Warden Song handed me two back issues of *The World of English*. After a year and three months, I once again had the great pleasure of reading this journal, which was like reuniting with an old friend. I couldn't help shouting out for joy in the cell. My cellmates had never seen such a journal as this, in fact had never heard of it. The attractively bound *World of English* quickly passed from hand to hand, and the novelty of Chinese and English on opposite pages had some of them leafing through it in fascination, though of course they ignored the English and only looked at the Chinese. Because the translation was also very elegant, they read with pleasure, and I had to wait my turn.

I recalled my long-standing relationship with this journal. When it was first published I was at the Beijing Institute of Aeronautics studying for my master's degree in aerodynamics, and I had bought the first issue from a bookstall on the street. From then on, I bought every issue, until later when I subscribed to it. In 1987 I went to England as a visiting scholar, and in a college in Wales, then at Oxford and Cambridge and in London, the language barrier caused me very little difficulty, and for this I must thank *The World of English*.

I had been locked up in Qincheng prison from 9 September 1989 to 6 February 1991. Every month I would put it on my book request slip, and my wife would bring it to the side gate of Number 44 Banbuqiao, and the officials would send it into Qincheng. During the days that I was in solitary confinement, reading it in a loud voice was a great blessing and pleasure for me. When the police guard, who'd had a middle school education, went past the door of my cell, he would pause and listen with an expression of happy enjoyment. After I was released I continued to read aloud every article in the journal in order to make up for my lack of opportunity to *speak* English. In every issue I found a few translation errors, and if I felt that they needed to be corrected, I would write to the editors of the journal, who wrote back to express their gratitude.

In the latter part of August 2000 I got the fifth and sixth issues of *Readings* for 1999. These had arrived in Section Seven at the end of July together with the two issues of *The World of English*. The reason they had reached me twenty days late didn't seem to be that someone wanted to read them but rather that they were anxious to inspect them carefully to make sure they didn't contain any inappropriate news from outside. The arrival of *Readings* also stirred up a lot of interest in the cell, adding some literary tone to the coarse little room. Again, almost none of my cellmates had had any contact with this journal on the outside; however, the caustic cartoons and incisive short essays quickly met with general approval. Although no one really wanted to read most of the other articles, everybody agreed that they were "very learned" and "of high quality." In present-day China, *Readings* is indeed an excellent journal. It not only provides a scholarly platform for the exchange of ideas, but also expresses the conscience of intellectuals and gives prominence to an ultimate concern for humanity. Naturally it has to avoid certain sensitive topics regarding some truths that are not supposed to be told. But what other journals across this great land would dare to publish Wang Ruoshui's writings arguing that Marxism is only one among many schools of thought? Still, in the past few years this journal has somewhat changed its flavor, often publishing articles of indifferent quality. Some of my very cultivated friends have stopped contributing to it. It's not a matter of standards being lowered, but just that they are no longer as sympathetic to the journal as they used to be. I continue to subscribe to *Readings* because it does still contain some good articles, and I like to hear both sides of the question.

Later on, issues 7 through 12 of *The World of English* and *Readings* also reached cell 404, and I continued to allow everybody to read them and copy excerpts as they pleased. However, after a while I discovered that one of the issues was missing. It had been quietly taken by a cellmate when his hearing was completed and he was sent to the Transfer Center.

After these journals had broken the ice, there was now hope that other good books would find their way within the walls. At the end of November I received Wei Junyi's *Record of Pain*, which is written with a depth of feeling and truthful language that shocks the reader into serious reflection. At the close of the twentieth century she said it was now time to cast aside contempt for human rights, and instead to recognize human rights as the cornerstone of society; time to abandon the treatment of people as tools or "strategic elements," and move on instead to a more enlightened doctrine where the well-being of the individual is paramount. Ms. Wei was suffering from a chronic illness and could not rise from her bed. As she slowly dictated these heartfelt words, we could only admire her devotion to her task.

In December of 2000 I had another happy surprise. Ms. Poole, a member of English PEN,* sent me an English book that gave a full and moving account of the past two hundred years in a Russian village. The book had been mailed to the "Banbuqiao Police Station, Beijing, China" and, having undergone multiple inspections, reached me complete and undamaged. It had made its way across the broad oceans and arrived carrying a breath of freedom from the British Isles and a sincere love and concern for humanity. Its arrival elicited many sighs from my cellmates.

---

* English PEN is part of a worldwide organization for the promotion of literature and freedom of expression, whose many activities include campaigning for the release of writers imprisoned for their beliefs.

There is one more book that must be mentioned. In January of 2001, *The Memoirs of Mao Zedong's Personal Physician*,* by the late Li Zhisui, appeared in the cell. Although this was a poor quality pirated publication, there was vigorous competition to read it, and it generated a great deal of thought and discussion. Cellmates had various opinions of the book, but there was one thing that all agreed on: the corruption that permeates officialdom began with Mao. Columbia University professor Andrew J. Nathan wrote an excellent preface for Mr. Li's book. And now let me mention that I have a special connection here. In 1991 I took part in translating Professor Nathan's *China's Crisis*, which was promptly brought out by Hong Kong's Mirror Publishing Company.

It seems as though in China it is becoming more and more difficult to keep the populace in ignorance. This is so not only in society in general, but also in the Detention Center. In Section Seven there are now several economic criminals in each cell, though there is only one political prisoner for about every ten cells. If there were political prisoners in every cell, to keep the people ignorant would be as difficult as climbing to heaven.

---

* Translated by Tai Hung-chao and published in London in 1994 as *The Private Life of Chairman Mao*, with a foreword by Andrew J. Nathan.

CHAPTER THIRTY-ONE

~

Blood on the Sleeping Platform

The atmosphere of the cell is definitely improved by the presence of books. However, a jail cell is not a library, and the smell of blood is very unpleasant.

Early one morning, after the doctor on duty finished making his rounds, Liu Deguo and Jiao Wenjie, who were sitting on the sleeping platform in their assigned places, started throwing outdated prescription pills at each other. Directly behind Jiao was the assistant monitor, who had been in a bad mood for several days. Seeing the disturbance, he angrily scolded Jiao, who flared up, "I was just returning fire." Offended, the monitor slapped Jiao on the back of his head. Jiao quickly turned around to "discuss" the issue, and the monitor hit him again and yelled at him, and the two of them started grappling with each other. The monitor was a big fellow and, with the additional disadvantage of his leg chains, Jiao was soon thrown to the floor in front of the sleeping platform. Seeing this, several men who held grudges against Jiao were on him like a swarm of bees, all punching him. Finally Jiao struggled to his feet. He said he would not hold anything against the monitor but he would certainly get even with the other men who had attacked him. The monitor pressed him to return to his seat, and finally, indignant and resentful, he sat down.

As soon as the monitor turned around and left him, Jiao jumped up and rushed at Liang Junzheng, one of the men who had attacked him. But Liang was prepared and stepped aside so that Jiao fell to the floor, and Liang attacked him again, while three or four of the others also lit into him. Liang suddenly started kicking Jiao, who tried to roll out of the way but still couldn't escape the assault. The monitor came over and stopped the fight, and Jiao was able to sit up, but blood was dripping from his nose and the corner of his eye, and dark smears of blood were all over the sleeping platform. Jiao ran to the cell door and pressed the red alarm button. A guard opened the door and called the warden. Jiao, his face covered in blood, called out the names of those who had attacked him, and the warden shouted an order, "Everyone involved, out!" Liang was slow to obey and, when he got out into the hallway, the warden boxed both of his ears. Blood spurted from his nose and didn't stop flowing for a long time. The upshot of this fight was that four men had their hands cuffed behind their backs and three others were transferred out of cell 404.

Similar fights occurred in the cell now and then. Once when Feng Jun and several others were playing cards, Chen Lianshun, who was watching the game, made some caustic criticisms of the card playing that offended Feng. The two of them started quarreling, coarse words were exchanged, and they entered into a fierce staring match. As his anger rose, Chen reached out to grab Feng, but before anyone could say anything, Hou Guanghui hit Chen, and Yang Zhongfa joined in. Within a minute or two, the three men had beaten Chen till his face was swollen and bloody. After the monitor and others had stopped the fight, they urged Chen to keep the matter private and not report it to the warden. Still gasping for breath, Chen didn't say anything, but then he suddenly leapt onto Hou and tried to gouge his eyes out. Restrained by his leg chains, he was only able to poke his fingers into Hou's face, as he received more heavy blows on his own face. Through the night Chen did not wipe the blood off his face, and he hardly slept at all. The next day he refused to eat. On the third day he did report the fight to the warden, and Hou and Yang had their hands cuffed behind their backs. Feng wasn't cuffed, apparently because there weren't enough handcuffs.

On another morning we were sitting in our proper places on the sleeping platform. Sun Bohe was in the middle of the first row, and Liu Kuijun was directly behind him in the second row. Because the rows were very close together, anyone in the back row could hardly shift his position without bumping against the person sitting in front of him, and although Liu was considered a well-behaved person, he couldn't help bumping Sun. Some of the men were reading, while others were chatting quietly or resting with their eyes closed. Suddenly Sun shouted at Liu, "Don't do that again!" Everyone thought this was strange, and Liu let it pass. But after a few minutes, Sun suddenly stood up, turned around, and started punching and kicking Liu who had unintentionally bumped Sun's back with his knee. Sun's overbearing rudeness irritated everybody, and the monitor hit him. Then several others got into it and started pounding Sun, chasing him into the toilet. I stood up and loudly scolded Sun, and none of the others came to his aid. The monitor pressed the alarm button, and when the warden came, he immediately took Sun into the hallway, where several guards beat and kicked him, cuffed his hands behind his back, and transferred him to cell 402. Afterward, we were all puzzled to see that the blameless Liu also had his hands cuffed behind his back. And he had to wear the cuffs for two weeks.

In Section Seven this sort of fighting and bloodletting probably occurred on average once a month in each cell. Insulting speech was an everyday occurrence, and from that to vicious slander and mutual humiliation was a short step. Anger quickly escalated to a black mood in which physically attacking someone became an irresistible temptation and the first choice for action. When people have no standard of decent behavior, such temptation becomes a fuse to ignite further violence, and when somebody felt like venting his fury, he would simply strike out at whoever was nearby. Or in the case of someone like Chen, his arrogance made him generally disliked, and there were people who were looking for an excuse to beat him up. Someone like Sun, whom others found perverse or obnoxious, would pick on other people, but then he himself would be viciously attacked. And yet, bloody fights like these in Section Seven were not nearly as serious as what happened in other districts and counties. They were not the typical oppression by prison bullies, but were mostly the result of lack of mutual respect and challenges thrown out among the prisoners.

In the detention centers of various districts and counties, such bloody battles are usually brought on by the sadism of prison bullies. Unlike Section Seven, the wardens and guards in those centers have an unspoken arrangement with the bullies, allowing or even encouraging their violent behavior. Furthermore, these bullies take pleasure in beating people to display their own strength and their dominant status. This kind of violence is a daily occurrence, and if the oppressed prisoners aren't actually left bleeding, they are bruised black and blue. They feel as though they have descended to Hades, and each day passes like a year. The most shocking thing is that a prisoner is sometimes beaten to death.

In April of 2000, in the Beijing Yanshan district detention center, sixteen-year-old Zhou Feng died after other prisoners took turns beating him. On entering the detention center, Zhou had had to undergo the usual ritual initiation in which he was yelled at, beaten, and repeatedly doused with buckets of cold water. Unable to bear this abuse, he called for the warden and was transferred to another cell. But in the new cell he was once again beaten and abused with no letup. When he was taken out for his hearing, he used this opportunity to complain to the hearing officer and to ask that he once again be transferred to a different cell. But a fellow prisoner who had been taken for his hearing at the same time told the monitor about Zhou's complaint, and when he returned to the cell, as soon as he stepped in the door, he was viciously beaten. He called out piteously, but no one showed any sympathy; on the contrary, a quilt was thrown over his head and, under the monitor's direction, cellmates formed into pairs and took turns jumping on him and beating him, until the life finally went out of him.

"Misfortunes come in pairs." In June of 2000, in the Changping district detention center, thirty-year-old Hao Chaofang was beaten and kicked to death by his cellmates. Hao had been an easy target for insults and abuse, suffering in silence whenever he was abused. Worse than that, the cell bullies wouldn't let him have even a drink of water. One time he was pushed into the exercise cage and a plastic bag was put over his head and fastened tightly, almost suffocating him. When he made a mild complaint, unexpectedly violating a taboo, the cell bully used his despotic power to organize cellmates to mete out punishment to him. He twisted and turned, jumped aside to avoid their blows, apologized and pled for mercy, and wailed in his misery, but all to no avail. He was beaten to death. When he died, his body was completely discolored with bruises, and terribly swollen, his head as big as a bucket—all too horrible to look at.

In 1994 a prisoner in the Chaoyang district detention center was surrounded by cellmates and severely beaten, and the next day he died in the cell. In 1995 another prisoner in the same detention center suffered a violent beating and died a week later. This case was thoroughly investigated and, after repeated complaints from the prisoner's family, the guilty parties were finally brought back for a new hearing in 1999. To my knowledge, the detention centers of the Eastern, Haidian, and Mentougou districts have all had cases of prisoners being violently beaten and dying in the lockup.

There are in fact many cases of "dead bodies in the lockup." The trampling of prisoners' personal rights and dignity, and even the basic right to food and shelter, occurs in the detention centers of the various districts and counties, and is in fact a very commonplace thing. The majority of prisoners are forced into a kind of abject slavery, while the privileged few are slave overlords or their accomplices. In my year and a half in Section Seven I heard many such gruesome stories. Not only that; from 30 May to 11 July 1994 I was held in the Western district jail. The reason for my arrest was that I had visited families of people who had been killed in the June 4th Incident, to give them contributions sent by overseas students. During those forty-three days and nights I witnessed several instances of verbal and physical abuse and heard piteous wails from within the prison, over which fluttered a triangular pennant displaying the slogan "Civilized Jail." This confirms that the authorities' obsession with maintaining "stability" even at the expense of the most basic human rights is immoral and inhumane.

Human rights, this concept that is so disliked and resisted from the depths of the hearts of the authorities, is something that Chinese society urgently needs to affirm and protect. If people suspected of crimes really had human rights, could the police be so generally violent and prone to torture? Could so many frightening incidents occur in the detention centers, and could the savage cruelties of the Middle Ages be replayed here at the turn of the twenty-first century?

CHAPTER THIRTY-TWO

~

A Small Society in a Narrow Room

In many detention centers it is only a minority who are prison bullies; the majority of the inmates simply exist in an abyss of suffering. Generally speaking, however, Section Seven was not like that. In the cells of Section Seven, a sort of class society had formed. A small number of people enjoyed special privileges, and the rest were able to get along fairly well. As time passed and we became more familiar with one another, we would help each other, make jokes, tell each other's fortunes, take someone else's turn on duty, repair each other's bedding, and so on. Time passed fairly quickly, worries were reduced, and friendships developed among us. Though it may be hard to believe, a place that from the outside seemed gloomy and filled with the laments of ghosts in torment could actually give rise to a certain nostalgia. I myself experienced such feelings on two occasions.

The first time was when I was hospitalized in the special basement section of the Beijing Public Security Hospital. My left ankle was locked to the steel bed frame twenty-four hours a day. Unable to get out of bed, I had nothing to listen to, no one to talk to, and no books to read. This extreme lack of freedom made me cherish the memory of the little society of cell 404, recalling the freedom to get up and walk about in the cell and the pleasure of jumping in *mogao** contests in the exercise cage. Another time was in April 2001 when I arrived at the Transfer Center, which was overflowing with the gloom of people who had been beaten down, degraded, and terrorized. This

---

* See final paragraph in chapter 8.

contrast made the relaxed atmosphere of Section Seven stand out, and all the "temporary prisoners" who had been transferred from there yearned for the past.

In cell 404 I had known five monitors. A monitor is like a stand-in club president, appointed by the warden to look after daily affairs in the cell. The monitor is the leader of a group of four to six people who have certain special privileges in the cell. For example, their allotted space on the sleeping platform is about twelve boards wide; when food is distributed, they are given larger portions; during periods of "sitting in place," they are allowed to chat; they can go to the toilet whenever they need to; someone washes their clothes for them; they can buy expensive cigarettes; and they can even use hot water for bathing. They do not usually oppress the other inmates, but get along peacefully with them. When there are extra wheat-flour buns, the monitors usually give them to those who ask for them, and especially to those responsible for cleaning the toilet and to the youngest of the inmates. And when there are special treats at festival time, they put them into cellmates' bowls one by one so that the distribution will be fair. On holidays, all those who smoke are allowed the luxury of a few puffs to cheer them up. After the homemade television antenna was installed in the cell, we discovered that we could get quite a number of channels, so we thought of asking the Detention Center to turn on the TV set outside the cell so that we could watch drama series and have more to talk about during the periods of sitting in place.

Zhang Jun came in August of 2000. At his initial trial, he had been sentenced to nineteen years for corruption and diverting public funds. Whenever a prisoner was brought into cell 404 after having been transferred from the temporary holding department in the Chaoyang detention center, if he wanted to appeal, I would usually write this up for him, following the standard form. Zhang drafted an appeal several pages long by himself, then asked me to look at it, and he also showed me his written judgment from the court and the section on corruption and diversion of public funds that he had copied from the criminal law code. After reading these carefully and thinking about them for two or three days, I discovered that his case was not really a matter of excessive punishment for the specified offense but that the charge should not have been sustained. I found that, according to the evidence, he had created false invoices to inflate sales so as to make it appear that the company's profits were rising. (Whether he could be prosecuted for tax evasion was a separate question.) If the company's finance officer had used him to cover his own corruption, Zhang should not have been charged with the crime. His case had been investigated by the redoubtable Eastern District

People's Procuratorate and heard by the Second Intermediate People's Court of Beijing. Seeing this absurd verdict, I couldn't help feeling suspicious. After I reported my opinion to Zhang, I came boldly to the point and asked him, "Has someone got it in for you on a personal basis?" He replied, "Yes. At first they alleged that I had received bribes from foreign companies totaling six hundred thousand US dollars."

Touched by my helpfulness, Zhang started telling his story. As he spoke, I was surprised to learn that he had special feelings for my hometown. After graduating from the Beijing Institute of Economics, he had worked in the government's Department of Chemical Engineering, and before his mishap, he had been the general manager of a state-owned company. He told me that in connection with his work, he had traveled all over the country, and there were two cities that especially impressed him with their warmth and beauty, of which one was my hometown, Changshu. He described the quiet streets and peaceful lanes of the Old City district, with its history of more than two thousand years. Once after a meeting in Changshu, his colleagues all rushed off to Shanghai, but he stayed on in Changshu for another week to absorb the poetic charm of the place. Late one evening, he had walked out from the Yushan Hotel and taken a stroll in the nearly empty streets of the city center. Before long a peddler with wonton on his carrying pole approached. He signaled and the peddler stopped and rested his burden on the ground and expertly served out the wonton while chatting with warm friendliness. Zhang felt such pleasure in the easy conversation late in the evening and the delicious aroma of the wonton that he felt almost as though he was becoming drunk. . . . When I had heard him out, I also felt a bit giddy with thoughts of my hometown, but I couldn't resist the temptation to try one more little test on him. I asked him whether he had eaten Changshu's fried dumpling noodles. He said he had not, which I felt was a great pity. With Changshu's shad almost gone and the famous "beggar's chicken" a thing of the past, only fried dumpling noodles were left as a true emblem of the city. For further emphasis, I said that in all of China it would probably be impossible to find noodles tastier than Changshu's fried dumpling noodles.

In August of 2000 Zhang became monitor. However, because of his years as a boss in a state enterprise, he couldn't help being a bit high-handed. For example, he would have others heat his instant noodles and get water for his footbaths, and would sometimes even ask someone to give him a massage. He seldom talked politics with me, though he did express some opinions on the June 4th Incident. We talked a lot about economics. He said that the allocation of resources on the whim of senior officials was very unreasonable and resulted in unimaginable waste. He agreed to meet me after we were released and to share firsthand information with me.

Once when we were watching television, the program *Stocks Unlimited* broadcast an interview with Fang Quan. Zhang had not played the stock market and did not recognize Fang. I told him that Fang had graduated from the Chinese Department of Beijing Normal College (now Capital Normal University) and then taught for many years in the Beijing Institute of Economics. I didn't tell him that Fang had been my fellow sufferer when we were locked up in Qincheng prison in 1990–1991. After I was released on 7 February 1991, he went into a small cell that I had occupied in area 204 of the prison and found a couplet that I had carved on the inside of a wooden door to the bathroom. Soon after Fang got out of Qincheng, he came to my home and, while we chatted, he mentioned this couplet. In the television interview, he spoke with ease and confidence, but I could tell that he was doing his best to tell the truth so as not to mislead investors in the stock market. Still, now that he was editor of *The Stock Market* magazine, there were things that he could not say directly. I had tried investing in the market, and on the basis of this, my evaluation of how it worked was quite low. Even aside from the strange practice of not allowing stocks in state enterprises to circulate, openness and impartiality were definitely rare in the Chinese stock market, and manipulation of individual investors was an undeniable fact. Granted that there are a few experts who have succeeded in riding the waves of the market, generally speaking, between grief and pleasure for the small investors, few are happy and bitterness is prevalent.

After Zhang had submitted his appeal, there was a long delay during which there was no action from the Beijing People's Superior Court. Then in January 2001 he left the cell to see his lawyer and came back with an expression of helplessness on his face. His lawyer had been summoned by the Superior Court and told to submit a request to the court that the time limit for Zhang's appeal be extended so that the court would not be censured for violating the "Code of Criminal Procedure." The lawyer had no choice but to comply. When I left Section Seven on the 30th of March, the Superior Court was still procrastinating, and Zhang's lawyer had submitted a request for a second extension. In the latter part of October 2001, when I was in Section Sixteen of the Number Two Prison, I ran into someone from cell 404 who told me that the Superior Court had still not acted on Zhang's case. The courts violate the law and commit fraud, trampling justice and transparency into the ground. Surely the judges are also subject to intervention by powerful interests, and they too suffer great bitterness.

In the cells of Section Seven small groups often formed according to where the inmates were from. Men from Beijing city made up one group, and those from the suburbs and nearby counties were also attached to this group. Uighurs, and men from Dongbei and Henan formed three typical groupings. We often saw men from other provinces but there were not enough of them to form groups. Although some came from as far away as Inner Mongolia, I never saw anyone from Tibet.

Men from Dongbei were mostly accused of serious or violent crimes. For example, Hou Guanghui had joined a gang and committed murder and robbery. Because he was a minor at the time, he was sentenced to life in prison, while one of his accomplices received a death sentence and the other a suspended death sentence. He and his buddies would pretend to be delivering fresh flowers, and when a door was opened they would rush in and rob and vandalize the home. Ma Ziqiang had been a laborer in the Benxi Iron and Steel Company. Several years earlier he was laid off because of company restructuring, and in 1999 he came to the Beijing area and became a robber, specializing in kidnapping bar girls and stealing from them. He was given a life sentence. He couldn't bear to hear Deng Xiaoping's name, and often criticized and cursed him. He said that in the spring of 1997, when Deng passed away, the family residential area of the Benxi Iron and Steel Company was filled with the sound of firecrackers being set off in celebration of his death. He had set off a lot of them himself. There were also some inmates who were in for selling drugs, such as Gong Renwei, who was given a nine-year sentence while his wife was sentenced to death.

All of the Uighurs had been arrested on suspicion of selling drugs. The oldest among them would wash themselves for prayers every morning. During Ramadan, the younger ones got hungry and ate regular meals during the daytime; only an old man in his sixties insisted on not eating anything until after sundown. They usually spoke to each other in Uighur and would get together to play cards, and didn't have much to do with ethnic Hans. There was one who spoke relatively fluent Mandarin. I made a point of asking him what he thought of Han people. Rather guardedly he said, "We Uighurs have lived in Xinjiang for many generations, but then you Hans came, and began to run things. When Hans set up factories in Xinjiang, they should give priority to hiring Uighurs, shouldn't they? But it's actually not that way. When they look for workers, they think first of Hans, but when it comes to laying them off then they think first of Uighurs. Isn't that very unfair?" Another man, who had lived in Russia for several years, said, "China is not democratic. In the future I want to go abroad again to live."

People from Henan are often denigrated by others. There is a story about Dong Cunrui that circulates in the world outside and also in the Detention Center. According to the story, Dong's fellow soldier, a Henanese, said he was going to look for a piece of equipment, but he didn't come back. As he was pulling a load of explosives, Dong yelled out, "Man from Henan, I'll screw your grandmother!" There were Henanese in almost every cell of Section Seven. When I was put into cell 313 back in May 1999, a Henanese named Chen Jun told me that the most important thing was to keep my skull safe. I since learned from television news that he had been executed, together with several others, and in cell 404 I met another Henanese who was executed in December 1999 for robbery. Later I also met several men from Henan who had been arrested for theft or robbery.

But people from Henan are not all alike. In the summer of 2000, twenty-year-old Song Jianxing arrived, who was not a bad kid. He had come from his home village to see his uncle who raised mushrooms in a Beijing suburb. On the day of Song's arrival, his uncle was in the workshop grilling one of his workers about the theft of five hundred yuan. He told Song to beat the "thief" with a strip of rubber and a tree branch. Of course his uncle was also vigorously beating the man. The next day the "thief" died from subcutaneous bleeding over a large area of his body. The uncle was given a suspended death sentence, and Song was sentenced to life in prison. This youth had no experience of the world and had never been in trouble. After the case was settled, his only thought was to use his time in prison to study. He quietly copied quite a number of articles in Chinese translation from *The World of English*, and he kept bothering me to tell him what the farm villages would be like fifteen years in the future.

Earlier I mentioned Liang Junzheng, a man from Qi County in Henan who had been sentenced to four years for starting a fight. While he was in the Detention Center he began reading and writing a lot. He had only graduated from middle school, but he borrowed my *Readings* magazine and took it away to study. I was startled to hear him say that the television program *Focus* was nothing more than a focus on regaining freedom. I asked him how he came to this conclusion, and he brought out an issue of *Readings* and turned to a critique of the program he thought was on the mark. He later produced a newly purchased notebook and asked me to write something in it for him to remember me by. I wrote the following two paragraphs:

In a democratic country speaking your mind is not considered a crime, but in China it is. Is this one of the variations of Jiang Zemin's "rich and varied" life in China?

A country governed by law does not implement literary inquisition, but China does. Does this represent progressive culture or backward culture?

Li Peng said "The rights of the state take precedence over human rights of the individual." This statement hardly needs to be refuted. The rights of the state that trample on human rights should be buried. How could the state's rights, which should be serving the well-being of the people, be higher than human rights?

After reading these paragraphs several times, Liang said with emotion that he understood what I had written and he was sincerely convinced that it was true.

Another person worth mentioning in cell 404 was a farmer from Hubei named Liao Lin. A member of the Tujia minority, he had not finished middle school, but he was intelligent and well informed. Every day, after the evening meal, he liked to express his views in a loud voice on all sorts of questions, and we would jokingly say, "The Tujia Station is broadcasting again!" He would often say, "'Shop around and compare'* is up for discussion. What is this 'one party government'?" Sometimes he repeated folk ditties that he had heard, such as "The Four Uglies":

Jiang Zemin's old lady, Li Peng's calligraphy,
Zhu Rongji's eyebrows, Rui Huan's face.†

When he finished, we always nodded in agreement and had a good laugh. Liao also had two other special tricks. He could do push-ups supporting his weight just on his thumbs rather than on the palms of his hands. And he could eat twenty boiled eggs at one go, without even letting out a fart. Once in a carefree mood, he asked me to write Li Yu's "Beauty Yu" poem‡ on a white undershirt, and he took red thread (torn from a shirt) and stitch by stitch sewed the characters into the cloth. In September of 2000 he was given a suspended death sentence for selling drugs. Within a few days a batch of written "comments" on cases that were in process arrived from the Beijing People's Procuratorate. For all of the others the decision was that "the punishment was too light"; only Liao Lin's was that the punishment was considered "disproportionately heavy." In the nearly two years that I was in the Detention Center, this was the only time I saw an official opinion that the punishment was too harsh. However, even here, on reconsideration

* Lit., *huo bi san jia*: "Compare the price at three different merchants" (before buying something).
† These were top leaders of the Party and government.
‡ A famous lament written by Li Yu (937–978), the last ruler of the Southern Tang dynasty while in prison after the fall of his kingdom.

of the case, the Second Intermediate People's Court of Beijing upheld the suspended death sentence.

In February of 2001 Zhou Jibin arrived in cell 404 with his written verdict of life in prison. A tall fellow, after being discharged from the Central Guards, he had worked for a while as a security guard at the Liangmahe Building but had soon resigned. One day in December 2000 he put on dark glasses and went to the Liangmahe Building to steal money, but was caught in the act. He said that when he was planning his caper he had overlooked a certain detail, causing him to "lose his footing" and be saddled with regrets for the rest of his life. I asked him where he had gotten the idea of robbery and why he had taken such a desperate risk. He said that his home area was very poor, and living in Beijing had opened his eyes. Seeing the way high officials, celebrities, and rich businessmen enjoyed the world of women and wine, he became too irritated and provoked. He imagined he could get a bundle of money in one night and take it home to build a nice house for his parents. Who would have thought his hope to get rich through theft wouldn't work and he would wind up in prison, leaving his father no peace and his mother's face washed in tears? He spent his time in prison in deep melancholy and dejection, feeling that a life sentence for one attempted robbery was unreasonably severe.

If we say that Zhou Jibin's poverty and desire for riches drove him off the path, then Ding Lan's wealth and desire for greater wealth led him astray. Ding had been deputy director of the Jingsong sub-branch and director of the Tiantan East Road sub-branch of the Beijing office of the Bank of China, and his wife also worked for the bank. Naturally, his family's standard of living was far above "comfortable." Through the muddy currents of partnerships formed to steal the wealth of the nation, he had gotten to know a man named Fu Rong, who was deputy director of the "Famous Fisherman's Club." This club had rented rooms in the Beijing Hotel for its office, and under the guise of "friendship" and "recreation" had become a broker for people seeking rentals for powerful interests. Fu was very close to certain government officials who had the prestige and influence to "cooperate" with the banks and benefit from high interest rates, capturing enormous funds for their own individual profit. Those who shared the fat profits were Fu's backers, Fu himself, and the banker Ding Lan, who arranged the deposits of funds into accounts of the policy makers. However, once the plot came to light, those hit hardest were Fu and Ding. Someone had to take the responsibility for a hundred and sixty million yuan. Ding went to Thailand and hid out for a year, but he was brought back.

He was transferred into cell 404 in October 1999, but he didn't at first tell me about Fu Rong's taking him to Yang Shangkun's* home till October of 2000. He said when he went to see his lawyer Fu smiled and said there was "no big problem." Ding felt that Fu Rong knew that the problem would be resolved and that high officials on the outside would take care of it for him. Later I heard from someone who had shared a cell with Fu that when the court convened for the first hearing, he was extremely anxious and quickly wrote a statement exposing the whole affair, including the parts played by the president's son and daughter. It wasn't clear whether he did this to make amends for his errors or whether he thought that he could scare the relevant officials into dropping the case. Still, we couldn't say that he was naive, or playing dumb; he was staking everything on this move. Of course it could be expected that the relevant parties would not believe his story, and furthermore, I felt that his "disclosure" had the effect of hastening his demise: such a "live witness" could not be allowed to survive. On 20 December 2000 both Fu and Ding were sentenced to death. In November 2001, when I was in the Number Two Prison, I learned that in the second hearing the court had upheld the original sentence. Fortunately, economic criminals get a third hearing, by the People's Superior Court. Perhaps Fu and Ding will still be able to see the new year in 2002?

I was an old hand in cell 404. From October 1999 until I left Section Seven, I was assigned the number two position on the sleeping platform and was one of the few men who enjoyed special privileges. The so-called number two position was right next to the monitor and was approximately twelve boards wide, or about 96 centimeters at 8 centimeters per board. In the latter part of each month, I was responsible for making a list of personal articles needed for the entire cell and collecting the appropriate contributions from those inmates who received money from outside. I also wrote letters for some of those who wanted to request money from family or friends, and prepared a calendar for the coming month listing any special activities. Beginning in September 2000 I was also excused from night watch duty. Then how was I different from the others who enjoyed special privileges? This made me very uneasy. Whenever it was time to clean the exercise cage, I would rush to carry the clean water out for mopping and carry the dirty water in to the toilet and dump it. (There was no drain in cell 404's exercise cage.) During Friday afternoon cell cleanups, I would quietly go into the bathroom for fresh water for the cleaning and dump the dirty water down the toilet, or I would grab a cleaning cloth and get busy

---

* Yang Shangkun (1907–1998) was president of the PRC from 1988 to 1993, and was permanent vice chairman of the Central Military Commission.

scrubbing the boards. I would never use the toilet in the morning because someone else would be brushing their teeth only a little more than a meter away from me. I often turned down others' offers to do my laundry, and I was always willing to be the one to ask the guards to turn on the television. When we were out for exercise, I would ask the guards to toss down a few cigarettes, or try to get cigarettes by some other means in order to ease the longings of the smokers. (I had sworn off cigarettes the evening before I departed to join a production brigade in 1968 and had never smoked again.)

The actions I have described above can be seen as ways of resisting special privileges that I never really felt were appropriate. Still, I wondered how long I would be able to resist the corrupting influence of special privilege. In December of 2000, when the water became ice cold, Li Jie repeatedly offered to do my laundry, and I finally gave in and let him do it. Beginning in January 2001, the work brigade started giving cell 404 an extra bucket of hot water, enough for five men to use for bathing, and I was happy to be one of the five. If things continued this way, would I not become just like the rest, standing aside and watching others do the work when it was time to mop out the exercise cage or clean the cell? Who could guarantee that I wouldn't lose my feelings of embarrassment and unconcernedly squat on the toilet while others were brushing their teeth beside me? Who could be sure that I wouldn't let others heat my instant noodles and prepare water for my footbaths, or even let them give me a massage? To "grasp the need to reform our world view"* seemed good, but it was not enough; we must change the system. A good system would be one in which those who had not yet improved their "world view" would not be able to do evil things; a bad system is one in which those who have done well in improving it can still easily engage in bad behavior. The corruption of power and the temptations of special privilege must be resisted by a combination of moral vigilance and built-in restraints. Holding firmly to the special privileges of class while opposing systemic corruption is no more than putting on a show and will never work.

On the matter of "world view," I have full confidence in the official doctrine of atheism. This is not because belief in God has been proven false or been refuted; belief in God actually cannot be proven false. The reason for my preference for atheism is probably due to earlier beliefs. In addition, I take the fate of humanity very seriously and do not want the machinations of devils and spirits to interfere with it. Nor do I want the gods to take responsibility for us. Unless there is irrefutable proof of the supernatural, I think that

* This is a motto that the Communist Party urges upon Party members and others for the improvement of modern society. Perhaps it is considered especially important for reform of prisoners.

the workings of the universe can best be grasped by human understanding, which alone can bring about the bright glories of the human mission. Aside from myself, another firmly convinced atheist in cell 404 was a forty-five-year-old farmer who had killed one person and injured several others in a dispute over homestead rights and was given a life sentence for intentional injury. The majority of the men in the cell believed in supernatural beings. They were all born after 1949. A full understanding of their resistance to the Communist Party's propagation of atheism would provide food for thought. For example, Hao Weijun, not yet thirty years old, who usually got along very well with me, believed in "butterfly spirits" and knew how to call them. I asked him to call one to show us how it was done. He tried for a while but didn't succeed. Some of the men insisted that there are ghosts. I said, "I have some 'devil money' (scrip issued by Section Seven). Call in some ghosts, and I'll invite them to a meal." They objected that ghosts don't eat food from the human world. I then said, "Invite them in for a chat," but they couldn't get them to come. I pointed out that Area Four of Section Seven is death row. Many people say that ghosts are often active over there. But how was it that I had been here almost two years and hadn't seen a single ghost? Besides, with almost six billion people on earth, why should we bring in ghosts to make it even more crowded and cause a lot of trouble? They were amused by this idea, but their faith in the existence of ghosts was not shaken.

One evening in November of 2000 I asked Liu Kuijun to check the status of my case by analyzing characters. He said, "Teacher Jiang, are you serious?" I replied "Yes," and he told me to select a character. I chose the character "yi," meaning "appearance, ceremony" and also "instrument." This seemed to displease him, as he frowned and became withdrawn. Then he entered into trance-like concentration for more than ten minutes. When he was finished, he told me, very seriously, "Your family and friends are spending money in a concentrated effort to help you." In his anxiety he had just given me a stereotyped answer. I couldn't help laughing, and asked myself what official would dare to accept money to help me? He saw what I was thinking and, changing course, said, "Well, whether they are spending money or not, they are trying hard to help you." I nodded my acceptance of this. I was certain that from my wife and son to my friends in Beijing and beyond, even to Hong Kong, Taiwan, and Macao and friends farther afield, also international human rights organizations, like the UN Commission on Human Rights and its high commissioner, Mary Robinson, would all definitely pay close attention to these cases of criminalizing free speech and trampling on human rights and would speak out on behalf of those who are suffering. He announced, "The resolution of your case is coming closer and closer." Hearing this, I laughed again, and he predicted that the court would hand down my verdict on 13 November. He said this with great assurance, and I followed up with, "It's not *approximately* the 13th?" He said, "It's not approximately. The date is the 13th." I glanced at the calendar and saw that the 13th was the next Monday, one year and twelve days from my court hearing on 1 November 1999. It seemed as though whether it was by reason, by law, or by fortune telling, it was time for my verdict to come down. The next day, Liu said to me, "If nothing happens on the 13th, the next date is the 20th." I didn't comment.

Both the 13th and the 20th passed. Liu's face reddened whenever he saw me, but I didn't criticize him. I felt that with the passage of time, people would gradually accept my view that the various means of fortune telling, by drawing straws, analyzing characters, and so forth, were all extremely subjective attempts to explain the multitudinous phenomena of the universe, which could not really answer these questions. I thought that all such attempts to extract information from the unknown, including physiognomy and palmistry, depended to a certain extent on the experience of the practitioners, but like the work of blind fortune tellers, they were fraught with ambiguity and linguistic tricks designed to avoid proof of validity or falsity.

Belief in ghosts and spirits, as well as fortune telling and other unscientific delusions, will undoubtedly be with us for a long time. In the restricted society of the prison cell, atheists and those who believe in gods and spirits, those who believe that "man's fate is determined by heaven" and those who don't, have to coexist. Isn't it the same in society at large outside the Detention Center?

CHAPTER THIRTY-THREE

Three Encounters with Falungong

After Sun Wei was transferred to the Haidian detention center, the newspapers and television continued to report occasionally on Falungong activities, but since then there had not been any practitioners in our cell. Of course I didn't hope that more Falungong people would be harassed or arrested. While there were serious disagreements between the adherents of the Wheel of Law and myself, they were, like me, merely holding to their beliefs and making their opinions known to others. One could dislike and ignore them, or analyze and refute them, but one shouldn't suppress them. Suppression is not only cruel, it is also illogical and ineffectual. To throw them into prison, and then "show solicitude" and undertake "reeducation by example," to expect frightened, otherworldly people to achieve "new life" just doesn't work. Indeed the Communist Party's efforts to achieve conformity in belief and thought have never really been successful, and this time it will be no different.

One Sunday, when we had had our naps and were relaxing with our shirts off and chatting or playing cards, a man was suddenly pushed into the cell carrying only a small plastic bag containing toothbrush, toothpaste, and toilet paper. He told us that his name was Liu Yongwang, and that after graduating from Tianjin University with a major in automation, he had worked for a subsidiary of Capital Iron and Steel Works. On a business trip to Shanghai, where he had gotten together with some fellow Falungong followers, he had been caught by the Shanghai police and held for a few days. Then he had been sent to Beijing and brought directly to Section Seven. Over the previous few months the government's attitude toward Falungong practitioners had undergone several changes. While the officials had originally provided food and bedding for Sun Wei, arranged for his priority at meals, and the warden had taken him out of the cell for interviews every day, there was now no bedding at all for Liu, and the warden basically ignored him. He didn't complain, and fortunately the cell monitor was quite considerate of him, finding him a quilt, which he used half as a bed pad and half for cover while he slept on his side in a space four boards wide. When we had both wheat-flour buns and cornmeal buns, he would quickly reach for the inferior cornmeal buns. If he was assigned to scrub the sleeping platform, he would finish his task and then start scrubbing the floor, and in the Friday cleanups, he would rush to do more than his share. Everybody agreed that he was a sincere "good guy."

Liu's home was in a farm village. When he started practicing Falungong, his parents also took it up, then his relatives. After he began to practice, his health and his disposition improved; he became more interested in things, and worried less. Naturally some of the cellmates didn't believe what he said, and controversy and arguments broke out. I was determined not to join in, but just to be an objective observer. The arguments with Liu were a replay of what had gone on before with Sun Wei, and what Liu said was amazingly similar to what Sun had said. However, in contrast to Sun's benign, imperturbable calm, Liu was an impetuous person and, in addition to having a defensive attitude, would often counterattack, which quickly earned him a nickname, "Wangwang," from the third character of his name, doubled, meaning "exuberant." For four or five days, I refrained from saying a single word in the squabbles between Wangwang and the other cellmates. But finally, one evening after everyone had lain down for the night, someone again engaged him in verbal battle and when he started theorizing about Newton, Einstein, and the fourth dimension, I could stand it no longer and sat up and loudly told him that he was talking nonsense. But Wangwang, in the clutches of Falun, had no fear of me, and we rapidly fell into a vigorous debate, after which I was unable to get to sleep for half the night.

The next morning we tangled again. I asked him why he never doubted anything said by the leader of the movement, Li Hongzhi. He said that when he first came into contact with Falungong he was skeptical, but after a while he started to believe what they said. I realized that it would be useless to continue the argument.

In addition to being more contentious than Sun, Wangwang was also bolder. He sought opportunities every day for meditation, and when he had a chance he would sit and do Falun exercises. Obviously, prison was not going to make a fellow so obsessed repent his errors. In the middle of July, without explanation, we no longer received newspapers and the television was turned off. After the evening meal on the 21st, Liu stopped drinking water. Nobody thought anything of that, but on the 22nd he neither ate nor spoke and ignored our efforts to find out what was the trouble. We were all puzzled by his behavior. On the 23rd he still didn't eat or drink, but sat quietly in his place with his head bowed. When the doctor made her rounds she told him he should go to the infirmary, but he pretended not to hear her and made no response. Then somebody remembered that July 22nd was the first anniversary of the government's banning of Falungong, and we realized that he was refusing to eat and drink in protest. On the 24th he continued his fast. His lips were chapped and a blister formed at the corner of his mouth, but he still forced himself to sit in his proper place, though he couldn't hold his head up and his body slumped forward in a shapeless heap. Late in the morning the warden took him out, and even gave him an English book, but when he came back into the cell he still wouldn't eat.

By the 24th he had had nothing to eat or drink for three days and nights. Cellmates gently wiped his lips with a wet washcloth, but he stubbornly pushed it away. He could no longer sit up but just quietly lay on the platform. He had obviously lost weight, but showed no sign of suffering. Those few days were very trying both for Liu and for the rest of us. While he withstood the torment of attempted suicide, we witnessed the willpower and stamina of a person who was completely devoted to his beliefs. A little later, several guards came to take him away, and he never returned. Not only I, but also most of the other cellmates, thought that at the end of the twentieth century such flagrant persecution of a believer who was at worst deluded, certainly not evil, was really primitive, brutal, and stupid.

Six months after Liu's departure, the colored streamers that the cellmates had made from instant noodle bags to celebrate the beginning of the Year of the Snake had already begun to come loose from the wall, but the seven-day New Year vacation was not yet over. To everybody's surprise, we heard the clang of the steel door, and we were joined by another Falungong adherent, Zhang Dakui.

Dakui was twenty-seven years old, from Wuhan, and had graduated from a technical secondary school. At the end of the previous year, he and his father, with some other Falungong colleagues, had unfurled a protest banner in Tiananmen Square. And the police had shoved them into a prison van and taken them to the Fengtai detention center. On the day they were moved, they had thought they were being released, but instead they were unexpectedly "posted" to Section Seven.

When he first came into the cell, Dakui's inarticulateness, together with his jaundiced appearance and scrawny frame, made it difficult for us to link him to the Falungong protestors whom we had known previously. Recalling the useless, heated arguments that I had had with Sun and Liu, I decided that this time I would listen and try to be more respectful and tolerant. Dakui quickly understood that in contrast to the reproachful questioning and ridicule of the others, my questions were sincere. In his Dongbei-accented Mandarin he told me that his father was from Wuhan but had gone at an early age to Liaoyuan for work and gotten married there to a Liaoyuan girl. He and his younger sister were born and had grown up there. After retiring, his father moved the family back to Hankou. When he was in middle school he had gotten interested in *qigong* and other bodily exercises, and he often bought books and took them home to do the exercises by himself.

For a long time his parents ignored all this. But his mother had a problem with her back that doctors had been unable to cure. At Dakui's repeated urgings, she had tried Falungong exercises, and her back problems mysteriously disappeared. His father, who had been assistant manager of a food processing plant, had no interest in *qigong*, but, happily surprised at its effect on his wife, he started reading Falungong books and began the exercises, with the result that his disposition and his health both improved. Soon his whole family, except for his sister, had become devotees. After moving to Wuhan, they were at peace with the world and with their neighbors, and they continued practicing Falungong.

They had not taken part in the April 1999 silent protest at Zhongnanhai and had never been back to Beijing. Once Falungong was banned as an "evil sect" and they could no longer do the exercises out of doors, they still did them in secret at home. Had it not been for frequent telephone harassment and surveillance by the Wuhan police, they would never have thought of coming to the capital to protest. He said that before they came to Beijing he and his father had made a few small posters, and on arrival at Tiananmen they had planned to display them. But when they saw that others were unfurling great long banners, they joined in and helped spread them out. Within a few minutes, the police had rolled up the banners and, together with those holding them, had taken them all away. He said that people like him did not come to Tiananmen to make a name for themselves or to create a disturbance; they just wanted to claim the right to hold their beliefs and practice their exercises.

My respect, understanding, and tolerance for Dakui was unusual in the cell. He could not ignore the probing questions about his beliefs and protest actions that were fired at him by other cellmates. The questions about his faith were the same as those that had been asked of Sun and Liu. But the latter category caused him a great deal of anguish and happened almost every day. People leveled two criticisms at him. First was, "If you're not allowed to do the exercises, just don't do them. You can still go on living, can't you?" And the second was, "Why come from so far away to demonstrate in Beijing's Tiananmen Square? Didn't you know you would be caught? Isn't this like throwing eggs at a rock?" The general feeling was that what he did was "not worth the trouble" and "foolish." The "sincere advice" that they gave him was: "Admit your mistake, plead guilty, curse Li Hongzhi, and ask the court for a light sentence. Do whatever is necessary to be released so you can go home." But my instincts were on his side of the debate because the same questions could be raised about my own position: "If they won't let you speak, just don't speak. You can go on living, can't you? But you not only speak out; you speak out over and over, and even carry it abroad. Don't you know you will be caught? Aren't you just throwing eggs against a rock?"

I felt that what was happening in cell 404 over the controversy about Dakui's beliefs and behavior was the kind of conflict between value systems that had gone on from time immemorial. . . . The accusers see the best course as "doing what saves your skin." As long as one can get by for the time being, dignity, rights, and preferences—everything that is not permitted by the political powers—can be set aside; even to live out one's life in shame is acceptable. And the defendants argue that "To drag out a shameful existence is as easy as lifting a feather." Personal dignity, however, has greater value. "An army's commander can be abducted, but a common man's ideals and his right to freedom cannot be taken from him." Was Dakui's unfurling a banner in Tiananmen Square like throwing eggs at a rock? I think not. He was only holding an egg in his hand and saying to the rock, "An egg may be fragile, but it has a right to exist." He wasn't attacking a rock with an egg, but merely demanding that the rock not smash the egg. In addition to myself, Dakui's fellow provincials had also expressed understanding and support for his resistance, and several others from Dongbei had refrained from criticizing him. This was only a minority of his cellmates, but it helped to relieve his anxieties.

One evening a few days after Dakui's arrival, the television news included a delayed official report of a shocking incident where several Falungong adherents had incinerated themselves in Tiananmen Square. The report said that under the influence of Li Hongzhi these people had been obsessed with the belief that through self-immolation they could rise to heaven and achieve wholeness. The atmosphere in the cell immediately turned somber. Liao Lin claimed that the government had created this false report to incriminate Falungong, but most of the men were shocked into silence. Dakui's eyes widened and he said he truly could not believe the report. After mulling it over, I told him that it must be true, but instead of thinking they were going to heaven, they were using this extreme measure to express their opposition to the government. Dakui replied, "Teacher Li has clearly said that suicide is a sin. Falungong practitioners would not commit suicide." I explained that while it was ridiculous to blame this event on Li Hongzhi, still, for people suffering from extreme depression, it was indeed possible. And besides, the government would not be so base and incompetent as to fake such a case. Dakui did not accept my explanation and nonetheless kept repeating that the Wheel of Law opposed suicide, just as it was even more strongly opposed to homicide.

I happened to be well informed on the official statistics: there were more than two hundred thousand suicides in China every year, and the number of attempted suicides was as high as two million. The number of suicides among Falungong practitioners was only a few hundred, or four in ten thousand, a rate that was far lower than the proportion of practitioners in the population at large, confirming Li Hongzhi's attitude toward suicide.

In spring 1994, I had gone to Changchun and had attended Li Hongzhi's "classes." The great majority of his followers went to hear him in the afternoon and then went to hear him again in the evening. I don't know who besides myself skipped the evening sessions, but for those in the daytime all seats were filled. On the final day of classes, after Li Hongzhi had answered a barrage of questions, the auditorium seethed with excitement and almost everyone stood up and cheered. It was very clear that, although what Li had to offer could not move or persuade me, his influence was obviously real and profound. I think that if he were to publish new scriptures in which he called on believers to make the ultimate sacrifice, many people would respond. Therefore, there was no doubt in my mind that those who immolated themselves in Tiananmen Square had done it on their own. A Falungong adherent, who had earlier incinerated himself in Beijing, left a will in which he stated very clearly that he could no longer bear government oppression and was taking his life in protest, and I suspect that others who had committed suicide previously had similar motives.

After that day, Dakui was more at peace. During the period of free activities he would play cards or chess, or sometimes do push-ups. Several times he wanted to do Falungong exercises, but the monitor didn't dare approve that. Later I learned that he had found a way. He would volunteer for night watch duty, and in the middle of the night when everybody else was fast asleep, he would faithfully do the exercises. I was away from the cell for ten days, having been sent to the Public Security Hospital for treatment of an eye infection. When I returned, I was told that Dakui had been asking after me and was very uneasy when I was away.

Dakui had written two or three letters to his family in Wuhan asking for money to buy bedding and personal use articles, but no money had arrived. Of course lack of material things was not important to him. Like Sun and Liu, the seeds of a simple and virtuous life had taken root in his heart, and he paid very little attention to physical comforts. On the 30th of March I left the Detention Center and went to the Beijing Transfer Center. Dakui still slept on the crowded platform with the others and stood watch duty for the latter half of the night. Before I departed, I left my army overcoat for him. Although spring had come, he was so emaciated that he really needed some protection from the cold winds that blew in just before dawn.

CHAPTER THIRTY-FOUR

~

When Would My Case Be Settled?

As fall turned to winter, the dried leaves of the cottonwood tree outside the exercise cage were blown away by the wind. In a little more than a month the year 2000 would be over and the twentieth century would come to an end. Why was my case still not settled? From 18 May 1999 when I was first detained to 26 June when my arrest warrant was prepared, to 21 October when I was charged, and finally to 1 November when I was taken to court for a hearing, everything had gone according to the regular procedures. But after the hearing something went awry. More than a year had passed without a verdict. The problem was obviously not with the court. Decision makers above the level of the court had not made up their minds, leaving me stuck in Section Seven, passing the time in the polluted atmosphere of the small cell.

In the middle of November, after the Detention Center had forbidden me to write directly to my lawyer, I wrote to Judge Wang Yan of the First Intermediate People's Court of Beijing asking her to tell Attorney Mo Shaoping that I would like to see him to discuss the authorities' serious violation of the law and their failure to bring my case to trial within a reasonable period of time. Mo arrived a few days later. He said that he had long ago submitted a request to the court for changes in my enforced detention, but the court, naturally, was unable to respond. And this time when he had telephoned Wang Yan, the court still had no clear information, saying only that they would try for a solution before the end of the year. I told Mo that I was sure that the authorities in control of my case were having difficulties, and I had no illusions that they might suddenly gain the wisdom and compassion of the

Buddha here on the eve of the new century. Of course they would continue to create prisoners of conscience. I just wanted to leave the narrow, restricted space of the Detention Center as soon as possible. Furthermore, once I arrived at the prison I would be able to see my family. However, Attorney Mo, and a female attorney who came with him, said something else that warmed my heart: I shouldn't hope that I would be declared not guilty and released, but there might be a possibility that I would just be detained for a specified period of time.

After I returned to the cell, my cellmates tried to speak in auspicious terms. Typically, if a decision was possible, it would be made. Such a long delay must mean that they didn't know what verdict was possible. "Teacher Jiang, you'll be home for the New Year!" To tell the truth, how could I not hope that this would be true? I longed for freedom no less than anyone else. However, both intuition and reason told me that if the probability of my being home for New Year's was not zero, it was infinitely small.

Another month and a half passed, and we were near the end of the year. On 20 December the court was finally clearing its accounts. Around nine o'clock in the morning Ding Lan was taken out of the cell. Then the guard turned around and came back and told the monitor to gather up his things. This was a signal that Ding was to receive his death sentence. Then just before noon we learned that he and Fu Rong had been sentenced to death. In addition, ten of the nineteen members of a robbery gang led by Li Yaping received death sentences, and there were also several other death sentences announced at that time. Leg irons and handcuffs were clamped on all of those who had just been condemned, and they were led toward area four. The corridor was filled with the metallic sounds of leg chains dragging on the concrete floor and steel doors opening and closing. It seemed as though the noise would never end. On the same day, Ding Lan was moved into cell 405. Early the next morning we heard three loud knocks on the wall of his cell, and we knew that this was Ding's final message to his former cellmates in 404.

December 27th was the third to the last working day of the year 2000 and of the twentieth century. When I got up in the morning, I made an exception to my usual practice and washed my head in cold water. A bit after nine o'clock a guard called me out of the cell and quietly told me that I was to go and receive the verdict on my case. The First Intermediate Court had sent a car to pick up three men. Two of them were going to exchange their verdict papers because of printing mistakes; I was the only one being taken to hear the actual announcement of a verdict. On arrival at the court we were put into the "cage" and told to sit and wait. At lunchtime we were each given a bun. I sat and thought about what my sentence might be. Surely it would be either a relatively light sentence of three years or a heavier one of four years. Whatever it was, I would simply have to serve it. Sitting with nothing to do, I dozed off.

About 1:30 p.m. the court policeman called me into court. I took off my army overcoat, inside which I was wearing my favorite dark red jacket, and within a minute I was in the courtroom. I nodded at my wife Zhang Hong, who was the only person in the visitors' section, and I cast a glance of recognition at attorneys Mo Shaoping and Wang Gang, who were sitting in the lawyers' section. Three judges and a secretary were already seated. The prosecutor's seat was empty. Once I was standing in my place, presiding judge Wang Yan called out "All stand," and began reading the court verdict. She spoke in a calm, businesslike voice, not with the moral indignation that we used to expect from the dictatorship of the proletariat. But the content of the verdict left me feeling scorned and unhappy. I felt a disrespectful, mocking smile form on my face. They were determined to keep me in prison. I could endure it; but how unreasonable, meaningless, and lamentable it was for those persecutors to undertake a literary inquisition here on the eve of the twenty-first century! When she had finished reading, Wang Yan asked me, "Do you understand?" I replied, "I understand." Then, without even asking the stipulated "Do you want to appeal?" she quickly announced the closing of the session. Suddenly furious, I shouted, "Speech as a crime, time to cease!" Inside and outside the courtroom, all was silence; no one said a word. I suddenly realized that the majority of people here would not understand my literary diction; so I angrily shouted again, "Bury the literary inquisition!" The two policemen stationed at either side of the courtroom recovered from their shock and came over and shoved me to get me moving. As I walked out, I saw a crowd of policemen outside the courtroom doors, and workmen, who had been renovating the building, stopped what they were doing and stared in my direction. I realized that people were thrown into a trance because for many years nobody had dared to shout out in court.

Returning along the corridor to the "cage," I was told to wait beside the court police duty desk, and soon Huang Xuan from the secretarial office appeared with a copy of the verdict, which she asked me to sign. She also asked whether I would appeal. I picked up a pen and, without thinking, wrote the following:

"Early on, I advised the court not to imitate Emperor Yongzheng, not to institute a literary inquisition, but you insist on persecuting Chinese intellectuals. Of course I will appeal and fight this case to the end."

While I was signing, Wang Yan walked over. Not wanting to vent my anger at her, I just chatted with her for a few minutes. It was obvious that the judges had to follow orders; they cannot make the decisions. If those in power want to create prisoners of conscience, the judges cannot disobey their orders.

The second day after I received the verdict, December 28, Attorney Mo came with his wife, Attorney Feng, to see me in Section Seven, and asked whether I wanted to appeal. I had three choices. I could decide not to appeal. It was not that I accepted the verdict, but rather that I wouldn't appeal because I knew it would be of no use. I could appeal but without the help of a lawyer. Or I could appeal with the help of a lawyer. I decided on the latter. I wanted to appeal in order to leave a clear account of the procedures leading to the resolution of the case. But my plea would be directed at the world and at history. In a case of political persecution such as this, the appeals court could only follow its orders. There was of course no hope that it could actually redress injustice. I wanted to continue to retain Mr. Mo as my defense attorney because of my gratitude and respect for his professionalism. We agreed that, after the new year, Attorney Mo would come to the Detention Center again to get the document that I would write and forward it to the Beijing People's Superior Court.

Through the final three days of the century I sat in the cell and worked on my appeal. In this special atmosphere I felt as though time had been rolled back to the end of the preceding century. Working on my theme, "Bury the literary inquisition," I felt like a condemned criminal waiting in the Ministry of Punishments for the Manchu Court's autumn executions. In my determination to leave for the world a decent record of events, I labored through mealtimes and into the night to write a document that could be understood by cellmates with a middle school education. On 1 January 2001, the first day of the new century, I completed the formal draft of my appeal.

The courts moved quickly. After I had signed the verdict on 27 December and written that I would appeal, the First Intermediate Court sent the file to the People's Superior Court before the end of the year. Shortly after the beginning of the new year, on the 3rd of January, secretarial personnel from the Superior Court came to the Detention Center for face-to-face interviews with those who intended to appeal. From areas six and seven together, there were more than twenty appellants to be interviewed on this day, with the interviews taking place in the western corridor between areas six and seven. These interviews had always gone off very smoothly. The court police, who did not treat the appellants as real people, and the appellants, who did not consider themselves real people, cooperated with each other. Like herding pigs, the police drove the prisoners to the interview station, and the prisoners went docilely along with their hands on their heads and their eyes meekly lowered. As they reached the station, looking like so many living corpses, they obediently squatted down facing the wall, with their hands still on their heads. When the secretaries called out a name, each appellant was taken by a policeman to the secretary's side, where he squatted down, looking up and answering the secretary's questions. Within a minute or two, the questions and answers were completed, fingerprints were pressed on the document, and the prisoner went back and once again squatted by the wall with his hands on his head. When all of the appellants had completed the interviews, the court police herded them back to the entrance to the corridor, where the prison guards took over and escorted them back to their respective cells.

On the afternoon of January 1st the court police taking appellants for their interviews had to deal with a most outlandish occurrence when they encountered an appellant who considered himself a human being. That afternoon there were seven or eight people being called for interviews. As the police were taking us upstairs I heard one of them yell, "What's the matter with that guy who doesn't have his hands on his head?" Actually I wasn't trying to make trouble; it was simply that my habit was not to put my hands on my head. I just kept walking, pretending not to hear. We were soon at the top of the stairs, and he had not taken the trouble to pull me out of the group. As we entered the corridor, everyone squatted down facing the wall, and with reluctance I also squatted. But while everyone else bent their necks down with their hands on their heads, presenting a nice uniform row, I kept my hands on my knees, my back straight, and faced forward, obviously taller than the rest of the row.

A policeman yelled, "Hands on your head!" I ignored him. He came over and pressed his knee into my back and angrily shouted, "I told you to put your hands on your head!" I still ignored him. If he had given the situation some thought and realized that there was something not right here, or just controlled his temper and used a little tact, nothing would have happened. But this court policeman followed his habit of not treating a man as a human being, and his coarse language, with his knee pressed harder into my back, set off an unexpected bomb. I suddenly straightened and jumped up, turned around and stared him hard in the face, shouting, "What right do you have to tell us to put our hands on our heads? What paragraph in the *Standards of Behavior for Detained Prisoners* sets the rule that we should put our hands on our heads? On the contrary, the *Detention Center Regulations* clearly states that police are not allowed to strike or curse prisoners!" This policeman, nearing forty years of age, was stunned. His jaw dropped and he couldn't get a word out. As he instinctively backed off a step, a younger fellow, apparently a squad leader, heard the disturbance and rushed over and said to me, "What are you yelling about? Who hit you?" I pointed to the man standing behind him and said, "It was him!" Maybe because this was such an unimaginable thing, or perhaps because I had spoken in such a loud voice, the man who had kneed me still couldn't get a word out. The corridor had already gone completely silent. Several of the secretaries, the group of court police, and twenty-odd appellants—nobody said a word. I continued in a loud voice, "Appellants are human! Why don't you treat us as human beings?"

One of the secretaries came over and asked me, "Are you Jiang Qisheng?" I replied "Yes," and he said, "Come on over for your interview." I followed him to the window and stood waiting. He opened his interrogation record book to begin questioning me. But the little squad leader walked over and shouted in my face, "Squat down!" He was so used to bullying people he couldn't drop the habit. I lost my temper and shouted back at him, "Why should I squat down?! I've lost my freedom to move about, but I have not lost my freedom to stand up straight!" The secretary saw the situation and quickly said, "Jiang Qisheng, you may stand," and the little squad leader angrily strode away. Before beginning the questioning, the secretary introduced himself as Li Kun. Then he calmly began the questioning, following standard procedures. I suppressed my anger and responded with a few of the most important points, and the interview was soon completed. I walked a couple meters away from Li Kun and confronted the squad leader again. Li, obviously a scrupulous person, quickly interrupted his interview of the next person and escorted me downstairs, turning me over to an area four guard. Unable to let matters rest, the squad leader followed us downstairs and on reaching area four, angrily said to the guard, "You'd better give this guy what he deserves!"

I waited in the area four corridor until the interviews were all completed and the appellants had returned to their cells. Warden Dai, who was in charge of death row prisoners, called me into his office. I entered and saw that there were three or four area four guards. I thought "These men in official uniforms will stand together. I'll see what they're going to do to me." But Warden Dai said, "Don't be so angry. Were you hurt?" and a guard asked, "Do you want to have a doctor examine you?" It was suddenly clear: the prison guards didn't want to be blamed for damage done by the court police. If I had really been hurt, they wanted to make clear who was responsible for it. I answered that I was not hurt, but the behavior of the police was quite unacceptable. I got angry because they so antagonized me. I went on to say that whether it was criminal suspects or appellants, though they had lost their personal freedom, they still deserved to be treated with dignity. With this, Warden Dai changed the subject and wanted to talk about my sentence and the stir-fry lunch boxes that the Detention Center was now preparing. He urged me to stay with them a few more days before moving to the formal prison.

When I returned to cell 404 everyone already knew about "the scholar's explosive rage." Fan Jiuxue, another appellant who had returned ahead of me, had recounted the whole episode to the men in the cell. While I felt that I was fully justified in my actions, I understood that for the secretaries, the police, and other appellants who were present it was like a rare and violent thunderstorm, and for the Detention Center, if not an especially important incident, it was at least unusual.

Once this event had passed, I was calm again, just waiting for my lawyers to come and take my appeal away. On the 9th of January, under clear skies after a snowfall, my lawyers arrived. A guard opened the door and I stepped out of cell 404. Suddenly an order was shouted from down the corridor: "Search him! And keep anything that has writing on it!" This was the first and only time I was searched when going to see my lawyers. The appeal that I had written out was confiscated along with a chapter, "Blood on the Sleeping Platform," from this book. This time the guards had turned hostile and negotiating with them was useless. They took the papers and held onto them. I was angry at myself. How could I have been so completely unprepared and let them steal the products of my labors? When I arrived at the attorneys' building and saw Attorney Wang Gang and a female colleague, I couldn't conceal the anger that still showed on my face. However, after ten minutes I grew calmer and recited what I had written in the appeal, and Attorney Wang wrote it down. We agreed to take a different approach and "following standard procedures," submit the appeal to the Detention Center. They would then pass it to the court, which would prepare a copy for the attorneys.

On January 11th I gave my appeal to Warden Song, hoping that they would handle it according to regular procedures. Song said, "After what you did on the 3rd, did you think they would let it pass?" Then I realized that the object of the search was to prevent me from getting a report on the police abuse out through my lawyer. They had unintentionally confiscated the thing that was important to me, my appeal.

At this point there remained the final two steps in my case: the court inquiry and adjudication. However, because of the long Spring Festival, followed by the meeting of the "Two Congresses" in early March, just when the inquiry and adjudication would take place was uncertain.

CHAPTER THIRTY-FIVE

~

From Detention Center to Transfer Center

On 19 January, as the Year of the Dragon gave way to the Year of the Snake, attorneys Mo and Wang, with their usual professionalism, came to the Detention Center to tell me that the Court of Appeals judge in charge of my case had contacted them, asking for my written appeal. I asked whether the Superior Court had received it, and Mo said that was not mentioned, but in principle, it should have been on the desk of the appeals court judge within a day or two of its receipt at the Superior Court. Eight days had now passed and the matter seemed not to have been settled. It seemed that the Detention Center was illegally holding my papers.

With Lunar New Year's Day two weeks in the past, the Lantern Festival had now arrived. This year the Detention Center was selling glutinous-rice dumpling soup for twenty yuan per bowl. As a southerner, of course I liked the dumplings, and I bought several extra bowls to share with cellmates who had no money. The Lantern Festival marked the end of the long spring vacation, and court activities should now get under way again.

Indeed the next day (8 February) the Superior Court sent officers to fetch two men, including myself. I had hidden the verdict from my initial trial inside my clothes, and I had written the draft for my appeal on the back of it. I felt that this was my opportunity to get the appeal out of the Detention Center. The Intermediate Court cuffs defendants in front of their bodies, but the People's Superior Court requires that hands be cuffed behind their backs. The little squad leader of the court police came over and stared at me, then cuffed me. I briefly returned his stare. We walked out of the building and, while we waited for female appellants to be brought over from area five, the fat man in charge of the fried foods stall walked by and called out to me, "Don't lose your temper again!" I smiled and said, "All right!"

The Superior Court and the First Intermediate Court are in the same compound, and defendants and appellants share the same "cage." However, a difference in the handling of the two types of prisoners is that appellants are searched before entering the Superior Court, and while they are being searched they have to put their hands on their heads. When the little squad leader came over to search me, he didn't dare tell me to put my hands on my head, but his search was thorough and he found the verdict from my initial trial. However, he didn't say anything, but just put it on a nearby bench. (If he had made any comment, of course I was prepared to respond.) When he turned away to search another person, I quickly picked up the verdict and put it in my jacket pocket. Later, it was he, together with another court policeman, who escorted me into the courtroom. Knowing what would happen if he told me to put my hands on my head, he didn't require me to do it. The others had to maintain that undignified posture until they reached the courtroom door, at which point they were told to put their hands down; otherwise, the incivility of the court would be exposed.

On entering the courtroom I saw a white-haired, middle-aged judge, the thirty-some-year-old presiding judge, a young female judge, and the secretary Li Kun. Below the bench there was a stenographer, and two court police stood behind me. There was no prosecutor, and no lawyers were present. This was a court enquiry, not an open court hearing.

The case was apparently to be presented by the white-haired judge, as he did all the talking. He first told me to be seated, then began with some trivial questions. When he asked whether I wanted to appeal, I responded with a question of my own, "Have you not yet received my appeal?" He looked through the papers in his file and asked, "Do you mean the several sentences that you wrote at the end of your trial?" I said no, it was more than two thousand characters long. He looked through the file again and found the copy of "My Defense" (which Zhang Hong had mailed to Judge Wang Yan) and asked me to identify it. I objected, "That's not it," and he said, "Then we haven't received it." This confirmed that after receiving my appeal on 11 January the Detention Center had not followed the law and submitted it to the court. This made me very angry, but at the same time I felt fortunate that I had learned another lesson.

I told the judges that I had brought my appeal and asked permission to read it out and let it stand as my statement. They quickly agreed.

I pulled the document from my jacket pocket, cleared my throat, and began to read in a loud voice. When I got to "and the court is not willing to emulate Deng Xiaoping and acknowledge its mistake and reverse the verdict,"* the presiding judge interrupted me. Further along, when I read, "the lies manufactured by the government about the War against Japan and the Korean War," he interrupted again, but the judges did allow me to read most of the document. Still I was disappointed in myself. I should have been able to recite a detailed defense and impromptu appeal, which would have been simpler and clearer and would have allowed me to watch the judges' expressions and get a better idea of their positions.

The judges told me to leave my written appeal with the court. I agreed and asked them to make a copy for themselves and to give the original back to me. After a few formalities the session came to an end. The judges had only done what the procedures required and, for my part, it was very different from my initial trial. I had not insisted on correcting the official errors, but had done what seemed necessary to get through the process.

On February 9th the court secretary Li Kun brought the appeal documents to me. He first gave me my draft, then handed me a printed copy of the court enquiry and asked me to sign it. But it was full of errors and quite inaccurate. With the utmost patience, I made some necessary revisions and corrections and told Li Kun that if he would take it back and have it printed again I would sign it. He complained about the trouble that my case was giving him, saying that he had, with difficulty, found the time to bring the document to me to read and sign. He wouldn't have done this in any other case. And to expect him to make yet another trip was really asking too much. He said he would guarantee that my corrections would be included in the final printing. I felt that Li could be trusted, and I had also become accustomed to accommodating other people in their difficulties. So I said that because of my trust in him, I would sign, but I hoped he would do two things for me: ask my lawyer to go to the court to get a copy of the appeal and, when the result of the appeal was known, ask the court to process the order promptly so that I could leave the Detention Center and go to prison. He said he had no objections and these two requests were entirely reasonable and feasible. Therefore I wrote a long note in the blank space on the transmission record, requesting the court not to manipulate the law in order to make things difficult for me but to allow me to leave a clear record as a victim of literary inquisition. And then I signed.

---

* Deng Xiaoping (1904–1997), China's paramount leader from 1978 to 1992, is often credited as the architect of the "reform and opening" policies that led to China's becoming an economic powerhouse. He was respected in China and abroad as a pragmatist who was willing to set aside communist doctrine in order to achieve economic progress. Among other things, he was known for his willingness to acknowledge past mistakes. After he ordered the military suppression of peaceful demonstrations in and around Tiananmen Square on June 4th, 1989, he lost much of the respect that his earlier leadership had earned for him.

After Li Kun left, I returned to the cell. Cellmates said that although I was innocent of any crime, there was nothing for me to do but wait to be locked up in prison. No one would have predicted that just as my time in the Detention Center was drawing to an end, there would still be an event of another kind.

On the 16th of February, at about eight thirty in the morning, the doctor was making his rounds of the cells when he unexpectedly called me to the door, saying, "You are Jiang Qisheng, aren't you? How are your eyes?" I said my right eye had been irritated and swollen for a long time. He said he would come back in a bit and take me out for treatment. My fellow prisoners congratulated me, "Lucky guy! Meat pies fall from heaven and you've got one." Since September of 2000, I had repeatedly asked the doctors and the wardens to let me go for an eye examination, but they had never approved my request. For the past couple of months I had given up and not raised the question again. So why were they now suddenly so concerned? Although I was happy for the opportunity, I couldn't help being a bit wary. Warden Song soon appeared at the cell door and called me out. I handed the army overcoat that I had used as a cushion, the pocket of which contained my appeal, to a fellow prisoner and got off the sleeping platform and walked out of the cell. I thought this would be an outpatient visit and I would surely be back by noontime.

I walked out of the building and got into the police car, together with a warden, the doctor, and two policemen. I was wearing handcuffs and leg irons, as the procedures required. When the car reached the gate, the armed sentry went through the usual inspection procedures and poked his head through the window to check the number of people in the car. We passed Tiananmen Square, entered a side street and reached the Beijing Public Security Hospital. My leg irons were removed, but the handcuffs remained on my wrists. I got out of the car and was taken to the emergency department; then they telephoned the head of the ophthalmology department. While waiting for him to come to examine me, I was surprised to discover that they had made arrangements for me to be admitted to the hospital. This seemed suspicious. How could they have decided to admit me for treatment before I had even been examined? However, I didn't think too much about it, but just assumed that they wanted to do what was best for me. A half an hour later the head of ophthalmology arrived, together with another doctor, and using instruments that they had brought with them, examined my eyes. When the examination was completed, it was the Detention Center doctor who told me that the hospital felt that I should be admitted for further examination. I felt a slight surge of happiness and nodded my approval. This seemed to be a good thing.

They led me to a special in-patient department in the basement. We took an elevator to the basement and then arrived at an unmarked steel door. When they pressed a doorbell, the door slowly opened and I saw a policeman open another steel door, and we entered a police duty room. We passed through this room and through yet another steel door and into a prisoners' in-patient section. Here my handcuffs were removed and I was given a haircut and allowed to take a shower before donning hospital clothes and slippers. The clothes, shoes, socks, and so on, that I had worn when I arrived were put into a black plastic bag and taken to the duty room. As Warden Song was about to leave, he asked me where I kept my belongings in the Detention Center. Thinking quickly, I said that I kept everything in a red plastic bucket, and the monitor, Zhang Jun, would know where it was. I thought this brief conversation was rather strange.

I was assigned to an empty ward containing four beds numbered 25 to 28. The policeman told me to take number 25, behind the door; then he used shackles to lock my left leg to the steel bed frame. I understood that this was a regulation procedure. But then he quickly took handcuffs and locked my right hand to the other end of the bed frame. It seemed that he did this just to put a new inmate in his place. At lunchtime the handcuff was removed and I was able to sit on the bed and eat, and subsequently the handcuffs were not used during the daytime.

About three o'clock in the afternoon the head of ophthalmology and another doctor came to examine me again. Although two policemen came in with the doctors, my leg was still chained to the bed. When the examination was completed the doctors didn't tell me what was the problem with my eye, though they did write a prescription for medicine that, according to the nurse, should relax the blood vessels. That evening, when the assistant head of the prisoner-patient department came by to chat with me, I made two requests. I asked that they wait until ten o'clock in the evening, rather than at eight, to cuff my right hand to the bed and that they use two pair of handcuffs linked together so as to allow a little more freedom of movement. He happily agreed, saying, "We'll take good care of you." Actually, my request was at the most basic level. Lying in a brightly lit room with my left leg and right arm fixed to the bed, unable to roll over, how could I expect to get to sleep? And if I did manage to sleep, with a leg and an arm chained to the bed, the slightest movement would wake me up. This was really inhumane. Furthermore, if I needed to urinate in the middle of the night, I could put my right foot on the floor, but then it was difficult to reach for the chamber pot with my left hand . . . really very awkward to take care of the need.

In this very restricted condition I managed to get through the first part of the night half asleep and half awake, adding a little to my experience of things that were hard to bear. Still, this was only the beginning. To be firmly fixed to the bed twenty-four hours a day, for a person who always liked movement and now only suffered from an eye ailment, this was really a challenge—a new lesson in asceticism for me. However, there was a small compensation through the first three days: I was able to read several different newspapers, which I had not been able to see in the Detention Center. A Falungong disciple from Hunan had come to Beijing and immolated himself, leaving a suicide letter, and my friend Hao Jian from the Beijing Film Academy had published his opinion of a current television series drama. I noticed that in addition to subscriptions by the hospital, nurses and other employees also subscribed, and these papers circulated around the building. However, on 19 February, without explanation, newspapers were no longer allowed in my ward. I asked the head nurse, who always had a smile on her face, to find some newspapers for me, but to my surprise, she ducked out without responding. And the other nurses, who came to dispense medicine or take patients' temperature or blood pressure and were normally taciturn, simply ignored me and continued on their rounds. The cleaning women were even more silent, leaving as soon as they had finished mopping the floor. Police seldom came into my ward and when they did come and I asked for newspapers, they would hem and haw and say, "There aren't any."

My days were increasingly grim. I was living a life of "four nos": nobody to chat with, no radio to listen to, no television to watch, no newspapers to read. All day long, except when my shackles were unlocked so I could go to the toilet, I was clamped to the bed. Fortunately, the leg irons allowed enough free play so that I could do sit-ups and push-ups, and sometimes I would put my right foot on the floor and do the "golden rooster standing on one leg" exercise. But gradually the only way I could pass the time through the long days was to sit and meditate, letting my mind travel as it would.

I thought of a conundrum that had long puzzled the scientific community: the "T transformation" problem. Physicists had disagreed about a definition for the T transformation ($t \rightarrow t = -t$), just what sort of transformation this was and how it was related to a time coordinate. I struggled with this for several days, then suddenly I seemed to find an answer. In my excitement I waved my hand in the air and brought it down hard on the bed and let out a yell for my good fortune. Surely the police who were watching me through the security camera in the corner of my room would be dumbfounded: what was this "prisoner-patient," who had only handcuffs and leg irons for company and is chained down like an animal all day long, so happy about?

This sudden insight in the basement was an unexpected bonus for me. During my time in the hospital I had become friendly with two orderlies whose care and concern left me with feelings of warm friendliness. One, whose surname was Shi, was in his early forties, and the other, named Liu, was about sixty. Hired from outside the public security system, their duties were to take care of the prisoner-patients' food, drink, toilet needs, sleep, and so forth, and they also ran errands and did odd jobs for the nurses. Among all the people I saw in the hospital, aside from the head nurse, Old Shi was the only one who always had a cheerful smile on his face. One day when he brought a wheat-flour bun to my bed, I whispered, "Oh, if only I could have some rice." Right away he said, "I'll go get some for you, and I'll tell them to give you rice with every meal." When he returned he also brought some newspapers and tucked them under my bedcovers. Just from these few minutes I felt his simple, unaffected sympathy, and this helped me endure the merciless cold of the steel handcuffs and leg irons. In the afternoon and evening, after I urinated, I'd call out "Old Shi," and he would come and take the chamber pot away and rinse it, and on his return he filled my paper cup with water. At bedtime he brought water for me to wash my face and brush my teeth, and then removed it and poured it out after I had finished. First thing the next morning, he would go through the same routine again. After breakfast he used to find fresh newspapers for me. One morning I ventured to ask if I might borrow his razor, and he brought it to me right away, along with a small mirror. For almost two years I had been plucking my whiskers out; what a comfort it was now to be able to get a clean, smooth shave. Unfortunately, as I proceeded with the shaving, looking right and left in the mirror, I forgot to turn my back to the surveillance camera; I soon heard a policeman call Old Shi out and scold him, saying this must not happen again.

Several days later Old Shi took leave and went to find another job to feed his family, and was replaced by Old Liu, a man from a village in Inner Mongolia. Liu's younger brother worked in a workers' cultural center in Beijing, but had been hospitalized for a long time due to an automobile accident, and Old Liu had left home to come to the city to look after him. When the brother was well enough to go home to recuperate, Old Liu was hired by the hospital. He was sixty years old but in very good health and agile, and he took on the various unpleasant responsibilities of the job of hospital orderly with proficiency and good cheer. He said his pay was far better than what he could earn at home. Though he did not go around with a smile on his face, he had the same feelings of sympathy and concern for others that Old Shi had exhibited. I had seen this quality in country people in several production brigades where I had lived when I had been "sent down" to work in the countryside in the 1960s. I hardly ever needed to call him. When he saw from the surveillance camera that there was something in my chamber pot, he would come in and take care of it and also fill my water cup, and each time he came in he stopped to chat for a few minutes. After I told him about my situation, he sighed and murmured about the injustice of my case. But he said that, although I had been accused of a crime, I had money to spend, while he would pass his life in poverty. He added that the reason he practiced the *xianggong* exercises was to stay healthy, because if he were to get sick, he could not afford to be hospitalized. And after the Falungong adherent Wang Jindong was assigned to the room opposite mine, he explained that *xianggong* was not like Falungong and was not designed for attaining Buddhahood. He would do the exercises whenever he had a chance.

Having been almost entirely deprived of our ability to take care of ourselves, we were fully dependent on the orderlies. At least I was able to go to the toilet for a bowel movement. Some of the prisoner-patients—for example, those who had been severely burned or scalded—could only lie on their beds and wait for the orderlies to catch their excrement and urine and then clean their bottoms for them. Wang Jindong had to have an orderly feed him. These circumstances made me think of the controversial adage "Unless a man looks out for himself, heaven will destroy him." In the 1980s this phrase was considered exceedingly offensive, but later it was very much in vogue. How, after all, should we think of this saying? Isn't it perfectly justified and proper that a person should look out for his own interests? Those high officials who don't want to look after themselves are actually well served by others, but we convicts can only depend on others to help us. So why not take care of yourself? Still, to look after your own interests but not do harm to others is only a basic requirement. It doesn't mean that you don't need to choose your actions. If you take care of yourself *and* benefit others, everybody is happy and that is in fact a very moral path. Viewed this way, looking out for oneself is fair and reasonable, and there is no need for harsh criticism of the aphorism.

As I lay in the basement ward, in spite of having solved the problem of the T transformation, being subject to the sympathy and consideration of the orderlies, and having two stir-fry dishes for each noon and evening meal, my desire to leave still increased with each passing day. I even began to long for the Detention Center! There I would at least have someone to talk to, newspapers to read, and television to watch, and I could jump up and move about and hum and sing. But here things were so inhuman as to be indescribably painful and suffocating. Beginning on the 23rd of the month, I started to pester the head nurse to have me discharged. On the afternoon of the 26th she suddenly gave me a slip for stool and urine analysis and, when I looked at the date, I discovered that the doctor had written it on the 16th. This was further evidence that the purpose of having me admitted to the hospital was not to cure my illness, and it also reminded me that they were now trying to cover up their subterfuge by discharging me. And this was indeed the case. After breakfast on the 27th, officers came from the Detention Center and I learned that I was to return there wearing only a sweatshirt, sweatpants, and slippers provided by the hospital. I was quickly handcuffed and taken up to the ground floor, and when I got into the car shackles were also locked onto my ankles. And yet perhaps heaven was smiling upon me, as I saw that a bright, warm, early springtime sun hung in the sky, and no cold winds blew upon us as we made our way back to Section Seven.

When I returned to the cell, all became clear. Everything that I had left in it (except for my army overcoat, which escaped the net) had been thoroughly examined and searched by the authorities. My sleeping pad and bed cover had been repeatedly folded and pinched, and everything with writing on it had been taken away. A cellmate said, "Teacher, what you wrote has been published in America!" The monitor told me that the warden had ordered that I was not to be allowed to touch a pen. I understood that what had been published must be "My Defense" and "My Final Statement," and also my letter of accusation against the inquest conducted by the Beijing Public Security Bureau. Fortunately, the first draft of this book, *My Life in Prison*, had already been taken out of the Detention Center by friends. Thus the authorities' arranging to have me sent to the hospital so they could secretly undertake a thorough search of my belongings had not really accomplished anything.

On the 16th of March, just after the closing of the Two Congresses, I went to the Superior Court to receive my "Criminal Adjudication" document. My wife Zhang Hong was present with Attorney Mo. The white-haired judge represented the court, and Secretary Li Kun was also present. The judge said, "There is no need to read the adjudication." In other words, it simply upheld the original decision. He went on to say that if I wanted to appeal further I could do so again to this court. I smiled and said, "What use would it be to appeal again to this court? If I make a further appeal, it will be to the UN Commission on Human Rights." I saw that Li Kun was holding a copy of the adjudication document and was preparing to bring it to me to sign, but that court police squad leader opened his mouth and insultingly ordered me to leave the courtroom. I turned toward Zhang Hong to say a few words to her, but the squad leader roughly obstructed me, and I was only able to call out to her, "See you soon!" After I returned to the cage, Li Kun brought me the copy of the document. I wrote on the receipt, "Repudiate the unjust verdict on June 4th, and bury the idea that free speech is a crime," and signed my name. Then Li Kun handed the document to me. I took it and, looking at the date, saw that it had been concocted on 16 February. In order to avoid the sensitive period of the so-called Two Congresses, they had withheld it from me for a full month. And the thing that most angered me and made me disdainful of the document was that it was so crudely written, falsely claiming that the appellant "did not consider his behavior a crime." What nonsense! I believe that any reasonable person, on reading "My Appeal," would understand that it was a dignified and coherent condemnation of the court's treatment of me. But in the words of the appeals court judges, it had been made to look like a groundless complaint and a weak entreaty for mercy. Those judges, sitting up and looking so imposing in their solemn robes, even if in their fear of the higher powers they had to announce a decision against their conscience, shouldn't be so unreasonable, unscrupulous, and absurd as this. I don't believe that language came directly from the powers that determined the verdict. Instead the words must have come from the judges who wrote the document, and they stand as a sign of their cultural and moral level. If one simply compares their adjudication order with the verdict concocted by the First Intermediate Court, this becomes very clear. Regardless of my extreme disagreement with the verdict, it at least spoke truthfully of my "defense on the basis of freedom of speech."

I returned with the nonsensical Document of Adjudication, and now my time in the Detention Center entered the countdown stage. Fourteen days later, on the morning of 30 March, a guard called my name and told me to collect my things and get ready to leave. I shook hands with my cellmates, telling each of them to "take care of yourself." Finally, at the doorway, I said good-bye to the monitor, Zhang Jun, saying to him, "When the result of your appeal comes down, your sentence surely will be greatly reduced." He replied, "Let's hope so." (In the fall of 2001, the People's Superior Court of Beijing handed down the adjudication, changing his sentence of nineteen years to three years and six months, and he was able to go home immediately.)

To my surprise, when I walked out of the cell and into the corridor, I was suddenly subjected to another search, and the draft of my appeal, which I had preserved with such difficulty, was once again taken from me. They just couldn't abide the fact that it still existed. Including the copy that they had taken on 9 January and the two copies that I had given up on 11 January, the Detention Center had now illegally swallowed four copies of the appeal. Finally, as I left the building and arrived at the vehicle that was to take me to the prison, someone hurried out of the administrative office to give me back the property that had been removed when I was brought in on 19 May 1999—my wallet, driver's license, key ring, shoes, and belt. After a quick glance at the items, I quickly signed for them, as there wasn't much time and also I was anxious about what other problems might occur. And then, to my fury, after I got in the car I discovered that my brand-new Triple A brand leather belt had been replaced by a worn and faded old belt. I gasped in amazement: power could really so corrupt a person that crooked police would steal even such a trifling item as this.

In spite of the two annoying things that had happened, my mood that day remained positive. Nor did the other convicted prisoners in the van show any sorrow in their expressions, although they were chained together in pairs or groups of three. To be moved from the Detention Center to the Transfer Center was generally considered a good thing. It was a victorious escape from the bitterest part of the bitter sea of confinement. As the men talked quietly and shared their relief at having gotten through that experience, the two vehicles made their way through the crowded streets, sounding their sirens from time to time to get past the heavy traffic as they headed for the Transfer Center, which was located in the Paradise River District of Beijing's Daxing County.

The Transfer Center was a special prison that was governed by the Beijing Municipal Prison Administration. Convicted prisoners from Beijing's various detention centers were sent there before being assigned to one or another of the jails managed by the Prison Administration: the Beijing Municipal Prison, the Beijing Number Two Prison, Liangxiang Prison, Yanqing Prison, the Women's Prison, and the Juvenile Training Center, or to one of a number of prisons located in the Tianjin Municipal Administrative Area. The term "Transfer Center for Convicted Criminals" was actually a misnomer because in addition to guilty and convicted criminals, the "convicted prisoners" held here (and in the other jails) included prisoners of conscience and those wrongfully convicted. A more accurate designation would be "Transfer Center for Persons Serving Their Sentences."

About 10 a.m. the prison vans arrived at the Transfer Center. From the window of the van we saw that this establishment, which had been in service only four and a half months, occupied a large area. The entry was a massive reinforced concrete structure that resembled a traditional gate in a city wall. After a ten minute wait, the steel gate slowly opened and the prison vans drove in under the watchful gaze of the armed sentry. The outer gate closed behind us and the inner gate opened so that they could drive into the yard of the Center. From inside the van we could only see that the area was broad and smooth with a blanket-like lawn. There were six or seven buildings placed here and there in the enclosure and, except for a few people moving about the parking lot, everything was quiet and peaceful under the spring sun. It was hard to imagine that this place, right next to lovely Tiangong Village and giving such a positive first impression, was in fact a real hell on earth. And I, a prisoner of conscience at the turn of the century and a witness to history, was to spend an unforgettable fifty-three days and nights here.

~

Epilogue to Part I

From 19 May 1999 to 3 March 2001, I spent 681 days and nights in cells 313 and 404 of the Beijing Detention Center, where I wrote the thirty-five chapters of *Random Notes from the Detention Center*,* though the last five were not completed until I was in the Beijing Number Two Prison. What I have written is a true portrayal of my life during my time there. My success in committing this record to paper was the result of both an awareness of my rights and a moral commitment. Of the several thousand people who shared my detention in Section Seven, or the more than a hundred thousand who have been held there over the years, how many have thought of writing about their experiences? How many have actually taken up the pen? And of those who have written something, how much of this has been published? Most people don't understand that they have a right to express themselves, and therefore they never even think of trying. Those who realize that they do have the right often give it up. Besides, whatever was written might not find a publisher and would lie at the bottom of a chest gathering dust. Thus, conditions within the high walls are seldom disclosed to the world. As a victim of China's literary inquisition at the end of the twentieth century, I understood that I had a right to express myself, and I felt duty bound to do so; I could not waive that right. Furthermore, I was confident that I would be able to get my work published. Meanwhile, I knew that in the Detention Center I could immediately write down my thoughts and produce an authen-

* This is the title of the book as published in Chinese, and is also the title of the first major section within the book. Thus the reference here is to Part I of the book.

tic record. This was possible, first of all, because we were provided with pen and paper. This "privilege" was granted so that some of the prisoners could undertake writing chores that the police were supposed to do—from filling out forms for other detainees to writing applications for the guards and police for admission to the Party and papers for graduation from the Communist Party School. Also, prisoners seldom told on each other, as carrying tales could do nothing to reduce their sentences and would result in humiliation in front of their cellmates. From the time I began writing in March of 2000 until I finished "My Defense" in February 2001, no one ever reported me to the authorities. Of course there were some problems. The first was dealing with unannounced inspections. Each time this happened, the guards would turn everything upside down, and they often made a special point of searching me. And I would have to find a place, within only a minute or two, to hide my papers. Also, I had to find ways to send my drafts outside the walls. It would be too bad if, after sitting with my pad on my knees and putting so much effort into my writing, the results of my efforts were all lost. I owe a deep debt of gratitude to those who took my drafts out for me, and in the future I surely must find a way to repay them.

For more than a year I wrote and sent out drafts of *Random Notes*. During this period my health significantly declined, while the sight in my right eye deteriorated precipitously. Now and then I would experience a bout of moodiness. But I never felt sorry for myself or became depressed. I knew that my hardships and suffering were nothing in the history of blood and tears that had been shed on behalf of struggles for freedom of speech. I knew too that I need not fear that I would be beheaded; I would merely be safely moved from the detention center to prison. Thirty-one years ago, twenty-seven-year-old Yu Luoke had been taken from this same detention center to the execution ground, where he gave his life for his beliefs. I am well aware that many people such as Yu, Lin Zhao, Zhang Zhixin, and Shi Yunfeng* were forerunners and martyrs who firmly closed off the road to hell for those who came after them and inspired many others to freely express their ideas and opinions. We have reached a point in today's China where those in power can no longer inflict the heaviest punishments for speaking out, or impose the death penalty for free speech. As one of the fortunate ones who have "come after" could I not forever remember those fearless heroes with their lofty ideals?

---

* These are individuals who were executed during the Cultural Revolution for speaking out against Mao Zedong or criticizing the Communist Party. Some of them were later rehabilitated by Party officials and declared "martyrs for the Communist Party."

In January 1999 some of my friends got together and published a book called *Posthumous Writings and Recollections of Yu Luoke*. In this, they did a very good thing for our nation, where people do not like to repent and are not necessarily good at thinking things over. Faced with a choice of telling the truth or preserving his life, Yu Luoke chose the former, exemplifying the motto "Live free or die." Through his robust character and the majesty of his soul, he exposed the backwardness of China's social system and culture. Is a society that requires a person to choose between freedom of expression and death not much more backward than one in which an individual can speak the truth without fear?

In order to confirm in this great land of China a system that recognizes the right to speak out and the right to disagree, and in which speech is not a crime, we must have people who will continually attack restrictions on free speech and challenge bad laws, and who, by suffering imprisonment, will close off the road to punishment for such "crimes." Before I was arrested, Fu Guoyong, Liu Xiaobo, and other brave individuals were accused for speaking out and thrown into prison, and after me, several more were put in chains and jailed for their writings. One can't deny that individuals who are willing to go to prison for speaking the truth are a minority, but this minority is indispensable. Given the size of China, with its population of 1.3 billion, if there are not a few upright and unyielding individuals who are willing to accuse the government in direct and uncertain terms, we should be ashamed of ourselves. Even more significant is the willingness of people to speak out in the face of danger; this will serve as a warning and an inspiration to the world and to our fellow Chinese. Mainland China desperately needs people who will choose to tell the truth and serve time in prison; it is a society in which the right to freedom of speech is trampled by the authorities; and thus it is a society in extreme need of reform. I firmly believe that in this land of ours, even the docile common people hope to see the day when telling the truth will be as commonplace as taking a walk in the park, going to a restaurant for a meal, or going to the movies—when this freedom from fear will not be restricted to the intellectual elite but will be something that any ordinary person who wants to say what he thinks can do so.

There are some scholars who defend the government's restrictions, saying that treating free speech as a crime has such a long history in China that changing it will be a slow process. Yet everybody knows that hoping for a "slow" process of change is equivalent to doing nothing. The twentieth century has already passed, with no change. Do we want to postpone the change for another fifty or a hundred years? Speech restrictions have long been abolished in Hong Kong and Macau, and the ban was lifted in Taiwan more than ten years ago. Why must mainland China still cling to the ban on free speech? In my opinion, the restrictions could be abolished with a simple courageous decision, just as the Qing government ended the punishment of dismemberment with the stroke of a pen in 1895, and as the Chinese government in the Republican period forbad foot binding, and castration for creating eunuchs. There is absolutely no excuse for further postponement.

I am not a naturally optimistic person; however, I keep thinking that in the present circumstances, the free speech restrictions are like a broken down old horse that is no longer capable of a long journey. May we ask, in the face of attacks by such people as Wu Zuguang, Xu Liangying, Wang Ruoshui, Ding Zilin, Bao Tong, and many others, how much longer can it be maintained? Challenged by the open, freely accessible Internet, how many firewalls can stand?

Abolition of the ban on free speech, which has been in effect for thousands of years, will mark a milestone of great progress, and we will celebrate China's merger with the main world current. From that time, China will welcome a new era in which cleverness and cunning in trivial matters will be transformed into intelligence and wisdom in great matters, the dignity of the Chinese people will be fully respected, and their creative abilities will flourish. This era will not be turned aside by the intransigence of either old or young obstructionists in the autocratic society, and will be a force that cannot be resisted by any emperor, president, chairman, or any other oppressive political authority.

Beijing Number Two Prison
Section 6, Subsection 16, Row 10
10 December 2001

PART II

IN THE TRANSFER CENTER

~

Prologue

The prison van stopped and we got out, handcuffed together in pairs or groups of three. The handcuffs were removed and one by one we stepped back into the van to retrieve our bedrolls, laying them on the ground in three neat rows. The police from the administrative office of Section Seven were now relaxed and, with a smile, the leader said, "Wait here for your physical exams. You don't need to squat down. You can sit on your bedrolls if you like, and you may talk quietly." Aware that we were now convicted prisoners, after the long time that we had spent in the narrow cells of the Detention Center, we were now out of doors. Although this "outdoors" was in fact a big bird cage; still to be in such a broad, open place, we at first felt that it was fresh and new, and there was a feeling of contentment. Now when the police showed us this little favor (though at no cost to themselves), we responded with light laughter and then quickly started chatting among ourselves. As we talked, I saw that one of the police officers had invited a prisoner into the van to chat about their common home district. There was a Uighur couple who had been convicted of selling drugs, and the police had permitted them to sit together and talk before being separated in the prison. One of the police noticed that I was more lively and sociable than the others and came over and asked me about my case and the length of my term. I said that for writing an essay commemorating the tenth anniversary of the June 4th Incident I had been sentenced to four years in prison. He was taken aback, then said with a grin, "Ah, what you wanted to say was that if you had just kept it to yourself, there would be no problem." I said, "Maybe you can keep your thoughts to yourself; I can't." That drew a laugh from those around us.

The hospital was in a four-story building in the southwest corner of the compound. Convicted prisoners brought from the various detention centers had to undergo a physical examination there to determine whether they would be kept in the Transfer Center. Those who were seriously ill would be sent back to the detention centers; those who were less seriously ill would be kept on here but put on the sick list; and those who were in good health would be sent on to various prisons as appropriate to their hometowns or districts and the length of their sentences. When our Section Seven van arrived, there were three vehicles from other detention centers already in the yard. After the prisoners from those three vehicles had been processed, our group of twenty-some persons was taken to the hospital. My weight was 66 kilograms, four kilos lighter than my original weight before entering the Detention Center. But my blood pressure had risen to 150 over 100, and the nurse told me that I should undergo treatment for this. They didn't notice my eye problem. We all felt that the examinations were conducted sympathetically. The surgeon was especially professional, carefully screening those who showed signs of possible venereal disease and advising them to get further screening or treatment. After the exams were completed, we each put any money that we had into individual accounts, and the Section Seven police said their good-byes to us while calmly escorting us back to the side of the van. Then they turned us over to the prison police and got into the van to return to the Detention Center.

On this sunny day, with white clouds in a blue sky, although the prison police didn't display the cheerfulness we were used to seeing on the faces of the Detention Center police, still they did not look ruthless or evil and angry. After lining us up for a roll call, they simply told us to pick up our bedrolls and move to the reception area. Those of us who were Beijing residents were to be held in Unit One, which was in a four-story building in the northeast corner of the compound, no more than two hundred meters from the parking lot. However, contrary to all our expectations, once we entered the Unit One building, passed through two electrically operated steel doors and walked into the corridor on the first floor, it was as if the sunny blue sky and white clouds had all been swallowed up by a demon, and we felt as if we had fallen into a hole in the ice. Our bodies were permeated by cold, and it was as if we had been plunged into a hopeless, shivering hell. How could we have thought that this would be better than the Detention Center? Here we would discover evildoers worse than any highwaymen on the outside. We would be humiliated, abused, and terrorized before we could finally be released to return home.

CHAPTER THIRTY-SIX

Encountering Prohibitions

Entering the building, we saw a large entrance hall. We put our bedrolls down by the wall, and an ashen-faced prison policeman appeared. Without any explanation or the slightest bit of sympathy, he shouted an order to squat down and put our hands on our heads. As usual, I did not put my hands on my head and, to my surprise, he said nothing to me. Then one by one he called out names, and as each name was called and the prisoner walked over and stood in place, the policeman asked him several questions in a stern voice, and told him to take all his clothes off and jump about several times. While this was going on, a "long-term prisoner" who had been assigned orderly duties nimbly searched the man's bedroll, leaving the bed pad and cover; washcloth, toothbrush, etc.; trousers, underwear, jacket, and socks; and putting everything else into a net bag to be picked up by family members when they came to visit. After each man put his shorts on and followed an order to put his jacket and trousers on wrong side out, a red paint marking was slapped roughly onto his clothing. If other pieces of clothing were still on the floor, they were also marked with red paint. Then each prisoner was thrown a set of cotton prison clothes and a pair of cotton shoes and ordered to put them on. After four of us had gone through these procedures, the guard sternly told us, "When you are in the corridor, stay close to the wall, and when you go around a corner, turn at a right angle. If you want to speak, you must first say "Report," and in response to an order you must call out "Yes Sir!" When your name is called, say "Present!" Then the orderly took us to Unit Two.

In the cell we saw about twenty people sitting on low plastic stools. The ashen-faced man at the door told us to put our bedding on the floor and wait for another round of questioning. Our questioner was the squad leader for Unit Two, another trustee prisoner. I was in second place among the men entering the cell. The man ahead of me was called over to the squad leader and told to squat down. Suddenly we heard the squad leader shout, "Don't look at me!" The prisoner appeared confused, and there was another shout: "Keep your eyes down!" This time he seemed to understand, and complied as if he were a slave responding to his master. I came out of my stupor and realized what was going on, but I was still astonished at this scene. I couldn't shake free from the thought that the crude and overbearing treatment that we had received from the moment that we stepped into the room must be designed to initiate us into the new environment, and now even the right to look at a person was taken from us. This was a new evil that we were being subjected to. I thought to myself, it's hard to understand this place, but the outlook is not good. After getting basic information on each "new prisoner," the next question was, "Do you acknowledge your guilt?" On hearing an affirmative answer, an equally mean-looking assistant standing beside the squad leader pulled out a paper on which the prisoner signed "admission of guilt and promise to repent."

Now it was my turn. At the order "Don't look at me!" I not only pretended not to understand; I also laughed. The assistant stared at me wide-eyed, and a look of fierce anger came on the squad leader's face. I quietly said, "I don't admit guilt." These four words had a profound effect. As soon as I spoke, the anger cleared from the squad leader's face, and he studied me carefully, realizing that he had encountered a "prisoner requiring special attention." He began to explain, rather awkwardly, "We have to send a letter of notification to each prisoner's family, so we need to have your mailing address." After I had replied to this question, he told me that he used to run a Muslim restaurant near my neighborhood. And finally he said that the "admission of guilt" form was not necessary for me.

But when the third and fourth prisoners came up for questioning, they still had to keep their eyes down, and they responded in low voices and obediently copied and signed the admission of guilt and promise to repent. Thus the spectacle of convicts being punished by a convict played out before my eyes. I couldn't help remembering the common occurrences from the Cultural Revolution, when it was not enough to label people as evildoers but it was felt necessary to divide the "evildoers" into grades of evil. The evildoers who were given power in this system destroyed what remained of the dignity of others.

It was already past lunchtime when we came into the corridor, and each person was given a wheat-flour bun, which we all slowly chewed on. But although we had passed the morning in difficult circumstances, we didn't really feel hungry; rather, our heads were filled with other concerns. After a while the squad leader lay down on his bunk for a nap. This was apparently a privilege reserved for him alone; the rest of us had only the low stools to sit on.

I began to feel a little sleepy, but suddenly I heard someone in the corridor shout my name. I was being summoned to talk with the authorities. I was taken by a trustee to the office of the section leader, where I was to have things explained to me as a "prisoner requiring special attention" by thirty-some-year-old "Big Brother." (A few days later I learned that this was what the trustees called the section chief behind his back.) He seemed to treat me with a measure of respect. In a gentle voice he said, "We hope you will understand that our policy is to ask that each prisoner reform himself and improve his behavior, but there will be some differences for you. Of course, this is not because your crime is special." I countered, "Of course the prison must accept everyone that the court has sent here as a criminal. I have no objections to this principle, and I will not blame you prison officials. However, I hope you will understand that I cannot consider myself a criminal." He nodded and said that if problems arose I could come to him. I asked him his name, and he told me I could call him Li Zhong. A little later, I was called out again. This time it was the police official who had looked so fierce when we arrived; he was the assistant section chief. But now his expression was much more relaxed than it had been earlier, and he even had someone get one of the low stools for me to sit on (while the other three men being questioned had to squat). He asked about my background and my family relationships. Then he slowly said, "Now that you are here, you must adapt to our rules. Don't cause trouble for us." I replied, "I am a sensible person. Some of the prison's regulations are clearly reasonable, and I will obey them. But I want to emphasize one thing: my dignity must be respected. As long as this is taken into consideration, there won't be any problems."

When the squad leader's nap was finished, he began to lay out the prison duties. He wanted all new prisoners to know the rules of the Transfer Center. Thus from my very first day, my ears were filled with the coarse voice of this squad leader berating and rebuking the other prisoners, and this uncouth man's repeated attempts to find every excuse to beat people down constantly played out before my eyes. I was a person who had seen his share of life. Over the past twelve years since 1989, I had been in Qincheng prison, Beijing's Western district jail, and the Beijing Detention Center, and now in the spring of the twenty-first century I had arrived at the Transfer Center. And yet, here the stench of the inhumanity of the Gulag assailed my nostrils. This was clearly worse than the Western district jail in the summer of 1994. In my own mind I quietly resolved that no matter how deep this hole was, I would wade through it. I didn't want to seek special privileges because of my status as a "special consideration" prisoner. A man's fate is determined by his temperament; I would be a genuine inmate of this purgatory, a fully qualified witness to history. I was sure that I was strong enough to carry it through because of the hardships that I had borne through ten years of labor in farm villages as a "sent-down" youth during the Cultural Revolution.

CHAPTER THIRTY-SEVEN

~

Unwritten Rules

When a verdict is carried out, an individual is deprived of his right to personal freedom and, for some people, their political rights are also stripped away. But in China, it would be naive to think that the deprivation of a convicted prisoner's rights goes only this far. An examination of the unwritten rules of the Transfer Center shows the extent of the desire to dehumanize those who are serving their sentences.

Among the many regulations of Unit Two, there are six that in my opinion exist only in the Transfer Center. I have reached this conclusion because these rules do not appear either in the *Prison Law of the People's Republic of China* or in the *Rules for the Reform of Criminals' Behavior* promulgated by the Ministry of Justice. (The latter is referred to as the "58 Rules.") The six unwritten rules are as follows:

Rule 1: Shout "Report!" "Yes Sir!" and "Present!" so loud that you make yourself hoarse. Rules 53 and 54 of the "58 Rules" do stipulate conditions under which, in responding to a warden's orders or seeking his attention, these three terms should be used, but nothing is said about how loud they should be spoken. However, in Unit Two, speaking them "loud and clear" does not pass muster. They must be shouted so loud that one is in danger of losing one's voice.

The men are told to shout these terms in five different orders, "Report, Present, Yes Sir," "Report, Yes Sir, Present," and so on. And for each of the sets of terms, they must first shout ten times as a group. The squad leader listens to the group recitation and picks out anyone whose shouting is not loud enough and makes him shout the set ten or twenty times. As the prisoners go through these five sets of orders, the leader would usually select five men for the repetition punishment. Sometimes there would be a man with a naturally small voice, who couldn't shout loudly no matter how he tried, or a newly arrived prisoner who hadn't yet realized the importance of this exercise and didn't want to draw attention to himself; such individuals would be called out for special punishment, insulted, and made to yell out again and again, until sometimes they sounded like a mad dog barking without pause, or a pig squealing under the slaughterer's knife, with the result that their voices would become so hoarse that they could hardly speak.

After morning roll call, each unit throughout the Transfer Center had to practice reciting these terms. In Unit Two there were additional sessions in the morning and afternoon, and special attention was paid to constantly calling out in the corridors, so that everyone became exceedingly sick of their own and others' shouting, and the rasping voices so grated on people's nerves that no one felt at peace.

Rule 2: No books or newspapers. Prisoners are only allowed to read—and recite—the Ten Prohibitions. Those held temporarily in the Transfer Center do not have a right to read books or newspapers. The only thing they are allowed to read—and indeed required to memorize and recite—is the second of the 58 Rules, to wit, the Ten Prohibitions. The Transfer Center has small wooden tablets on which the Ten Prohibitions are inscribed. At about 7:45 every evening these tablets are distributed to the prisoners. While each prisoner stands at attention and holds a tablet in both hands, one person reads the inscription and the others read after him. They are required to memorize the Ten Prohibitions within a few days and recite them fluently. Those who fail to memorize them are reprimanded and beaten.

Rule 3: Do not talk to each other. This is an astonishing rule. It doesn't just deprive us of our right to free speech; it takes away our right to speech itself. If it was a great crime for slave masters more than two thousand years ago to treat their slaves as tools with the ability to speak, how much greater is the crime now of making prisoners into dumb animals. What could be worse than this humiliation and debasement of human nature? How can a human being, even one who has been enslaved, bear not being allowed to speak to his fellow men? Some wanted to test this completely alienated squad leader. They found that his hearing was extremely acute. If someone quietly said a few words, they were sure to be scolded and cursed, and if the offense was repeated, a beating would surely follow. In Unit Two, in addition to the squad leader and assistant squad leader, there was a trustee who ten days earlier had been the squad leader of Unit Six. But he had committed an "error" and lost that position and been sent to Unit Two to receive "stern" training. Once when we were sitting side by side, he very quietly started to chat a bit. When he spoke he continued to face straight ahead and carefully watched the squad leader, but the leader gave him a contemptuous stare, and he immediately stopped talking.

Rule 4: If we have a moment of free time, we are required to stand facing the wall; we must not look out the window or peek through the door. For example, if everyone is sweeping and mopping to clean up the cell and some of us have completed our work but two or three men are still finishing the job, those who have completed their work are not allowed to look for a place to sit down or even to choose where they would like to stand. The squad leader's orders are very clear: everyone must line up and stand facing the wall. Anyone who gets out of line will be cursed and insulted, and if he complains, he will be taken out of the cell and subjected to severe excoriation by the corridor monitor.

While the barred windows serve as the hardware that strips away the prisoners' personal freedom, these rules are the software that locks them into the position of having constantly to stand and face the wall. The obvious purpose is to let you know your status: you are a pitiful wretch without any independence or self-respect.

Rule 5: Prisoners in the Reception Unit cannot go to bed until 11:00 p.m. This is another rule that is designed to make people suffer. After getting up at six o'clock every morning, the day is filled with tension, fatigue, and fear. There is nothing like the noon naptime of the Detention Center, and the afternoon is filled with abuse and torment, so that by evening one feels utterly disheartened. At 9:30 p.m., prisoners in the other units go to bed, and before ten o'clock the squad leader in Unit Two retires. But under the supervision of the night-shift assistant squad leader, the men in Unit Two are still sitting on the low stools, with their backs straight, reciting the Ten Prohibitions. If anyone's sitting posture departs from the standard, or if his eyes close, the assistant squad leader will almost certainly see him, and the corridor monitor, who watches through a transparent door, will also come down hard on him.

Rule 6: Every morning prisoners must review and confirm their status. This rule was established especially by and for Unit Two on the second floor. Those of us downstairs heard clearly that after the morning roll call, during the period for "reviewing the rules," each of the men on the second floor had to recite in a loud voice, "I am prisoner so-and-so, sentenced to so-many-years for the crime of such-and-such. I acknowledge my crime and am determined to follow the law, serve my sentence, and reform my behavior. I ask for instruction from the squad leader." Apparently the purpose of this rule was to make the prisoners remember their status at all times.

In April of 2001 the Transfer Center came up with another nonsensical rule. This was invented in the Reception Unit of Area One. I will describe it separately in the next chapter.

CHAPTER THIRTY-EIGHT

~

A True April Fool's Day Story

Sunday, the 1st of April, 2001, was my third day in the Transfer Center. It was bright and sunny out of doors, and inside everything was neat and clean. Here, just as in the Detention Center, there were only two meals on Sunday, with no breakfast, and therefore the time devoted to cleanup was extended. The squad leader had said that everything had to be done to the highest standard today. It must be so clean that if the section chief came by, he could touch any surface and not find a speck of dust. I was responsible for cleaning the tableware cabinet. I wiped it down with a wet cloth, then wiped it with a dry cloth, and finally went over it again with my bare hands; then I went through the whole process a second time. Because it was only during cleanup that we could be in control of our bodies—how we stood and how we moved—nobody complained about the work. We all just quietly went ahead with our tasks.

In the Reception Unit, on Sundays after the cleanup was done, prisoners still had to practice the assigned commands. First they shouted "Report!" "Present!" and "Yes Sir!"; then they practiced "Left face!" "Right face!" and "About face!" followed by marching in place. The thing that was a bit different was that the exercise period was shortened, and after it was over, the squad leader brought out the little tablets with the Ten Prohibitions inscribed on them and, with each prisoner holding a tablet, we sat up straight and attacked our "studies." As usual I also sat on a low stool, but I did not participate in the recitations. Furthermore, like a blind person, I held the tablet upside down. Of course I did this on purpose, in keeping with my statement to the squad leader when I had arrived that I was not guilty of a crime and therefore had no need to reform or to read the *Rules for the Reform of Criminals' Behavior*. The squad leader understood this. He said, "You political prisoners are all like this." On the day of our arrival we were told to sing the prison song, "Call out 'one, two, one'; Hold your head high!" The squad leader had told me that I didn't have to sing. I said that when they were not calling out "one, two, one," they always looked down, but when have I looked down? There is an old saying, "Look down and admit your guilt." But I am not guilty, so why should I look down? The squad leader said, "Forget it. You are you, they are them. They must recite and must sing."

Before long the trustee on duty in the corridor came to report that there was a party from the banking profession coming to tour the prison. At the time I didn't know what this was all about, but later I learned why those upper- and middle-class white collar professionals are sent to visit the prisons, which house the lowest levels of society. It is to let those handsome men and pretty ladies see with their own eyes what prison life is like so that they will be forewarned and will not play fast and loose with the money that passes through their hands. However, the people who set things up for the visitors were not really in sync with the purposes of the visit, as they wanted to save face by making prison life look as presentable as possible and showing that it is "civilized and humanitarian."

Shortly before ten o'clock we heard the electrically operated steel doors open and more than seventy neatly dressed bank personnel came in, one following another in orderly procession. Due to the careful planning of the Transfer Center, they saw no electric prods and heard no screams of pain. As they walked along the clean corridor they saw rooms labeled "Library" and "Psychological Counseling Room," and, in the northwestern corner of the main hall, a big 34-inch color television. Then there was the shining clean toilet and washroom. The prison dormitory contained identical bedroom-and-study suites labeled "Unit One" to "Unit Eight." In each of these rooms, prisoners sat quietly, with good posture, concentrating on their "studies." No one turned around or looked right and left, or whispered in his neighbor's ear. The work tables and equipment that was ordinarily used for prison shop work had been moved away and completely hidden. No matter where one looked, there was not a trace of the work that usually went on here. Perhaps because they were relatively young, as the visitors moved through the area chattering away, the only expressions of surprise that we heard were such remarks as, "The mattresses on the prisoners' bunks are all the same size and laid out so neatly with checked sheets, and the blue quilts are neatly folded with squared off corners." "The atmosphere is like an army barracks but even better." What these kind and good young people did not think of was why every bunk was surrounded with bed curtains, and they had no idea that stuffed beneath the bunks was the worn and mismatched bedding that the prisoners actually slept on. Sadly, the prisoners' pitiful bedrolls couldn't speak, and the prisoners—who of course really knew what was going on—sat in the rooms with fear in their hearts and didn't dare to speak. Thus those intelligent young men and women were brazenly deceived on this April Fool's Day. They would go home from the Transfer Center and would probably give lively descriptions to their family and friends of what they had seen.

Every newly arriving prisoner was subjected to the same deception that was worked upon these young people from the banking profession, but the difference was that for the prisoners, when evening came, they would know that they had been deceived. I remember very well that when I entered the reception area on the 30th of March and saw the rows of double-deck bunks with mattresses and quilts on them, having been a stranger to a proper bed for so long, I couldn't help feeling pleasantly surprised. I thought at the time that since we had been issued shirts, pants, and socks, surely mattresses, sheets, and quilts would also be provided for us. We couldn't complain if we had to spend a little time straightening things up, or if the organization was rather militaristic. But that evening, after nine o'clock—bedtime at the Detention Center—I felt sleepy, and it was only with difficulty that I stayed awake till eleven. Then just as I was preparing to pull back a blue quilt and enjoy the luxury of sleeping one man to a bed, I suddenly saw an entirely unexpected scene: directed by the assistant squad leader, the prisoners took the neatly arranged bedding off the bunks and laid it on sheets that were spread on the floor. Then someone who was assigned to the task pulled our own bedrolls out from under the bunks and each man took his bedroll and spread it on the bunk to which he was assigned. But there were more men than bunks, so the prisoners who were in temporary detention had to double up, three men occupying two bunks. If there were yet more men, some would have to sleep on the floor. One can imagine how disgusted I felt on seeing this. What marvels are produced under the leadership of the Communist Party! And among those who participated in the production of these marvels, there were many who were so accustomed to these procedures that they were insensitive to them.

Early on the morning of the 31st, as the monitor on duty called out the order to get out of bed, the men in each unit got dressed within a few minutes and put their bedrolls on the floor, and a man especially assigned to the task came around and pushed all the bedrolls under the bunks, kicking them with his feet to stuff them in tightly so that nothing would disturb the bed curtains that obscured them. While this was going on, another crew spread the showcase bedding on the bunks so that they would be ready for visitors to see the "high quality" accommodations.

The close-up view of this falsity made me feel nauseated. On the first of April I even had the impulse to follow in the footsteps of Wang Hai* and pull the curtains aside and disclose this fakery. The reason I didn't actually do this was not that I was afraid of what would be done to me but that I didn't want to suddenly cause the Transfer Center such extreme embarrassment in front of so many young men and women from the banks. On the day that the group of visitors left, I spoke out and criticized the Center's fabrications, and a few days later I wrote a strong protest. I said that for an organization that was responsible for the reform of criminals to involve the men they were supposedly reforming in such fakery amounted to dragging them deeper into corruption. I asked, with China's economic growth number one in the world, why is it that the prison system cannot afford to provide bedding for the inmates? If there was really no money to buy bedding, it would be a hundred times better to take the effort to make the prisoners' own bedding more presentable than the falseness of the present procedure.

The Transfer Center's response to my questions was silence. There was probably no alternative, both because there could be no good argument against what I said and because it is difficult to change corrupt customs. Chinese people's habit of fooling each other was really not a once-a-year April Fool's Day performance, but was a never-ending show that went on from day to day and year to year. As far as I know, that show of putting things up in the morning and taking them down in the evening still plays out every day. Also, the library, that "deaf man's ear," is still completely silent. When has it been opened to a temporary prisoner, and what prisoner has ever borrowed a book from it? Later, when I was in Unit Three, I ran into a prisoner who went into the library occasionally on cleanup duty, and he said that there were indeed many books there, including hardback books and multivolume sets, but none of them were available for checkout or for the intellectual improvement of inmates; rather they existed simply for decoration and as stage props for fooling people. The library was maintained to satisfy those in charge and for display toward the outside world, but its real function was completely ignored.

Fellow citizens, when will we stop fooling ourselves and fooling others?

---

* Wang Hai was a young man who in 1995 discovered that there was a law for protection of consumers' rights that stipulated that anyone who could prove that he had bought fake goods could demand that the merchant from whom he had made the purchase reimburse him double the price that he had paid for the goods. He discovered that the law really worked and made a great deal of money by buying fake goods and demanding reimbursement. Others followed suit, and for a time Wang Hai became a folk hero, until courts ceased to enforce the law.

CHAPTER THIRTY-NINE

~

A Frightening Interlude

There was also another true story that took place on the 1st of April 2001.* A Chinese J-8 fighter plane collided with an American naval reconnaissance plane over the South China Sea. The Chinese pilot, Wang Wei, parachuted from his plane and was lost at sea, while the US plane had to make an emergency landing at Yulin Airport on China's Hainan Island. Naturally, everything that we could hear and read in the Chinese government-controlled media was inflammatory reporting of the Chinese view of the incident. Ordinarily, in situations like this, aside from reports that followed the official line, one could also seek information from other channels and, through independent reasoning, could come to one's own conclusions. But in the Detention Center, we had no choice. We could only hear the Chinese government version, and furthermore, we were ordered not to think about the incident or discuss it among ourselves. We were not even permitted to be silent about it, but were required to express our opinions according to the official account.

* What follows here is a straightforward account of an incident that occurred on 1 April 2001. There were conflicting claims on the Chinese and American sides regarding the location of the accident ("in Chinese airspace" or "seventy miles off the coast of Hainan Island") and its cause (whether the reconnaissance plane "veered into the path of the fighter jet" or the fighter pilot, in an attempt to intimidate the crew of the US plane, made a misjudgment that resulted in wing-to-wing contact). The twenty-four crew members of the reconnaissance plane were detained by the Chinese authorities for eleven days and finally released after the United States published a carefully worded "apology" for the accident. The author's analysis of the likely cause of the accident is close to the US version. Wang Wei, the deceased pilot, was made a patriotic hero by the official Chinese press, though many Chinese at the time expressed opinions similar to our author's, some of them noting that Wang had a reputation as a "hotshot" pilot likely to be involved in such an accident.

Under pressure from the prison authorities, sentiment in the Detention Center quickly became very agitated. All the prisoners vented their feelings, and everything that was said was written down and sent up through the various layers of authority. The essence of these expressions of opinion was that whatever the higher authorities said was parroted by all those below. The more dull-witted simply shouted slogans, while the glib-tongued took the opportunity to show off their ability to rouse emotions. Soon an atmosphere of bitter hatred of "the enemy" spread throughout the prison. However, while these "performers" followed along thoughtlessly, as an observer I couldn't help giving serious consideration to what was occurring. I found this incitement of the prisoners a frightening reminder of the mass movements of the 1950s, 1960s, and 1970s. The crucial aspect of this action was that it treated the prisoners as people without souls and without any will of their own, only able to speak with a high degree of agreement with the official view. No spirit of independence or freedom of thought was possible. If anyone was silent he was assumed to be in opposition. Any expression of an opposing opinion was considered treason and treated as plotting rebellion. Although the authorities were no longer capable of achieving their goals outside the prison walls, their suppression of the human spirit of the prisoners here in the twenty-first century was more than enough to cause one deep heartache.

In the first meeting of our section on the question of the airplane collision, I didn't speak until everyone else had stated their opinions. Then I began by quoting an old saying, "Listen to both sides and be enlightened, listen to only one side and you'll be in the dark." I went on to say that I would have to hear both sides and then use my own judgment in order to know the true story of the collision, and I could not express an opinion until I knew the true situation. No one could reasonably find fault with what I said, but the squad leader's "class struggle" constraints were very tight, and he immediately went out to make a report. As soon as he returned, the assistant brigade chief called me out and quizzed me about what I had said. I repeated this and added that, if we heard only one side, there was no way we could "seek truth from facts."* He angrily retorted, "You don't have to take part in these discussions. There is no need for you to state your opinion." Obviously he couldn't tolerate any expression of a differing view, regardless of how reasonable and equitable it might be.

To tell the truth, the idea that a reconnaissance plane carrying more than twenty personnel knocked down a jet fighter leaves one quite suspicious.

* Here the author is using one of Deng Xiaoping's favorite quotations as a lightly sarcastic jab at the prison officials.

The prisoners were not idiots, but they did not dare speak out for fear of being scolded, criticized, or subjected to the electric prod. For my part, if I had committed an offense through speaking out, why should I object to verbal criticism? In addition, as a student in the Beijing College of Aeronautics, I had gone in June of 1981 to visit the big airplane factory in Shenyang and had seen the J-6 jet fighters and the J-8 fighters that were just going into production. Twenty years later I still had a clear impression of the powerful twin-engine jet fighter planes and their designers' description of their capabilities. Two J-8 jet fighters had gone up to "escort" the US reconnaissance plane, and one of them had fallen into the sea and the pilot was lost. How persuasive was the Chinese government's blaming the collision on the much slower and less maneuverable reconnaissance plane?

While the affair of the airplane collision continued to play out on television, the curtain was raised on another "crackdown" that was to continue for two years. It had begun with an explosion in an apartment building in Hebei Province. This unusual case of violence greatly agitated the inner circles of the government, causing them to roll out the time-honored magic weapon of "crackdown" as a means of keeping the country under control. And while that was happening on the outside, how could things continue in a normal fashion inside the prison? The Beijing People's Superior Court, People's Procuratorate, Public Security Bureau, and the Justice Department put out a "Joint Public Notice" saying that all prisoners should admit their crimes and also report the crimes of others. Those who informed on others would have their punishments reduced and would also receive rewards, while the people who were reported would be severely punished. Then the processes of a "movement," so familiar to older and middle-aged people, got under way, with orders passed from one level down to the next. The Detention Center held a big meeting, followed by brigade level and section meetings, again requiring all prisoners to state their opinions and come clean about their crimes, swearing an oath that they were being truthful, that they were not hiding any unreported crimes, and that if anything they said was found to be false they would willingly accept appropriate punishment.

A few days after the first round of statements were collected, several men who had "guaranteed that they did not know of any other people's crimes" now went to the prison police and reported such "crimes." This resulted in a redoubling of encouragements to inform on fellow prisoners, "not withholding even a tiny bit of information," and prisoners were required to write yet another guarantee of truthfulness. All this was frighteningly similar to the Cultural Revolution, when everyone had to feel that "the revolution erupted from the depths of their souls" and they had to confess their own transgressions and inform on their colleagues, friends, and even family members in order to "ensure that the Party and the nation would not change color" (that is, would remain loyal Communist *red*). While the others were submitting their pledges, I wrote to the administration of the Detention Center laying out my criticism of the crackdown. My view was that this was a product of senior officials' willfulness and was a symbol of personal rule rather than rule by law. It dealt only with symptoms rather than root problems, and acting on impulse and meting out heavy punishments for light offenses was seriously harmful to the administration of justice. Law enforcement and the dispensation of justice should not arbitrarily swing back and forth between strictness and laxness. I suggested that crackdowns should be permanently abolished and the government should act according to the law.

The authorities responded to my criticism only with silence. It seemed to me that this was a matter of yielding, or compromise, but if someone wanted to consider it progress, I would not object to that either, because I couldn't forget how many men and women with lofty ideals had, since 1949, continued to express their beliefs from prison and as a result been labeled "obstinate oppositionists" or "arrogant counterrevolutionaries" and had their punishments increased, even to the point of being sent to the execution grounds. Wasn't this the way Lin Zhao, Yu Luoke, Zhang Zhixin, and others had met their cruel fates?*

* Lin Zhao was an outspoken dissident during the Hundred Flowers Movement of 1957. In prison she wrote hundreds of pages of criticism of Mao Zedong using her own blood. She was executed in 1968. Yu Luoke wrote an essay in 1966, at the beginning of the Cultural Revolution, titled "Theory of Class Origin," and wrote additional essays that were widely read, but in 1968 he was accused of "making vicious attacks" and "organizing a counterrevolutionary group," and was executed. Zhang Zhixin was a dissident during the Cultural Revolution who became famous for criticizing the idolization of Mao. In 1969 she was imprisoned for six years and was executed in 1975.

CHAPTER FORTY

~

Visitors Day

Life in the Transfer Center was much more difficult than it had been in the Detention Center. We were not allowed to sleep past 5:30 in the morning, when we had to crawl out of bed and quickly stuff our bedding under the bunks and replace it with the "for show" quilts and bedspreads. Next was cleanup of the quarters, followed immediately by the prison police coming in to call the roll. Then we lined up to go to urinate, wash our faces, and brush our teeth, all of which had to be completed in three or four minutes. Then we returned to "recite the rules" and shout "Report!" "Present!" and "Yes Sir!" After breakfast the recitations resumed and continued until lunchtime with only a brief midmorning break to go and urinate again. There was no nap after lunch. The recitations went on without letup except to line up and go and relieve our bowels, and for this we had only five or six minutes before being herded back to continue reciting until supper time. After eating, it was more recitation, until 6:30, when we watched television news for an hour. Then, yet again it was reciting the rules and shouting commands from 7:30 to 8:30, followed by "study the Ten Prohibitions" until eleven o'clock. During this period the prison police came back to take the evening roll. This routine, together with verbal and corporal punishments, made life truly unbearable. It was no wonder that all new arrivals in the Reception Unit couldn't wait to be transferred to the Production Unit, where aside from calling out "Present" when the roll was called, they merely had to shout a token "Report" and "Yes Sir" when entering and leaving the dormitory, and at 9:30 they could lie down to sleep.

The only pleasure for prisoners in the Reception Unit of the Transfer Center was the imminent hope of seeing family members from whom they had so long been separated. For those of us who had arrived on 30 March, our day to see family was the 5th of April. Needless to say, the person who would come to see me was my wife, Zhang Hong. My son was studying in America, and other family members were all in Changshu. We were not allowed to have visits from friends. It was now almost two years since 18 May 1999 when the police had come in the middle of the night and taken me away from home. During this time, on the 1st of November 1999, I had seen my wife in the First Intermediate People's Court of Beijing, when she had heard almost all of my court hearing. When the prosecutor had been unable to find proof that I had written "Light a Million Candles to Commemorate the Souls of the Heroes of June 4th" and I had willingly acknowledged my authorship, I felt that she approved my admission. My lawyer, Mo Shaoping, had read out a bit of that essay and asked me whether it represented my views, and I said, "Yes, this is indeed my view of the 1989 Democracy Movement." I felt that Zhang Hong was in accord with my position. In order to avoid interruptions of my defense by the judges, I had been quite restrained in what I said, but at the end of my final statement I couldn't help showing some emotion in expressing my ideals, and at this point there was an unexpected burst of applause from Zhang Hong. This outburst from one delicate woman was much more golden than the so-called thunderous applause that one reads about occurring in the Great Hall of the People on Tiananmen Square.

Almost fourteen months later, on 27 December 2000, we had once again seen each other in a courtroom, and she had witnessed my angry criticism of the literary inquisition. And on 16 March 2001, in the People's Superior Court of Beijing, we had seen each other a third time, and she had heard my lighthearted ridicule of the adjudication of my retrial. Most regrettably, however, in none of these three instances over the period of two years were we able to speak to each other. This time, although we would be separated by glass and have to speak through telephones, at least we would be able to talk to one another for half an hour.

When the day arrived, the sky was alternately clear and cloudy, with brief periods of light rain. The interview room was at the southeast corner of the courtyard and, as we left from the northwest corner, we made our way diagonally across the entire Transfer Center. The five of us who were scheduled to meet family members formed a small column as we walked slowly forward. I carried a woven net bag in each hand containing personal belongings from the Detention Center that I wanted to ask Zhang Hong to take home. We were escorted across the courtyard by a guard in his twenties. As we entered the interview room, the five of us took our assigned seats, and the outer door quickly opened and the family members came rushing in. In spite of my nearsightedness and the serious decline in the vision of my right eye, I immediately recognized Zhang Hong and, to my surprise, I saw that a friend whom I had called "Xiao Yi," or "Auntie," was with her. Upon seeing Zhang Hong and Xiao Yi, the resentment that I had felt for several days over having to wear prison clothes and being forced to shave my head quickly dissipated. I raised my hand in a V signal to them, and Zhang Hong and I picked up the telephone receivers simultaneously. She brought me up to date on our various family members and friends such as Xu Liangying and Ding Zilin.* Then Xiao Yi and I chatted. With a sad catch in her voice, she told me that another "Auntie," Su Bingxian, had passed away. I had great respect for Xiao Yi and Su Bingxian and was very close to them. Both of them had children who had sacrificed their young lives for their ideals in the 1989 June 4th massacre. They had not only suffered the greatest sadness that mothers can bear, but had also braved danger and great pressure by undertaking to locate and visit other mothers bereaved by the June 4 tragedy and had issued protests against the government action. In the spring of 1999 family members of more than a hundred people who had been killed on June 4th had submitted a formal statement to the International Court of Justice accusing Li Peng† of crimes against humanity. Xiao Yi had personally taken a copy of that accusation to the People's Highest Procuratorate. Su Bingxian had worked in the Marxist-Leninist Compilation and Translation Bureau, and it was through her that I had become acquainted with Bao Tong.‡ Auntie Su had been in poor health, but I had no idea in the fall of 1997, when she took me to Bao Tong's home, that that would be the last time I would ever see her.

When Zhang Hong picked up the phone again, I told her about the ten days in February that I had spent in the Public Security Hospital. She replied saying that the "Five Pieces" had already been published before that time.§ The "Five Pieces" were my "Accusing the Preliminary Hearing Department of the Bei-

* Xu Liangying (b. 1920) is an eminent physicist, historian, and translator of Einstein's works who has been active in civil rights movements in China. Ding Zilin was a professor of philosophy at People's University in Beijing until she was forced into retirement after establishing the organization Tiananmen Mothers to press the government to apologize and account for the deaths of their sons and daughters in the June 4th demonstrations. Her seventeen-year-old son was one of the first demonstrators shot to death by People's Liberation Army (PLA) soldiers on the night of June 3–4. Both Xu and Ding wrote prefaces for the Chinese edition of *My Life in Prison*.

† At the time of the Tiananmen demonstrations, Li Peng was premier of China and a leader of the hard-liners in the top leadership. As premier, he had declared martial law in Beijing on 20 May, and many hold him primarily responsible for the decision to "clear Tiananmen Square" and the ensuing June 4th massacre.

‡ Bao Tong was a high-level official who opposed the crackdown on student demonstrators and was arrested a week before June 4th and later sentenced to seven years in prison.

§ Thus she let him know that he need not be further concerned that the prison authorities had found and confiscated these documents when they sent him to the hospital so they could undertake a thorough search of his prison sleeping area.

jing Public Security Bureau," "My Defense," "My Final Statement," "Attorney Mo's Defense on My Behalf," and the People's Procuratorate's "Indictment." Of course we couldn't list these items in our conversation but could only refer to them indirectly. I was especially gratified to learn that she had obtained my "Statement of Appeal." The Detention Center had not hesitated to defy the law and hold my four attempts at appeal instead of passing them up the chain of command, and this had made me all the more determined to pursue the appeal. The authorities had forcibly created a literary inquisition and then, to pretty it up even more, had tried to smother the objections of the injured party. It would be hard to find a more unbalanced contest than this.

I only lightly touched on conditions in the Transfer Center. It wasn't that I was afraid of offending the officials who were carefully listening to our conversation, but rather that I didn't want to cause my family unnecessary worry. How could I explain that the Reception Unit was like a bridge to hell, that there was absolutely no respect for the human dignity of the prisoners there, or that, corralled within the buildings that they could see from the outside, were people who spent their days in fear because they were blamed for every word they spoke and every movement they made. I only mentioned a few aspects of our life inside, saying that our workload was not heavy. We were only assigned such tasks as occasionally helping the Production Unit make shopping bags. I didn't say that we were yelled at and abused seventeen hours a day, treated like animals being trained in a circus. I mentioned that the section chief used to be in the restaurant business in the West Balizhuang area, and he looked out for me. This "looking out for me" was true. I didn't have to recite the prison rules, sing the prison song, or shout the commands until I was hoarse, nor was I required to stand stiffly at attention like a soldier in training. But finally I did divulge one fact that would cause worry for my family: my blood pressure was rather high, 150 over 100.

Thirty minutes passed in the blink of an eye. The dreaded bell sounded suddenly, announcing the end of visiting time, and our voices were cut off in the telephone receivers. I stood up and waved my arms and moved my legs to show that I was in good health. Zhang Hong and Xiao Yi raised their right hands with the V signal and backed away, waving. I was pleased that my overstepping the boundaries of usually permitted speech had not brought a reprimand from the squad leader, and in fact, when we lined up to return to the Reception Unit, he let me bring up the rear of the group and fell in beside me for a chat, quietly urging that in future I should keep my thoughts to myself so as to avoid trouble. I concluded that he was actually a good person, and then I realized that the meanness that he and other squad leaders usually displayed was simply what was required by the rules of the Transfer Center.

CHAPTER FORTY-ONE

~

Guinness Record Levels of Suffering

When prisoners spoke with their family members on these telephones, the prison authorities could very conveniently listen and record what was said. Therefore, in addition to holding back unpleasant information so as not to cause concern to their families, prisoners didn't want to report the bad aspects of the Transfer Center for fear of reprisals. Still, they couldn't help but feel discouraged at the knowledge that no matter how far they went against their consciences and hid the darkness and evil of the Center, presenting a smiling face to the visitors, the cold, inhuman system and rules awaited them in the corridor. There was no concept that one good turn deserves another. The Center would not show them any appreciation or favors; its established principle was to thoroughly remold all prisoners, and the first step in this process was to let them know the taste of despotism. This was the main source of the Transfer Center's evil and the Reception Unit's ruthlessness.

In the evening of 6 April the chief of the Reception Unit was called into the corridor and spent a half an hour in the prison police office. When he returned, he quietly called me aside and, with an unhappy frown on his face, asked me what I had said about him in my family interview the previous day. I replied that I had said some good things about him. "That," he said, "is what's causing me trouble! They say that I am not keeping a proper distance from you, that I am treating you with special favor." When I replied that anyone could see that there is nothing special between us, he said, "The higher-ups don't see it that way. They say I should be tough with you. It would be better for me if you would say bad things about me." I understood. The chief of the Reception Unit had heavy responsibilities. He was charged with suppressing and controlling all of the temporary prisoners who came through the section and all of those who were sent back because of offenses in Unit Two, and he also had to deal with long-term prisoners. Given these considerations, it was not surprising that the prisoners under his charge would be made to suffer maltreatment and abuse.

Let's begin with the two questions of getting boiled water to drink and taking care of our toilet needs. Newly arrived prisoners have to shout "Report!" "Present!" and "Yes Sir!" throughout the morning and afternoon, and at the same time they must march in place and then stand at attention for long periods of time, and they have to help with the work of the Production Unit. They have very limited opportunities to get boiled water for drinking. Only after the squad leader and assistant squad leader have drunk all they want is it possible for the other prisoners to get drinking water. Temporary prisoners are not given cups, so when they have a chance at drinking water, they have to wait their turn, using a plastic food bowl. (Spoons and bowls are not issued to individual prisoners; everybody uses the same ones, regardless of any concern for hygiene.) Anybody who is the least bit polite simply won't get anything to drink. When the drinking water is limited and everyone is very thirsty, some of the men will simply have to drink cold water from the spigot. But there is a sign above the spigot saying, "In order to avoid diarrhea, drinking faucet water is strictly prohibited." When people go to the bathroom to wash their faces, the monitor, squad leader, and assistant squad leader, who have no worry about getting enough drinking water, watch carefully, and if anyone sneaks a drink of faucet water, he will surely be caught, scolded, told to stop his washing immediately, and made to stand at the door awaiting further punishment. Sometimes a prisoner will get so thirsty that he will wait till the group goes to urinate and, while standing there, catch a mouthful of water in his hand from the small pipe that brings water to rinse the urinal, and drink it. But to succeed at this, one must be very alert and dexterous so as not to be seen by a monitor watching through the transparent door of the toilet and put to shame as if he had been caught at a theft. Like a seven-foot-tall man going through a six-foot door, once someone has been sent to the Transfer Center, he has no choice but to suffer torment and indignity just to get a drink of water.

Defecations are classified as minor and major. The time allotted for lining up and going for a minor one is barely enough to accommodate the biological need. More problematical is the major defecation, for which only five or six minutes are allowed. It would probably never occur to those on the outside that when a person arrives at the Transfer Center, for the first three days there is usually no inclination to have a bowel movement. The move from the more relaxed atmosphere of the Detention Center to the despotic discipline of the Transfer Center throws a person's involuntary nervous system into confusion and, although he continues to eat, there is no inclination to have bowel movements. The most annoying thing is that when the appointed time comes, even if you know that you won't have a bowel movement, you still must go to the toilet and squat over a hole. You can't even stand to the side and wait, but must squat with the others until they are finished, then line up and go back to the cell with the group. Then on the fourth, or maybe the fifth or sixth day, you finally feel that you want to have a movement, and you try to get a forward position in line hoping to find a place in the toilet, where there are never as many holes as there are men. But then to solve this problem, believe it or not, the squad leader might order that two men use the same hole at the same time. Of course men who had just arrived at the Transfer Center and were getting used to being treated as slaves would not dare disobey the squad leader's order, so we had the unimaginable spectacle, worthy of the *Guinness Book of Records*, of two men as if joined in one body, back to back and buttock against buttock, squatting over one hole to defecate. In this age of globalizing humanitarian civilization, can anyone imagine a more revolting spectacle? And when two men are put together like this, especially given the limited time allowed for the chore, one man will always be stronger than the other, and the weaker one gets pushed off and has to fight his way back over the hole with loud curses. The first time I saw it happen, I was filled with nausea and immediately lost my inclination to defecate. This procedure was invented by the number two squad leader and is the rule that I referred to above as worse than any other. In my opinion, the ability to invent such a "rule" as this is not ordinary wickedness but is evil in the extreme. It was not until 4 April, my sixth day in the Transfer Center, that I managed to squat over a hole by myself and with great effort, and beads of sweat rolling down my face, complete the much needed evacuation.

One more inhuman thing that I must mention is the way the prison authorities sacrifice the prisoners' basic health precautions in the name of "hygiene." As the temporary prisoners don't have drinking cups, they also, of course, don't have cups to use while brushing their teeth. Each person has only a small plastic bag for his toothbrush, toothpaste, and washcloth, and all these plastic bags are supposed to be stuffed together into a wash basin just like we have to stuff our bedding under our bunks. As the temperature rises, these wet washcloths quickly develop a repugnant odor, and thus something that should be used to maintain good hygiene soon becomes a breeding ground for pathogenic germs and bacteria—another item for Guinness. Later

I learned that the blueprints for the Transfer Center sleeping areas did not include any place for drying washcloths. Of course, with a little flexibility, the wet washcloths could simply be hung on the radiator pipes, but this was not allowed because it would not look good, and the cell "hygiene" would not meet the required standard.

In early April the Transfer Center's surveillance system was completed and put into operation so that the prison police could sit in their control room and, with a glance at the monitors, see what was going on in the cells, the toilets, the washrooms, and the main entryway. They could also call out to the squad leaders, who could stand by the speakers and immediately respond to the calls. So now the squad leader of Unit Two had one more thing to add to his announcements: "Everybody listen to me! I am a person who likes to lay everything out clearly. If anyone does not obey the rules and gives me a hard time or interferes with my hopes of getting rewards and having my sentence reduced, I promise I will make you regret it."

The high walls, electrified netting, iron-barred windows, electric prods, and surveillance cameras can be taken for granted. But the failure to provide for the most basic biological needs of prisoners and deprivation of their human dignity are nakedly inhumane and must be exposed, denounced, and eradicated.

CHAPTER FORTY-TWO

~

Others May Be Biased, but I Am Impartial

Having spent time in the Detention Center, the Transfer Center, and the Number Two Prison, I can vouch for the fact that whatever curses might be directed at the Transfer Center, they will never be excessive. My time there was spent in Unit One, while most of the people who arrived at the Number Two Prison with me on 22 May 2001 had been assigned to Unit Two, with a few sent to the Infirmary Section. Later, when I was in the Number Two Prison, one man who was assigned, with me, to Squad Ten of Unit Sixteen had been in the infirmary at the Transfer Center. On the afternoon of our arrival, while we were bathing in cold water, he kept splashing it on his body and happily shouting, "I'm home! I'm home!" One shouldn't be too surprised at this young fellow's attitude, as temporary prisoners never had a chance for a good cold water bath in the Transfer Center. We were only allowed two or three minutes a day to dip our washcloths in the water and rub our bodies with them. The men from Unit Two in the Transfer Center cursed it as a devilish, dark place that they would remember the rest of their lives. On the day of their arrival at the Center, even before changing into prison clothes, they had been subjected to electric shocks, for imagined offenses or for no reason at all. If they were in for a second offense: electric shock. Multiple charges: electric shock. Failure to shout "Present!": shock. Failure to look straight ahead: shock. Speak to a fellow prisoner: shock. In Unit Two, men were punished by the requirement of shouting "Report! Present! Yes Sir!" not ten or twenty times as in Unit One, but fifty or a hundred times. And the last five men to report for duty in the Production Unit were required to scrub the entire corridor of the unit fifty times.

When those who had arrived at the Number Two Prison earlier than my group heard the Transfer Center mentioned, they expressed extreme hatred for it and cursed it in the strongest possible language. Those who were a little more cultured said that character, dignity, and human rights were all worthless there and were completely trampled underfoot. Some who had an interest in history said that the Transfer Center was a holographic facsimile of China in the 1960s and 1970s,* and that it should be considered "sacred ground" for historical review and study.

When those who had arrived at the Number Two Prison later than my group spoke of their experience in the Transfer Center, they would shudder and be reluctant to talk about it. In April of 2002 I was cited for "talking back to a warden" and sent to Unit Ten of Number Two Prison for "group training." Aside from the "strict," "ordinary," and "lenient" classes organized by the group training personnel, Unit Ten also had a "reception" or "new" class made up of prisoners who had just arrived from the Transfer Center. Although the men I met from this "new" class were no longer so terrorized that from morning to night they didn't dare take a deep breath, they still walked furtively, with their heads down and taking care not to look to either side. I chatted with a number of them in the water room and, without exception, they all had terrible things to say about the Transfer Center and felt that they were fortunate in not having had to stay there more than a few days.

Then, was there no way in which the Transfer Center was better than the Detention Center? And if the Transfer Center was better in some way, would I acknowledge it? I could avoid addressing this question. As long as I didn't blindly say, "There is absolutely no way in which the Transfer Center is better than the Detention Center," I was on safe ground. But what would be the practical result of suppressing a bit of truth? People would be easily misled into believing that the Transfer Center is black to its roots, an inhuman morass with no positive aspects. Obviously, this would be less than completely objective and would not be fair and equitable, and it would also mean that I was falling short of my goal of honest and fair reporting of what I had seen and experienced. I will uphold the principle that, even if others are unfair, I will be impartial.

On the basis, then, of what I have seen and experienced, there are six ways in which the Transfer Center is better than the Detention Center, as follows:

1. Prisoners are not physically restrained. Except for an extremely small number of men who are held in close confinement, prisoners do not

* The turmoil, terror, and disorder of the "Great Proletarian Cultural Revolution" lasted from 1966 until Mao Zedong's death in 1976.

have to wear restraints. This is an important liberating feature for those who have had to wear handcuffs or leg irons in the Detention Center. And those who had not worn handcuffs or leg irons no longer needed to feel that they were caged together with wild animals or savages. In cell 404 of Section Seven there had been as many as thirteen men who wore leg irons. In the afternoon, when they were taken out for inspection, they had to be taken in two groups.

2. No requirement for night watch. Suspects held in the Detention Center, except for monitors and assistant monitors, had to take their turn standing night watch. With two or three men given this duty each night, when the number of men in a cell was relatively small, this duty would come so often that one would lose out on a lot of sleep. A person on night watch duty would often nod off, and if he was caught by a guard patrolling the cells, he would be punished the next day, either with a severe scolding or by being turned over to the warden and having his hands cuffed behind his back, in addition to being given extra night watch duty. In the Transfer Center, certain long-term prisoners were assigned to special night watch duty, so short-term prisoners no longer had to interrupt their sleep for this duty.
3. The cells were less crowded. At the Detention Center the cells were supposed to accommodate eighteen people, but sometimes as many as thirty-six were crowded into one cell. Then the floor would be covered with sleeping prisoners and, as those on the sleeping platform struggled for more space, fights would break out. One of the most trying duties of the monitors was to assign sleeping space and to stop these fights before they became serious. In the Reception Unit of the Transfer Center there were fourteen bunks, and to the best of my knowledge there had never been more than twenty men crowded into the room, nor had anyone had to sleep on the floor. Later, after I had been moved to the Production Unit, it was also no more crowded than this, and I never saw anyone sleeping on the floor.
4. There was more variety of food. In the Detention Center the staples were wheat-flour buns and cornmeal buns, and later it was only wheat-flour buns throughout the whole year. In the Transfer Center wheat-flour buns were the main staple, but on Sundays there was rice. Breakfast was rice congee, with deep-fried dough cakes once a week, and once every two weeks the noontime meal was baked wheat pancakes. The supplementary foods (things other than the grain-based staples) were also better and more varied in the Transfer Center. In the Detention Center we had in the main had only cabbage, potatoes, or

napa cabbage, rotated according to season, with celery or winter melon substituted occasionally. But in the first week in the Transfer Center we had napa, carrots, rape, and spinach, and sometimes we could get a little tofu or bean-flour noodles. Furthermore, the vegetables did not seem to have been overcooked in a big pot, but had more flavor and seemed to be more nourishing.

5. Twice a month we could have a hot bath. In the Detention Center there had been no hot baths; people detained there could only take cold baths throughout the year. Of course this was not a problem between the end of spring and midautumn, but when the weather got cold it was excruciating. And given that the heating in the building was not really adequate, using water that chilled one to the bone was hard to bear. At the Transfer Center a bathhouse had been built that was large enough to accommodate a whole company of prisoners at once, and from October through April we could go there for a hot shower twice a month. Of course there would sometimes be three or four men under one shower head, and the time for a shower was limited to fifteen minutes, but still a hot shower always put one in a better mood. Even more comforting was the fact that the noise of the showers made it possible, while keeping a sharp lookout for the guards, to chat a bit with fellow prisoners, to express ourselves more naturally, and even to get to know men from other sections of the prison. This was really the only chance for normal human contact within the Transfer Center. Even after finishing our showers, out in the dressing room we could still have a few minutes to talk, quickly shake hands, etc., while getting dressed. This was really a precious opportunity for release from the usual condition where we had to sit and stand like wooden men and move like automatons. Like a tiny oasis in a vast desert, the bathhouse was the most pleasant place in the whole Transfer Center.
6. We could play basketball. On the day I arrived at the Transfer Center I saw several basketball courts, but for the first ten days that we were there we were shut up in the prison building and had no chance to get outside, even for a short walk. But then on April 9th, a Sunday, not long after breakfast, we were taken for showers, and after the showers, we were herded out to the basketball courts. After marching around the courts several times, we were ordered to sit down on the ground. Suddenly the principal monitor shouted, "Each squad select five men to play ball. First, squad two will play squad three. There were shouts from squad three, and five men stood up, but only three men volunteered from squad two. After a few more shouts from the squad leader,

> a fourth man stood up. I had not touched a basketball during the seventeen years since I had left college in 1984, and I was fifty-three years old, while the rest of these men were in their twenties, so I thought it might not be appropriate for me to bump and struggle with these young fellows. But the monitor continued to shout, saying that if squad two couldn't turn out five men, we would forfeit the game. Provoked by this speech, I jumped up. I was wearing a padded jacket, pants, and shoes, but I thought, "Heck with it! I'll give it a try." After getting on the court and going through several exchanges of offense and defense, I discovered that I still had some ability. My feeling for the game and my technical competence were actually a little better than that of the other men. When I made the first basket for squad two, not only my teammates but all the men on the court broke out in applause. However, although I was stimulated by this encouragement, the two years I had spent confined to the small cell in the Detention Center had taken a heavy toll on my health, and I found that after running a few steps I was left panting for breath and had to pass the ball to someone else. Before long I felt a burning sensation in my throat and my leg muscles began to cramp. The crowded conditions and lack of exercise in the Detention Center had caused me to lose weight and a great deal of strength, and my lung capacity was seriously reduced.

Subsequently, I did participate in several more games.

One more thing I'd like to record is that in the Number Two Prison there was a man who had arrived there at the same time as I did, who spoke in strong opposition to the generally held view of the Transfer Center, saying a lot of good things about it. When others complained that the Center didn't give them enough food, he said that they gave him more than he could eat, and when they then complained about fatigue and loss of weight, he countered that he felt that life in the Center was quite comfortable. Later, when I questioned him more closely, I learned that what he said was indeed true. When he had arrived in Unit Two of the Center, he had struck up an acquaintance with an orderly called "Porcelain," who after their first meeting always gave him extra-large portions of food. He was also a very crafty fellow. Whenever he was given heavy work or anything that would make one tired, he would respond with psychologically induced vomiting, and after he had thus contaminated several products, they excused him from the work details. However, I had no respect for this kind of behavior, and I couldn't believe that such people really had a more pleasant life than the rest of us.

CHAPTER FORTY-THREE

When the Cock Crows at Dawn, the System Is Even More Cruel

The population of the Transfer Center was less stable than in any other prison. Convicted criminals were sent in from the various detention centers every Monday, Wednesday, and Friday, and once or twice a month, on a Tuesday or Thursday, prisoners were transferred out to local prisons either in Beijing or outside the city. Within the Center, the Reception Unit (Unit Two) had the most fluid population. A prisoner would usually stay there between two and five or six days. It was extremely unusual that a person would be kept there for two weeks, as I was, before being transferred to the Production Unit (Unit Three). I saw repeated scenes of abuse and persecution and heard howls of protest and pain time after time. Growing increasingly impatient and angry, I finally sent a request to the prison police that I be transferred out of Unit Two.

After supper on April 13th I was moved to Unit Three, which was right next to Unit Two and was where "prisoners requiring special attention" and juvenile offenders were usually assigned on their first arrival. I was moved there after a space opened up when a "special attention" prisoner had been moved to the infirmary a couple days earlier. The squad leader in Unit Three was not as intimidating as the leader of Unit Two, and his voice was also somewhat more gentle. Seeing this, it suddenly occurred to me that perhaps the most extreme treatment was meted out in the Reception Unit so as to put the newly arrived prisoners in their place and make them more docile for the remainder of their stay, and that the Production Unit might be more civilized and sympathetic. By chance, on the evening I was transferred, the chief of Unit Three came in to speak to the men in the section. His manner was indeed quite mild and contained none of the stern admonitions that I was used to hearing. He was a man nearing sixty years of age. On entering, he gestured to the squad leader to indicate that there was no need to shout "Attention!" Thus we continued to sit on our low stools. He chatted with the squad leader for a few minutes, then walked over in front of us, and we rose to attention, but he immediately gave the "At ease" order. Then he spoke for about twenty minutes without any of the scolding, curses, or abusive language that we were used to hearing. Having just come from the other side of the wall, I felt as though I were suddenly in a different world.

After the chief left, all the men in the section got to work making paper shopping bags in an assembly-line process. Each person went to his usual place on the line, and the work got under way. But now I faced a decision: to work or not to work? As a "prisoner requiring special attention," I could refuse to work. But I quickly chose to comply. As we were all living together, I didn't want to turn a blind eye to the ongoing work and sit to one side and relax. This was partly because of my temperament and partly because I was determined to gain experience. I remembered that during the busy fall season of 1970, after I was "sent down" to the countryside, the commune had selected me to participate in class-struggle sessions and told me to gather materials on the dictatorship of the proletariat and put them in order. While the other youths had to get up before daylight and do hard labor till after dark, I only had to do a little light work after the sun was up, and yet I received the same work points as the others. But I didn't feel that this was my good luck; on the contrary, I was unsettled by the unfairness of the arrangement. I felt as if I had done something shameful, and was afraid to talk to people. When I had to go to the team headquarters or the commune offices, I would often take a roundabout route in order to avoid contact with those who were working in the fields. When I returned, if the others were still in the fields, I would find a place to dawdle until they had finished for the day and gone back to the village, then I would hurry back home. This was in my nature. It was not that I was being sly or malingering. I felt bad for having been given special privileges for no good reason. Also I had confidence in my own ability to stand hard work. Thus it was no problem for me to join in with the other men in the Transfer Center.

As I was new to the work, the assistant squad leader taught me how to "fold the opening" of the bags; this was the second procedure of the assembly-line process. This work was not difficult, and before long I had mastered the essentials, although I was still much slower than the others. I took my position on the line and slowly began work. The others on the line did not complain or urge me to work faster, and I didn't press myself either—even when I heard the squad leader scolding the others and urging them to speed up. I felt pretty good about my progress in learning the ropes.

Around nine o'clock we stopped working, cleaned up the work tables, and swept the floor. Then we took the "for display" bedding off the bunks and pulled our own bedding out from under the bunks and replaced it with the display quilts and sheets. Finally, a chamber pot was placed in the middle of the room for use if anyone needed to get up in the night, as all the electric doors had been closed and could not be opened except in special circumstances. Then around 9:30 we went to bed. Although three men had to crowd into space designed for two, when I thought of the men next door having to study the Ten Prohibitions for another hour and a half before they could go to bed, I felt pretty good about my situation.

When the order to get out of bed was called out at dawn the next day, I got up from my bottom bunk and quickly dressed and pushed my bedding under the bunk. However, there were always some who were slower than others, and the squad leader soon started scolding. Although his voice was not especially loud, it was very disagreeable. While one group of people anxiously stuffed bedding under the bunks, another hurriedly replaced it with the display bedding. As this was going on, I saw that the squad leader was watching with an expression of disapproval, and when he saw someone whose movements displeased him, he was quick to scold the culprit. The next task was to mop the floor and wipe down the doors, windows, and cupboards, while two or three men climbed onto the bunks to arrange the bedding. Just as in Unit Two, this had to be done with great care, leaving the bedding with straight edges and square corners. It seemed that the squad leader had a special mania for scolding people. Anyone who was just a bit slow was sure to be scolded, and even punished by having to redo the job two or three times. At morning roll call, the squad leader warned that "Anyone who fails to shout 'Present' will have to answer to me!" I began to feel that it was not all that different here from what I was used to next door.

Over the next few days I gradually came to understand the situation. From the time he got up in the morning till he went to bed at night, this Unit Three squad leader wore a hungry look on his face and never cracked a smile. He always frowned severely at the people around him and was eternally ready to reprimand and rebuke the men under his charge. It seemed as though the main thing that made him act this way was pressure from his duties in charge of production under superior officers who insisted on ranking the various units engaged in it. But his unreasonable attitude was both oppressive and hateful.

In the Production Unit, work was everything. There were no books, newspapers, chess, or cards. Talking was forbidden. Inmates were treated as mute tools. In terms of time and the intensity of the work, no quarter was given. We were expected to constantly carry an overload. It was not unusual to be required to start before breakfast, and we weren't even allowed to wash our hands before eating. When we had eaten half a bowl of congee and were still chewing a bun, the dishes were taken away and the cloth was spread for the work to begin. Through the morning, except for a group toilet break, we had to work right up to lunchtime without any rest. At lunch everyone grabbed a bun with one dirty hand and picked up a broken plastic spoon with the other and tried to scrape a few mouthfuls of food from the bottom of the bowl. After drinking half a bowl of water, we had to get back to work, while two men took all the dishes and washed them.

In the afternoon there were two toilet breaks, the longer one for three to five minutes, including washing our hands and rinsing our mouths, then we worked right up until the evening meal was brought in. After eating, we resumed work until 6:20, then from 6:30 to 7:30 we watched television news. After the news, we went back to work until nine, or sometimes ten o'clock. Because the production line had been meticulously designed, and furthermore was constantly being "improved," there was no chance to get even a little rest during work time. We were forced to keep going until we were exhausted. If work piled up at some station on the assembly line, affecting overall progress, the squad leader would quickly intervene, striking out at the person who had slowed it down. The leader and assistant leader also checked product quality, and if a fault was discovered in a completed or partially completed item, the leader would ridicule and criticize the person responsible for the fault and make him immediately redo the item.

Some products didn't have to be done on the assembly line, and these were handed out and counted on a piecework basis. After everyone had gotten their pieces and begun work, the squad leader served as a supervisor. Regardless of whether he was standing or sitting, he kept a careful lookout on all the work. Anyone who was slow would be ridiculed, and the slowest of the group was sure to be reprimanded. Thus the squad leader's role was not easy either. Even though he could get large helpings of food at the noon and evening meals, his countenance was always gray and his eyes dull. When the day's work was tallied, the two men who had been slowest had to go over to Unit Two to "study and consider their errors," and they didn't come back to go to bed until nearly eleven o'clock.

Thus the work was heavy and tense, food and boiled water for drinking were scarce, and during rest periods the inmates were subjected to scolding and humiliation. Initially the juvenile offenders felt that they must simply bear it. Most of them quietly voiced their complaints to me, saying it would be better to go back to Unit Two. But one boy, who couldn't stand the pressure and openly talked back to the squad leader several times, was sent to Unit Two for "strict training." The great majority of the others restrained themselves and were careful not to give voice to their anger, though one, who repeatedly quarreled with the leader, was sent to Unit Two to "consider his errors."

Except for the squad leader and his assistant, all the people in Unit Three were so fatigued that they became psychologically unbalanced. Because constipation from the time spent in Unit Two wasn't relieved, there was extra toilet paper from what had been issued to individuals, and this was useful in catching the phlegm from our throats and nostrils that resulted from our unhealthy condition. The bathroom sink collected so much phlegm and snot that it couldn't be scrubbed clean. Some of the inmates became so weak that they lost their appetites and would only eat one of the two buns that were distributed at each meal. These were all typical results of excessive fatigue and the rise of internal heat in the body. Everyone was losing weight.

Anyone over the age of forty would be familiar with the story "The Cock Crows at Midnight." There was a landlord named Zhou, who thought of a sneaky plan to get more work out of his laborers. He would creep to the chicken coop at midnight and make a crowing sound so as to get the rooster to crow. Then he would go to the laborers' bunkhouse and get them up, saying, "The cock has already crowed. How come you lazy bums aren't out in the field working?" Because they felt that this black-hearted landlord was flaying them alive, they gave him the nickname "Skinner Zhou." But, following the old adage "The authorities promulgate their policies, but we have our countermeasures," although the workers had to get up in the middle of the night, they quietly made up their lost sleep after they got to the fields. And then they got even when they saw him going out to the chicken coop and, pretending to think he was a chicken thief, gave him a good beating, after which he never again made the cock crow in the middle of the night. The Transfer Center prisoners weren't required to get up in the middle of the night, but after arising at dawn they could not lie down again until late in the evening. Of course there was no way to get even with the squad leader. If they lost their temper and dared to cross him, they would be reminded that the prison policeman's electric prod was very real. And after being shocked by the prod, they would have to write a detailed self-examination and solemnly promise not to misbehave again.

In the Transfer Center work began at dawn, but the system was even more cruel than on Mr. Zhou's farm, where the laborers had to get up and go to work at midnight.

CHAPTER FORTY-FOUR

~

I've Never Been Afraid of Hard Work

I was perhaps the only person in the Transfer Center who had ever volunteered to be "skinned alive." I not only voluntarily chose to work, but also carried an overload. During my almost two years of confinement in the Detention Center my weight had declined from 70 to 66 kilograms, and during my fifty-three days in the Transfer Center I lost another 4 kilos, my weight further declining to 62 kilos. In the work assignments, not only did I not ask for special consideration, I was determined, too, not to fall behind the others. Among more than ten workers, most of them young men, I usually maintained third or fourth place, while the first- and-second-ranked men were twenty and twenty-one years old.

There were three events that illustrate the extreme fatigue I experienced in Unit Three of the Transfer Center.

First, like my fellow workers, at the end of the day I was so tired that I was fast asleep as soon as my head hit the "pillow" formed by folding my padded jacket and pants. But in the middle of the night I would awaken with a feeling of suffocation from phlegm obstructing my throat and mucus blocking my nose. Therefore, before going to sleep I would have to make sure that I had toilet paper to spit phlegm and blow my nose into when I woke up during the night. Of course, this accumulation of phlegm and mucus was the result of extreme fatigue from the long hours of work. The second example was one day when I was especially exhausted, I had difficulty breathing and my hands and feet felt numb. After trying a number of times to overcome these symptoms, I finally asked the squad leader for permission to rest for half an hour. After sitting quietly on my low stool for a while, I felt fairly normal again. And third, when I would go to the toilet in the afternoon, because of unrelieved constipation, I sometimes felt that I didn't have the strength to finish the chore. I tried taking laxatives, but they didn't help, so I would just skip going to the toilet. (In Unit Three this was permitted. If someone didn't want to go to the toilet with the group, he could just sit at his work station, under the watchful eye of the assistant squad leader.)

Still, although the Transfer Center challenged my willpower and caused me physical misery, I did not regret my choice. If I had sat to one side and relaxed while the others were working, how could I have fully known the disgraceful, evil reality of the Center? Also, my position was somewhat better than that of the other prisoners. The squad leader would only complain to me about my behavior; he wouldn't humiliate me as he did the others. And the assistant squad leader also looked out for me. When I first came into the Transfer Center, he had overheard the group chief talking to me and, from that, learned something of my situation. Then after I was moved into Unit Three, he would sometimes give me a little of his food or tell the man from the kitchen who distributed food to give me a little more. Considering that our usual portion was no more than three or four mouthfuls, these small increments were significant. Furthermore, he would publicly call me Teacher Jiang, which in the atmosphere of the Transfer Center, required a considerable amount of courage. I also got on well with the great majority of my fellow inmates, and they respected me as a "special attention prisoner" who didn't put on airs and was willing to sweat together with the rest of them. There was one prisoner with whom I got on especially well. I used to let him see the pieces that I wrote criticizing the Transfer Center. And, when I chatted quietly with him, the monitor, apparently because of my status and the fact that this man was an unusually good worker, would ignore us, or at most, say, "All right, that's enough." I will always have fond recollections of this man and other workers and officials of the Transfer Center who were good to me.

There had also been a supervising squad leader in Area One who was kind to me. He had been convicted of economic, or fiscal, crime. When I was still in Unit Two, he had ignored the danger of arousing suspicion on himself and come in to talk with me. When I wrote criticisms of the Transfer Center, or suggestions for improvement, he had usually passed them to the authorities for me. He would sometimes call me into the squad leaders' office and patiently try to explain the Center's policies and problems to me. On learning that I was troubled by constipation, he said that I could ask permission to go to the toilet whenever I felt the urge. I had seen others ask permission to go to the toilet, but the result depended on the whims of the squad leader. Some requests were readily accepted, while others were denied or ignored, or the individual was told to withdraw the request. So I was reluctant to step out and make such a special request. However, there was one time when I thought I really must take action. I made the request and got permission, and went into the toilet alone and squatted for a full half hour before finally clearing all the dry, hardened stool from my guts. When I finished, my legs were so cramped and numb that I could hardly stand. The orderly on duty had come into the toilet twice to check on me, and seeing the soybean-size beads of sweat dripping from my face, had thought I must be ill.

At the end of April the work became increasingly tense. Not only were the leaders constantly trying to speed things up, but the evening news session, which had been inviolate, was scrubbed. I thought that this was a decision that Area One had made surreptitiously (i.e., without the knowledge of the overall administration of the prison system). My speculation was based on a strange thing that happened on the 27th, 28th and 29th of the month. At 6:25 p.m. on each of these three days, the section chief had told the orderly on duty to call me out, alone, to watch an hour of news with Li Wenzhang, who was in charge of turning the TV on and off. Thus the 34-inch color TV sat in the spacious entry hall with only the two of us watching. As was his habit, Li sat with a notebook on his lap and wrote down the main points of the news broadcast as he watched. Meanwhile, throughout the Center, work went on at an accelerated pace. As the long May Day holiday period approached, the authorities wanted to get as much done as possible before the men would have to be given some rest.

CHAPTER FORTY-FIVE

The Long May Day Holiday

Everyone who had spent any amount of time in the Production Unit understood that the Transfer Center was absolutely determined to squeeze as much unpaid labor out of them as possible, and this meant that the inmates would be flayed to the utmost. It was not just that work was the top priority objective; it was the only objective. I had submitted a written criticism to the authorities, suggesting that when short-term prisoners first arrived, they should be assigned to study *The Prison Law of the People's Republic of China.* Many people broke the law because they didn't know what the law was or didn't understand it. Wouldn't this be the perfect time to make up that lack of knowledge? The prisoners could at least become acquainted with the superficial explanations that the Communist Party is so good at producing. But the authorities ignored my recommendation. Their overriding methodology was "Reform through labor," which meant making as much money off the prisoners' labor as possible.

Still, the transfer center did have to ease up on their unreasonable policies before the long May Day holiday.* On the morning of 30 April they began to check the equipment and inventory the products on hand and put them into boxes. In the afternoon each unit got its preholiday cleanup under way, and inmates were told to write out promises to respect the regulations and maintain discipline. As the sun went down, I noticed that the expressions of the prison police, orderlies, and squad leaders became more relaxed. The

* The length of the various government-declared holidays has varied over the years. At the time of writing, the May Day, or Labor Day, holiday was a full week, beginning on May 1st.

unit chief told me I would soon see that a holiday was more real here than in the Detention Center. And two recommendations that I had written up for the holiday received unprecedented responses. My suggestions had been that during the holiday, the unit should organize (1) a ping-pong tournament, and (2) a chess competition. I had said that a ping-pong table was not expensive and could easily be purchased with money from sales of the products made by the Production Unit. The table could be set up for use in the big entry hallway, and when it was not in use it could be folded up and placed by the wall, out of the way. The chief's response was that there wasn't enough money to buy a ping-pong table, but a chess competition would be arranged. They would also organize a singing competition, and he hoped that I would show my singing voice.

From my personal experience I could say, without exaggeration, that a prisoner in the Transfer Center could indeed celebrate a long holiday. Surely this was a bit of good fortune passed to us by the accumulated good deeds of our ancestors. And my own experience and close observation of the holiday gave me a more objective and complete view of the Transfer Center and enabled me to write a more comprehensive, accurate, and unbiased record.

On the morning of May 1st everyone slept a half hour longer than usual, but that short thirty minutes seemed to bring magical results. After morning roll call, as if he had suddenly taken off a mask, the squad leader broke out into a smile. The prohibition against speaking evaporated, and quiet conversation was no longer met with interference or reprimands. As if by magic, the squad leader produced old newspapers, playing cards, and chess pieces. He said that in the morning we would have a section meeting; then we could take baths. From the afternoon of the 1st through the 7th we would not work, and there would be various kinds of entertainment, including VCDs. We would have better food for these seven days. There would be two meals a day, with rice in the morning and wheat-flour buns in the evening.

The main purpose of the meeting on the morning of the 1st was to have each prisoner share his thoughts, and secondarily to guarantee that during the long holiday he wouldn't cause disorder in the Center or trouble for the monitors. In this obviously warmer atmosphere, everyone still maintained a uniform attitude. The inmates all said that they would "remember their status," and no one uttered a word of dissatisfaction. When finally it was my turn to speak, I had decided that I would loosen things up by trying to bring about a break with the jailhouse rigidity that had been maintained without weakening for the past half century. I spoke in a way that was not in the least provocative, offering only constructive criticism, though with a bit of sarcasm. I said that ordinarily we all had to work very hard and our food was neither sufficient nor very good, and now that the holiday was here, work had stopped and we were getting better food. This was our good fortune. I said I was thinking that perhaps the Transfer Center could be a little more generous and give each person half a bowl of meat. The three or four little pieces of meat that we were each getting were not nearly enough to satisfy our craving. At this point there was an unprecedented burst of laughter and some of the men spoke up with calls of "Right! Good!" I continued, saying, "There is a strange thing in the Transfer Center. We are allowed to trim our fingernails but not our toenails. This is unreasonable. For the May Day holiday, could the Center make an exception and show more mercy?" This brought out another burst of happy laughter. Finally I said, "There is another thing that is even stranger. We are not allowed to hang our wet washcloths up to dry, but have to pack them up and let them become a breeding ground for germs. Such an unscientific, unhygienic procedure should not be allowed to continue." This got everyone to whispering among themselves, then excitedly discussing the matter, and the juvenile inmates especially supported my suggestion, calling out, "Let us hang our washcloths up to dry!"

My three suggestions were obviously directed at the Transfer Center administration, but to my surprise, the squad leader showed his anger. He loudly disagreed: "I have not prevented you from trimming your toenails." However, no one chimed in to support him, and several people backed me up. In a very stern voice, the squad leader said, "I have never forbidden you to hang your washcloths up to dry." He then told his assistant to get a nail trimming knife from the orderly, adding, "Anyone who wants to hang their washcloths up can put them on the radiator pipes." I was very happy on hearing this, and had no inclination to argue with the monitor about his denials. I went over and pulled the wash basin out from under my bunk, took the washcloth out of it, and hung it on a radiator pipe. Several young inmates followed suit, and one of the older men did the same, but the rest of them didn't move. They couldn't break the old habits.

On this day the noon meal was two stir-fry dishes. Each person was given two and a half times the usual helpings of food, and it was quite tasty. I felt good and ate a big bowl of rice. After the meal, everyone enjoyed an hour's nap, and then some of the men started playing cards or chess. The chess competition would get under way the next day. Each squad selected an individual to play in the competition, and I was chosen to represent Squad Three. One fellow squad member was disappointed that he was passed over and challenged me to two games, saying it was to "help me warm up for the competition." I won both games. On the morning of May 2nd the Unit Two player was brought into Unit Three to play against me. On the afternoon of the 3rd the competition came to a close, with me as the champion. The atmosphere in the section was cheerful. The squad leader magnanimously congratulated me and played a game of chess with me. Then the brigade chief came to play with me, and after several hard-fought games, I came out on top. The Unit Eight monitor won third place, and later he often invited me over to his section to play, brewing tea for me when I came. Thus I became the only short-term prisoner in the brigade who had the privilege of moving about among the various units.

In the afternoon of May 4th the singing competition was held on the basketball courts. Each unit entered two individuals in the contest. Four orderlies served as judges. In contrast with the chess tournament, I had no idea that I would win this competition. I could carry a tune, but singing was not my forte. I had just thought that among the 160 or so inmates in the brigade I had had a chance to come into contact with only about 20 of them, and this would help to let others get to know something about me—much as had been the case when I went out to play basketball. I was prepared to sing two songs. The first was "Happy May Day," which was based on "Happy New Year," with a few necessary changes. I would sing this in English. The other was "Ode to the Plum Tree," through which I wanted to express my dread of the bitter winter weather. From the time I was a small child I had always been fond of the "three cold-weather friends"* and had a special liking for the plum. But thinking of plum blossoms also always reawakened sad memories of a close friend who had died in Changshu's Plum Blossom Hospital when he was a young man.

We were performing in reverse order, with Unit Eight first and Unit Two last. When the competition got under way, all of the young men sang popular songs. Some of them sang very well and won applause and cheers. But there was another thing that they all had in common: they couldn't forget their status. They couldn't open up. They didn't stand up straight. They didn't dare show emotion, and instead of looking directly at the audience they let their gaze fall on the gray concrete in front of the performance area. They were unable to project their voices and they made no gestures with their hands, but stood without any variation in their posture. I understood this. In the first place, they had guilt feelings from their crimes, and the severe treatment in the Transfer Center just strengthened these feelings. Naturally there was no way they could hold up their heads and show high spirits.

---

* The three friends are the pine and the bamboo because they remain green through the winter, and the plum tree because it blooms in the winter. These "three friends" are often depicted in Chinese painting.

When my turn came I slowly walked forward and took my position, then I let my gaze move over the entire audience, making eye contact with them. Then after brief opening remarks, I started singing. I sang "Happy May Day" twice in English. I did it with a cheerful expression on my face and moved around as I sang, then ended with gestures. When I was finished there was a big round of applause and cheers. When I sang "Ode to the Plum Tree," I cast my eyes upward, letting the blue heavens know my resentment at the miscarriage of justice in my imprisonment for a literary work, and expressing my loyalty to the principle of righteousness. I let myself go and put everything into the singing, and when I was finished the whole crowd broke out into even louder applause.

Much to my surprise, when the results were announced the judges had given me first place. Still, I didn't feel that the brigade had arranged it beforehand, nor was it possible that the judges had given me first place because of special feelings of sympathy for me. The most likely reason was that while all the others had sung as if they were kneeling, I had stood straight and sung out without restraint. This was surely the factor that created a distance between my singing and that of the others.

In the evening of May 6th, there was a meeting of the entire brigade. The brigade chief reviewed the activities of the holiday period and passed out prizes for the first three places in the chess and singing competitions. First prize was an exercise book and two ball-point pens. As a dual champion, I received two sets of prizes.

According to the law, the next day would be the final day of the May Day holiday. While everyone complained that the time had passed too quickly and the "good times" were about to come to an end, we all had a common hope for the coming day, expecting that it would be similar to the last day of holiday periods in the Detention Center, when we were allowed to relax and chat, play chess and cards, and read books and newspapers. After we went to bed, everyone probably had the same pleasant dreams.

CHAPTER FORTY-SIX

~

The Unchanging Transfer Center

On the 7th of May, our last day off work, the Transfer Center once again showed its exploitative nature, this time with an announcement that the May Day holiday was at an end and production was resuming. This was a naked case of power overshadowing the law, and of the authorities trampling personal rights.

The prisoners had no choice but to "cooperate." No matter that it was common knowledge that government authorities habitually take advantage of the people, and regardless of the fact that none of us wanted to see our legal holiday activities forcibly supplanted by corvée labor, still everyone understood that there could be no appeal for justice from officialdom. Officials had all the power. Anyone who failed to cooperate would be labeled "recalcitrant," "resisting reform," and would surely be punished. On the other hand, when the authorities break the law in the name of "law enforcement," there is nothing that can be done about it.

While everyone was reluctantly getting back to work, I asked the squad leader for pen and paper and began writing a letter of complaint to the Transfer Center authorities. I said that over the past six days, the inmates had enjoyed the legally designated long holiday and had appreciated living in a humane environment. I couldn't understand why on this final day of the holiday the Center would risk being labeled "illegal" by abandoning something important for an insignificantly small monetary gain. In the face of such arbitrary maltreatment, others could swallow their anger and remain silent, but I had to speak up. I had to offer criticism.

The squad leader gave my letter to supervising squad leader Bian Yi, who quickly passed it on to the prison police, and before long the orderly on duty called me into the Squad One office. Soon the company commander came in, but he remained silent. I could tell from the sounds coming from upstairs that in the other squads the last day of the holiday had been swallowed up just as in Squad Three. As he couldn't raise an argument against my protest, nor could he criticize the Transfer Center, there was nothing he could say. He told the orderly to bring in a chess set and said that he had come to challenge the champion. We played until dark, with a break for me to go back to Squad Three for supper. Thus on 7 May I was the only prisoner in Area One who continued to enjoy the holiday, while everyone else was illegally forced to toil through its final day.

Actually, the Transfer Center's habit of enslavement had already been demonstrated at the start of the May Day holiday, and it had cast a shadow over the whole week. After the meeting on the 1st of May, we had gone out for showers. As usual, all the groups had filed through the security door, one after another, and once we were all outside, we had lined up in four ranks to count off and double-check that everyone was present. Normally, right after the count-off, we would all squat down for a further count so as to make sure there was no error. But this time, after counting off and squatting for the additional count, the section chief suddenly gave the order to spread our legs and bend our heads down as far as possible, with our hands on our heads. The men who were so used to doing this in the Detention Center accepted the order without question. (They knew they would get a shock from the electric prod if they didn't.) I was in the rear rank, and seeing all the men uniformly sitting with their hands on their heads and their heads pushed toward their crotches, I couldn't help thinking that they looked like a flock of oversize farm fowl trussed up for slaughter. My disgust and anger steadily rose, like the numbers on the meter of a taxicab, with no way to stop the upward progression. I had thought that the police ordered suspects to put their hands on their heads when making arrests in order to prevent them from destroying evidence or pulling out a weapon, and that was reasonable. But inside the high walls and electrified fences of the Detention Center or the prison, was there any reason at all for this order? The only possible explanation was that stripping away one's personal freedom was not enough; they also wanted to insult and humiliate the prisoners.

Throughout the month of April, the Transfer Center had not done this. Why were they suddenly doing it now? But the count-off was coming close, and I wouldn't make the choice; there was nothing I could do but ignore it. When it was finished, there was a moment's silence. Bian Yi did not give the order to stand at attention. Instead, we heard Li Zhong call out: "Who is that who didn't put his hands on his head?!" The orderly on duty quietly answered Li Zhong's question, and Li asked me, "Why didn't you put your hands on your head?" When I explained that I never did this, he responded, "The rule here is to squat down and put your hands on your head." I objected, "This rule is unreasonable. When I was in Section Seven, I didn't follow it." At this point, Bian Yi interrupted: "Section Seven is Section Seven. The Transfer Center is a prison, and the circumstances are different." I said, "To me they are both the same." Bian spoke up again: "While you're here you have to obey our rules." My anger rose and I said, "There are fifty-eight articles in *The Rules for the Reform of Criminals' Behavior*. Tell me which article stipulates that prisoners must squat down and put their hands on their heads." Bian was at a loss for further words, and Li took over again: "Jiang Qisheng, do you mean to challenge me?" I replied, "I don't want to challenge you, but to cover my head with my hands is something that I just can't do." We had reached an impasse.

There were about 150 "big turkeys" squatting on the ground, and standing around the group were seven or eight orderlies and three or four prison police. Commander Cao quickly walked over and stood in front of me and said, "Jiang Qisheng, when you first arrived here, I told you that whether you admit guilt or not, you have to obey the rules and regulations of the prison. Didn't I say this to you?" I answered calmly but sternly, "Commander Cao, you know that during the month that I have been here I have been sensible and reasonable. There is only one way that you can make me obey these rules. Bring four men to force me to do it. I cannot put my hands on my head." He did not say anything more, but backed off and stood to one side. Later, one of the inmates told me that some of the orderlies had quietly spoken to Li Zhong, saying, "Let's use the electric prod on him." I don't know what Li's thoughts were at this point. He had gotten astride the tiger and there was no good way for him now to dismount. There was another moment of silence before he gave the order, "Stand at attention!" and after a "Right face!" everyone marched off to the bathhouse.

This sudden disturbance brought about a change in the atmosphere of the bathhouse. Many of the men found ways to tell me how they felt about it, and there was concern about the future retaliation that was likely to be directed at me. Amid the noise of the showers, I pondered the situation. This was a clash that I did not by any means want to see. What had brought it about during this important holiday? I thought of three factors: First was that the Transfer Center had once again invoked an illegal rule, imposing an uncivilized, harsh demand on the prisoners' squatting posture. Second was that

Li Zhong had not responded to my resistance in a flexible way; he could have just "watched with one eye open and the other closed." And third was that I had been very firm in adhering to my basic principle of conduct. I was not a person who liked to make trouble, but if trouble arose I was not afraid to deal with it. I was willing and able to pay the price for defending my dignity.

Not long after lunch, I was called out alone and left sitting in an empty interview room. Everyone knew that the morning's affair was not over. The men in the squad felt that things did not look good for me. I myself was uncertain: in the morning Li Zhong had let me off, but what would he do now? Would he punish me, or was he prepared to compromise, with each of us yielding something? Either way seemed possible. When he entered, he came directly to the point: The requirement that prisoners squat and cover their heads with their hands was not his idea; it was in a written order from the administration. It should have been put into effect ten days ago. Furthermore, I should understand that he had not done anything to exacerbate the situation this morning, but if the matter were just dropped now, I must realize that he, after all, would have to remain here and would still have to manage more than a hundred inmates. As a person willing to respond to persuasion but not to force, I broke in and said, "Why don't you just tell me what you would like me to do?" At this, he made his proposal: after a while there would be a general meeting of the section, and he would like me to make a "self-criticism" to save a little face for him.

Not surprised at this request, I replied that I could say a few words that would save face for him, but I could not admit error and apologize, nor could I promise to thoroughly reform my behavior and in the future follow the rule and put my hands on my head. He asked, "Then what would you say?" I responded that I would say three things. First, I would express regret for what happened this morning. Second, that although I had expressed my anger at the "company," I now realized that the order for us to squat and cover our heads with our hands came not from it but from the top administration of the Transfer Center. The third was that in order to prevent similar clashes from occurring in the future, I would do my best to avoid being present on such occasions. When I had finished, he had one more question: couldn't I say a little more than that? I replied that I couldn't. He hesitated, but did not insist on pursuing the matter further. Ten minutes later, at the general meeting, he pulled out the confidential order, which had come from the Transfer Center on 11 April, and read the rule about prisoners' standing, sitting, and squatting posture, and he followed this with a restrained comment on the morning's clash. Then, keeping to our gentlemen's agreement, I stood up and said my three sentences—no more and no less.

Later, I did not succeed in my plans for "avoidance" of such occasions. At the singing competition on the afternoon of 4 May, when all the men in the company came out of the building, the usual order was given for us to squat down and count off. Of course, I did not put my hands on my head, but Assistant Commander Liu and the other police ignored me. (Li had gone home for the holiday.) Subsequently, this pattern was followed throughout the remainder of the time I was in the Transfer Center. The Center's 11 April order had no effect on me. When Area One illegally made the short-term prisoners get back to work before the end of the holiday, the 11 April order was put into effect at the same time, and whenever the prisoners left the building they had to hold their heads down. When they went to watch television, and when they left the TV room, they also had their heads down. This resulted in an interesting scene: every time the "Heads down!" order was given, row upon row of men's heads would be uniformly lowered, but there would be one prisoner of conscience whose head remained proudly erect.

In April of 2003 the Transfer Center once again restored this outworn policy, requiring prisoners to hold their heads down and put their hands on them. An inmate in Squad Two had told me about his stay in the old Transfer Center, saying that prisoners had been required to bow down with their hands on their heads and squat; they were not allowed to look human, and anyone who stepped over the line, even just a little, would be scolded, shocked, and beaten. Under those agonizing circumstances, his hair had suddenly begun to turn gray. With a sigh, he told me that after the Center moved here, conditions had been much better. He no longer had to bow his head or cover it with his hands, and his contact with the electric prod was also much less. But right after he told me this, the Transfer Center suddenly revived its old hostile policy and gave up the more civilized direction that it had been following. Hearing this story motivated me once again to write a letter of criticism to the Center. I said it promoted the prison ditty, "Call out 'one-two-one,' keep your head up!" (In Chinese the two lines rhyme.) The purpose of this was to allow the inmates to have at least a basic level of self-respect, and I thought this was good. But why did the Center then insist on depriving them of the freedom to stand up straight with their chests out and their heads held high when they were not chanting "one-two-one"? The order that they had sent down stipulates an extremely uncivilized squatting posture that forces inmates into self-humiliation. And yet when ladies and gentlemen come to visit the Center, it trembles in fear and doesn't dare display its masterpiece to the honored guests by allowing them to see the prisoners crouched down in this degrading squatting posture!

From the 8th of May the heavy workload continued without letup. "We are the Transfer Center, and we are not afraid of anyone. We cancelled the holiday on May 7th. What are you passing geese (short-term prisoners) going to do to stop us from plucking a few more of your feathers? If we pluck all your feathers, what's so special about that?" In the middle of May the weather got warmer and we changed our padded clothing for unlined shirts and pants; then received short-sleeve shirts. Unfortunately, however, we were only issued one shirt, so washing it was a problem. Although the ceiling fans were turned on, the time for washing our faces was not increased and drinking water was still very limited. (When the temperature rose sharply on the 17th and 18th of May and our sweat poured like rain, Li Zhong did allow an additional time for face washing.)

Of course the "passing geese" received absolutely no compensation for their labor—not a cent in monetary compensation, nor any points toward prizes or reduction of their sentences. Their labor was thoroughgoing uncompensated "tribute." This was unique in the prison system. And in addition, what made the men really angry and resentful was the expectation that "the horses would run fast but would not be given hay to eat." Even in spending their own money, the short-term prisoners were allowed to buy only ten yuan of goods per month. This policy meant that not only was it impossible to augment their diet and gain a little more strength, but also daily necessities like dish washing liquid, laundry powder, and even toilet paper were in short supply. This was in spite of the fact that the regulations of the Beijing Prison Administration clearly stated that short-term prisoners were to be allowed to spend up to eighty yuan per month.

Civilized? Humane? Reasonable?—in describing the Transfer Center, where would one begin?

A few weeks earlier these convicted criminals had thought only of leaving the Detention Center, but now their most heartfelt wish was that they could leave the Transfer Center a day, an hour, or a minute sooner. They wanted to get out of this abyss of suffering and go somewhere fit for people to live. In trying to think how I could be extricated, I remembered the "crackdowns" that were so hated by the prisoners. If the latest crackdown of 2001 could quickly bear fruit, perhaps the detention centers would become so overcrowded that they would have to speed up the movement of prisoners to the Transfer Center, then it would soon become so crowded that it would have to move people on out.

The day finally arrived. On 22 May, around ten a.m., area one juvenile inmates were transferred to the Juvenile Reformatory, and I was one of two people who were sent on to the Number Two Prison. The two of us boarded a prison van to join twenty-some prisoners from area two, and as the van drove out of the Transfer Center gate I said to myself, "The fifty-three days that I have spent here, together with the first three days in Section Seven, were the most difficult and unforgettable of my four years in the prison system."

Written in Section Six
Subsection Sixteen of
Beijing Number Two Prison
April and May 2002

Epilogue to Part II

I completed my draft of *Notes on the Transfer Center* a year ago. Now, as I take pen in hand to write an epilogue for the account, we are in the fifth day of the sealing off of the Center because of SARS.* With firm assurance I can now tell the world that among the nearly twenty institutions of confinement under the authority of the Beijing Prison Administration, there is no other unit that is as inhumane as the Transfer Center. It is an unusual, special case and my account is an authentic description of the abuse and humiliation meted out to the short-term prisoners. However, I want to add a word on behalf of the prison police and the long-term prisoners in the Center: to be assigned to work there, or to continue their confinement there, is their ill fortune, and basic survival for them is very difficult. The time that they spend there is likely to shorten their lives.

The thing that I don't understand is what has caused the Transfer Center to sink to such a disgraceful state. Is it a conscious policy of the Beijing Prison Administration to forcibly reduce prisoners to a submissive state so

* SARS is an acronym for "severe acute respiratory syndrome." Early in 2003, this unusual and highly contagious variety of influenza had become a serious concern in Hong Kong, but the Chinese government denied that it existed in the mainland. By late April and into May, as the number of confirmed infections grew into the thousands and deaths into the hundreds, the government was finally forced by publicity and attention from the World Health Organization to admit its existence in Beijing and other cities and regions of the country, and to take measures to control its spread. Schools and other institutions and offices were closed, public transportation had to be disinfected daily, and the streets, buses, and subways became almost deserted as most people stayed in their homes. When people did go out, they wore surgical masks. The outbreak spread around the world. In July 2003, WHO declared it contained.

that they will be "easier to manage," or is it just that these unauthorized rash actions, deceiving and exploiting the short-term prisoners, are undertaken entirely without reason or hope of any useful result? Or is it both of those things together?

At any rate, regardless of how it came to be in that state, it is imperative that the Transfer Center be thoroughly remolded. In terms of darkness and cruelty, of course today's Transfer Center cannot be compared to the Gulags of the twentieth century, but is there any reason why it should not be called a part of the Gulag of the twenty-first century? Although the maxim "The people should not struggle against officials" is said to represent the wisdom of the common people, it might be more realistic to say that it is the condensation of their blood and tears. Where lies China's hope? What is the way out for China? In plain language, it is to reverse that maxim and make it "Officials must not tyrannize and oppress the people." Government officials of all ranks should instead revere the people and must conduct their business in light of the desires of the masses, taking care not to violate any of the sacred rights of citizens.

Human conscience and the desire for justice require that the "Gulags" be abolished and that the Transfer Centers be moved onto the path of respect for human dignity and transformed into civilized and humane institutions of confinement. When prisoners' freedom has been legally taken from them, there is absolutely no reason to subject them to further maltreatment and abuse.

As a transcentury prisoner of conscience, put simply, I served the twentieth-century half of my sentence in the Beijing Municipal Detention Center and the twenty-first-century half in the Transfer Center and the Beijing Number Two Prison—53 days in the Transfer Center and 726 days in the prison. Yet, after writing a thirty-thousand-character account of the 53 days in the Transfer Center, I have not taken up my pen again to describe my experiences during the almost two full years that I spent in the Number Two Prison. The principal reason for this is that the Number Two Prison was not like the endless unspeakable misery of the Transfer Center, where each day passed as slowly as a year. Therefore I decided that for the time being I would set the Number Two Prison aside.

~

The Day I Was Released from Prison

All those who have spent time in prison know that the most common method of keeping track of time is by "reverse countdown." How many years, months, and days must pass before I will be released and can go home? The Beijing Number Two Prison mostly holds individuals convicted of serious crimes, foreigners, and prisoners of conscience. When I first arrived, because the remainder of my sentence was relatively short, the envious long-term prisoners immediately began a reverse countdown of months for me. And when I wrote "A Summary of Thought Reform" and my "Pledge," they began to do the reverse countdown in days.

Reaching the point of counting in days is both a happy thing and troublesome. From morning roll call till evening roll call, there is a constant stream of people coming by to offer congratulations—prisoners and police, members of one's own and other units. "You lucky guy; how many days before you go home?" And most of them add, "Teacher Jiang, once you get out of here, don't come back. This is definitely not a good place to be." A man from Taiwan who was serving a suspended death sentence for espionage, said, "I'm sure you will continue to speak the truth." Another man, who, ten years ago, had been a regimental commander in the army and was serving a life sentence for economic crimes, said, as we were parting, "I hope that after you get out you will continue to work for democratization in China." I assured him that I would. This was right in the midst of the SARS epidemic, and several people teased me, saying, "Don't you want to write up a request that your release be delayed? It's safer in here." I played along with the joke, asking,

"What would you do if it were you?" The answer was clear. Not a single person would want to stay even one day longer, even with SARS raging outside.

On the evening of 15 May 2003, less than two full days before I was due to leave, I was playing basketball when Brigade Commander Xu called me out to tell me, with some embarrassment, that the Public Security Bureau had called to say that the day after tomorrow, when I was ready to go, I should not bother family or friends to come to collect me, as the Bureau would send a car to take me home. If I accepted their offer, they would notify Zhang Hong that she needn't come to pick me up. When I heard this, my anger rose, and I said to Xu, "This is ridiculous! While I've been in prison, I've thought day and night about my family. I certainly haven't thought of the Public Security Bureau. Please tell your bosses that even if my family could not come to get me, I would rather walk home than ride in the Bureau's car."

Knowledge of this affair quickly spread among my fellow prisoners. They thought it was quite fascinating, but also worrisome. Why would the authorities suddenly come up with such a lousy idea? I said they had probably thought of such an unreasonable and offensive plan because they were afraid that the foreign media would be willing to brave the SARS scare to interview me as soon as I left prison. I told them that I knew how to deal with it.

The next evening Public Security called the police office of Unit Sixteen and asked to speak to me. The person on the phone was a policeman whom I had previously known. I picked up the telephone saying, "Wasn't what I said yesterday clear enough?" He explained that the higher-ups had ordered him to call again and talk it over with me. I insisted that there was nothing to discuss, and asked him if he were in my place, would he accept the offer. He said, "We are doing this for your own good. We will send a high-class car that has been thoroughly disinfected. We guarantee that we will deliver you safely home, which will save your family the trouble of looking for a car." On first hearing it, this sounded like a reasonable suggestion, and it seemed to have kind intent. But in fact, it wasn't so. I said, "I don't doubt that you will send a high-class car and that it will be disinfected, but do you think that this would tempt me to ride in your car? Aren't family and friends more important than these two conditions? Furthermore, tomorrow is not an ordinary day; it is the day I leave prison. Four years ago, when I was arrested, I had no choice. I had to get into the police car. But now, having regained my freedom, would I want to ride in one? What in the world are your higher-ups thinking?"

There was a long pause, then the caller spoke again: "Let me put it this way. There is something that you still have to see to at your local police station. After your release, your political rights will not be restored for another year. We would take you by the station to take care of that, and then drive you home. Wouldn't that be very convenient for you?" When I heard this, I angrily objected, "Let's first set aside the fact that I was wrongly accused and have served an unjustified sentence. I ask you, which article of what law says that a person must register for the accessory penalty on the day that he is released from prison?" He hesitated, then said, "Well no, there's no such law. We just thought it would be more convenient for you to deal with it all at once." Not wanting to hear any more of their lies, I raised my voice: "Please tell your superiors that whether or not they send a car tomorrow is none of my business and what car I get into to leave the prison is none of their business!" With that, I hung up the phone. A prison policeman, who had been monitoring the conversation, exclaimed, "Really! How can they be so meddlesome!"

After morning roll call on the 17th, many of my fellow inmates came to say good-bye. A friend from Unit Seventeen came to the window, and we wished each other well. He said, "I'm sure you will still be in Beijing five years from now. When I get out, you will be the first person that I'll look up." There had been a shower during the night and the early summer sky was especially clear. After breakfast everyone went out for exercise. Because of SARS, no vehicles could enter the prison, so the prisoners didn't have to work and could go out for exercise every day. This was very much in contrast to ordinary times, when the men spent most of their time working and seldom had a chance to go out of doors. As the clock marked the final minutes of my countdown, more than a hundred men from Unit Sixteen, who were in the exercise yard, saw that I was all set to leave and sighed for my repeated victories in the competitions for shooting baskets that we had organized.

Soon, officials from the prison administration came to perform the final procedure for me. As a "prisoner requiring special attention," I had to be thoroughly searched so as to ensure that nothing, not even the smallest scrap of paper, would be taken out of the prison. When the search was completed, they returned several dozen books to me. These had been handed over for examination two months earlier. Because of SARS, clothing that had been sent to me from home was not allowed into the prison, so I was still wearing prison garb. Accompanied by three men from the prison administration, I left Unit Sixteen and walked slowly to the main North Gate of Number Two Prison. The outside police at the gate were wearing face masks, and the prison police turned the books over to them for inspection, and then, as they couldn't go through the gate, I was finally left alone and I walked out carrying a bag of books in each hand.

As I stepped through the gate, I saw that a group of people were standing two or three hundred meters beyond the administrative area outside the prison. Before I was released I had been told that I could change into civilian clothes in the dispatch office just outside the gate and that I could pick up my "Certificate of Release" there. I walked ahead a little way and stopped and turned around for a final look at the armed guards standing by the forbidding steel gate, and the large characters, Beijing Municipal Number Two Prison. Then I walked on forward. When I was several dozen meters from them I made out Zhang Hong, together with our friends Professor Zhang Xianling and Zhu Rui. Then I saw ten or twelve more well-wishers, one or two of whom I had not previously met. We all greeted each other with a nod.

Not surprisingly, I also saw the unwelcome police car and policemen. I handed the books to Zhang Hong and took the clothes and shoes that she had brought. Then I walked back to the dispatch office. Two policemen entered the office with me, and before I had a chance to begin changing my clothes, they started to pester me, insisting that I reconsider and accept their kind offer of a ride in the police car. In spite of my extreme irritation, because I was acquainted with these two officers, I did my best to control my temper and said, "Beginning two days ago this is the third time! You are officers of the law. Does the law require that you prevent me from taking my family's or friends' car home? As human beings, can you justify such behavior in terms of sentiment or reason?" Unable to give me a direct answer, they said, "You are a sensible person. Surely you understand the difficult position that we are in." I countered, "Aren't these difficulties of your own making? Your bosses have given an unreasonable order, and you have run into my insistence on holding to my principles. I suppose you must be very annoyed to be caught in the middle." At this they sighed, saying, "You go ahead and change your clothes while we ask for instructions."

From the inside to the outside, from undershirt to socks, I made a complete change of clothing, leaving the prison uniform for the guards to collect. But when I had put on the leather shoes that I had not worn for four years and was about to step outside, the two policemen still insisted that I get into their car. Seeing this, I lost all patience and flew into a rage, shouting at them, "Have you got water in your brain? Your bosses have water in their brains? When someone has hoped so long for something happy, you still insist on making trouble for him! I'll tell you once more: every day, for 365 days of the year, I have longed for my family and friends. Believe me, I have never once felt any longing for the Public Security Bureau or the police station! Today I have come out from between the high walls of the prison. Haven't I regained my freedom? If I can't even decide which car I want to get into for the ride home, I might as well change back into prison clothes and go back inside!" And I started to undress. The prison guards in the dispatch office had been standing aside, listening without saying anything. But now they interceded in an attempt to smooth things over: "No, no. Wait." Seeing that the situation would soon pass the point of no return, the police said, "Teacher Jiang, don't be angry, don't be angry. Go ahead and get in your friend's car and go home. But, when you get home, can you please not answer the telephone? If you are not careful, you'll say the wrong thing." The first sentence caused my anger to subside a bit, but the second made me even angrier, and I replied, "What are you talking about? Is it any of your business whether or not I answer the telephone in my own home?" They were at a loss and said no more.

Because of official interference, something that should have taken no more than a few minutes was stretched to a full half hour. My friends had just seen me emerge from the solid walls and electric fencing of the prison, and then they were witnesses as I was immediately besieged by intangible walls and fencing. They had become anxious and somewhat agitated while waiting. They knew that an argument was going on in the dispatch office. They had heard me shouting. But they had no way of knowing what the outcome would be. Finally I walked out. We exchanged loud and happy greetings, and with a feeling of elation, I got into a car with friends. With some difficulty, I controlled my excitement and told them about the struggle that had been going on over the past three days. My account was accurate but was also tinged with sarcasm and humor, and it brought sympathetic understanding from my companions; and their laughter spilled out onto streets that were almost empty because of the SARS scare, and onto the police car that was following closely behind us.

16 October 2004

Index

Note: Page numbers followed by "n" refer to footnotes.

~

About the Authors

Jiang Qisheng (pronounced Jang Chee-shung) was born on 5 November 1948, in Changshu City, Jiangsu Province. In October 1968 he was "sent down" to the countryside to work among the peasants. In the spring of 1978 he entered the Beijing Institute of Aeronautics, earning a master' s degree in aerodynamics in 1984. From 1985 to 1988 he held a teaching post at the branch campus of Tsinghua University. In the autumn of 1988, he started studying for his Ph.D. at People' s University and was involved in the 1989 Tiananmen student movement and the Tiananmen Mothers Group. He was a member of a delegation that met with national leaders in an attempt to resolve the protests peacefully but was jailed for eighteen months in 1989 because of his activities in the protests. After his release he was denied regular employment and became a freelance writer, publishing numerous articles in American, Japanese, and Hong Kong journals. He also cooperated on translations of *The Structure of Scientific Revolutions* by Thomas Kuhn and *China's Crisis* by Andrew J. Nathan. In April 1999, he wrote an open letter entitled "Light a Million Candles to Commemorate the Souls of the Heroes of June 4th." On May 18 he was arrested and was held in the Beijing Detention Center for nearly two years. On 27 December 2000, he was convicted of the so-called crime of "incitement to subvert state power" by Beijing First Intermediate People's Court; on 16 February 2001, Beijing People's Superior Court passed final judgment upholding the original verdict, and he spent two months in the Beijing Transfer Center before being sent on to the Beijing Number Two Prison, where he served the remaining two years of his four-year sentence. Jiang was one of the drafters of Charter 08 and has been subjected to continued harassment by the authorities ever since. *My Life in Prison* was published in Chinese in Hong Kong in 2005, as *Kanshousuo Zaji*.

James E. Dew taught Chinese language and linguistics for many years at the University of Michigan, directed advanced Chinese language programs for American students in Taipei and Beijing, and was founding director of the Language Teaching Center at Johns Hopkins University. He was Chinese Language Consultant for the Peace Corps in China in the summers of 1995, 1996, and 1998. His publications include *City of Cats* (translation of Lao She's early 1930s satirical novel *Mao Cheng Ji*), *6000 Chinese Words: A Vocabulary Frequency Handbook for Chinese Language Teachers and Students*, *Classical Chinese: A Functional Approach* (coauthor with Kai Li), and articles on Chinese language pedagogy. Born in Montana and brought up in Florida, he has lived a total of twenty-five years in Taipei, Beijing, and Hong Kong. He now lives in Santa Barbara, California, with his wife, Vivian Ling.

Andrew J. Nathan is Class of 1919 Professor of Political Science at Columbia University and co-chair of the board of Human Rights in China. His teaching and research interests include Chinese politics and foreign policy, the comparative study of political participation and political culture, and human rights. He is engaged in long-term research and writing on Chinese foreign policy and on sources of political legitimacy in Asia, the latter research based on data from the Asian Barometer Survey, a multinational collaborative survey research project active in eighteen countries in Asia. He is the author of numerous books on China and co-editor with Perry Link of *The Tiananmen Papers*.

Perry Link is professor emeritus of East Asian Studies, Princeton University; Chancellorial Chair for Teaching Across Disciplines, University of California, Riverside; and chair of the board of the Princeton China Initiative, a human rights advocacy group. He teaches and publishes on Chinese language, literature, and cultural history. His most recent books are *No Hatred, No Enemies: Essays and Poems of Liu Xiaobo* (2011) and *Anatomy of Chinese: Rhythm, Metaphor, Politics* (2012). He is married to Tong Yi, who was a colleague of Jiang Qisheng on the student "dialogue delegation" at Tiananmen in 1989. Tong and Link hosted Jiang's son, Jiang Feng, for study in the United States while the father was in prison.

Naomi May is a writer and artist. Born in Glasgow, Scotland, she studied at the Slade School of Fine Art, London, where she won the History of Art Prize. She has exhibited in solo and mixed shows and taught art in inner-city schools and the history of art for the extramural department of the University of London. She has published three novels, a number of short stories, and written for major newspapers on life during the Troubles in Northern Ireland. A member of English PEN's Writers in Prison Committee, she became a "minder" for Jiang Qisheng near the end of his sentence in Beijing Number Two Prison.